The Dialectical Behavior Therapy Skills Workbook

— *for* —

Bipolar Disorder

Using DBT to Regain Control of Your Emotions and Your Life

SHERI VAN DIJK, MSW

New Harbinger Publications, Inc.

Publisher's Note

This publication is designed to provide accurate and authoritative information in regard to the subject matter covered. It is sold with the understanding that the publisher is not engaged in rendering psychological, financial, legal, or other professional services. If expert assistance or counseling is needed, the services of a competent professional should be sought.

Distributed in Canada by Raincoast Books

Copyright © 2009 by Sheri Van Dijk
New Harbinger Publications, Inc.
5674 Shattuck Avenue
Oakland, CA 94609
www.newharbinger.com

The Mood Disorder Questionnaire, © 2006 by R. Hirschfeld, is used by permission of the publisher.

Acquired by Tesilya Hanauer; Cover design by Amy Shoup;
Edited by Carole Honeychurch; Text design by Tracy Carlson

Library of Congress Cataloging-in-Publication Data

Van Dijk, Sheri.
  The dialectical behavior therapy skills workbook for bipolar disorder
: using DBT to regain control of your emotions and your life / Sheri Van Dijk ; foreword by Zindel V. Segal.
     p. cm.
  Includes bibliographical references.
  ISBN-13: 978-1-57224-628-7 (pbk. : alk. paper)
  ISBN-10: 1-57224-628-6 (pbk. : alk. paper)
  1. Manic-depressive illness--Treatment--Popular works. 2.
Dialectical behavior therapy--Popular works. 3. Manic-depressive persons--Life skills guides. I. Title.
  RC516.V36 2009
  616.89'506--dc22

                         2009014664

14 13 12

10 9 8 7 6 5

"Finally, a straightforward and compassionate resource for anyone wanting to understand more about bipolar disorder. The combination of personal stories and practical exercises provides a powerful guide to living a balanced and joyful life."

> —Susan Philpott, M.Sc., MSW, mental health supervisor at York Support Services Network in Sutton West, Ontario, Canada

"In this thorough and engaging workbook, Sheri Van Dijk breaks new ground by adapting dialectical behavior therapy for people living with bipolar disorder. This workbook provides patients struggling with this illness with a clear program and real-life day-to-day tools for coping. This workbook will help many people with bipolar disorder find order in their lives. A welcome addition to the helping field."

> —Paul Cappuccio, MSW, RSW, clinical manager of outpatient mental health services as Southlake Regional Health Centre and lecturer at Queens University

"Medication is the foundational treatment for bipolar disorder. However, medication use alone often results in failed relationships, financial demise, and continued symptoms of depression and anxiety. Van Dijk's *Dialectical Behavior Therapy Skills Workbook for Bipolar Disorder* can help to increase readers' personal serenity, interpersonal harmony, and intimacy in relationships, and optimize their quality of life. This book is clear, concise, and very readable, filled with wise guidelines that are rewarding and practical to implement."

> —Stephen B. Stokl, MD, FRCP, chief of psychiatry at Southlake Regional Health Centre in Newmarket, Ontario, Canada, and author of *Mentally Speaking*

This book is dedicated to my mother and father, Paulette and Rinty Van Dyk. From the two of you I learned that I can achieve whatever I put my mind to. Thank you for being my teachers, mentors, and friends.

Contents

Foreword

If you have bipolar disorder (BD), you know that it can have a huge effect on your life and even put your life at risk. The typical treatment for BD involves medications that are pretty effective in curbing the extreme mood swings that define this condition. Still, there is a growing recognition that BD is not something you simply get over and never have again. In fact, relapse and recurrence are common. Living with BD in the long run involves managing it the same way you would manage a chronic disease such as asthma, high blood pressure, or diabetes. You combine medical treatment with lifestyle changes to reduce the risk of aggravating your symptoms and bringing on an episode. You learn to recognize the moments in which you have a choice about something that's going to affect your emotions, and you learn to choose the behavior that's going to help you cope and regulate your mood, even when you're in the midst of the uncomfortable symptoms of bipolar disorder. This involves learning new skills and attitudes.

There is, however, an interesting paradox that arises when you use psychological strategies to manage the difficulties of BD. The very tool required for this work—the mind—is often touched by the disorder itself. The behavioral school of psychology has responded to this by sidestepping the mind, instead focusing on behavior and relying on the consequences of that behavior to bring relief. A second approach, cognitive therapy, uses logic and evidence to change the degree to which you believe in your thoughts, which ultimately changes your behavior. Either way, the result is that you come to know your mind and recognize its capacity for choice and change within moments of feeling bipolar symptoms.

The approach presented by Sheri Van Dijk in this clearly written and practical book combines the best elements of behavioral and cognitive work with the fruits of mindfulness training to acquaint you with both the territory of BD and the possibility of coping differently. This workbook starts from the premise that we are often unaware of how unspoken attitudes and beliefs can influence our view of the world around us. To help you cultivate a greater awareness of these silent influences on your behavior, the author provides a number of exercises that help to build awareness of present-moment experience and its corollary, the inevitable mind-wandering and daydreaming that occurs when we attempt to do only one thing at a time. An important theme that is returned to throughout the book is that managing the ups and downs that go along with BD involves learning how to survive a crisis.

Regardless of whether a difficulty is personal, interpersonal, or financial, you can determine whether your reactions will make it better or worse. The first step, that of acceptance, may seem counterproductive or even feel like resignation; perhaps it seems like the last thing you would choose to do. In fact, acceptance is the first step toward responding effectively rather than simply reacting to challenges. Because acceptance requires you to let go of some habitual tendencies to push away or minimize unpleasant experiences, you are able to see more clearly what it is that you are up against and choose healthier action.

Additional sections on emotional intelligence, distress tolerance, and interpersonal effectiveness offer you a wide repertoire of new skills and abilities. A later chapter considers the needs of family members. This is important because the quality of care received by people with BD is often determined by those around them.

Bipolar disorder continues to present a challenge to both its sufferers and the mental health community. There are too few workbooks such as this one, in which the needs of people with BD are placed foremost and an approach for helping them learn how to manage overwhelming emotions is so clearly articulated. I expect it will be a valuable resource for years to come.

—Zindel V. Segal, Ph.D.
professor of psychiatry, University of Toronto
author of *The Mindful Way Through Depression*

An Overview of Bipolar Disorder and Dialectical Behavior Therapy

You've picked up this book, which likely means that you or someone you care about is having emotional problems. You're wondering if it's bipolar disorder, or even more likely, you're wondering "What *is* bipolar disorder?" Let me help.

You may or may not have heard the term *manic depression.* Bipolar disorder used to be known as manic depression because this illness is characterized by extreme highs and lows in mood. In other words, people with this disorder go through cycles when their mood is either elevated (manic) or depressed.

The following is a screening tool to help you decide if you or your loved one may have bipolar disorder (Hirschfeld et al. 2000). It is not a diagnostic tool; only a professional can make an actual diagnosis of bipolar disorder. However, this screening tool can help you to decide if this workbook will be useful for you or your loved one. If some of these symptoms sound familiar, the skills taught in this book will be helpful, whether there is a diagnosis of bipolar disorder or not.

Mood Disorder Questionnaire

1.	Has there ever been a period of time when you were not your usual self and…	Yes	No
	…you felt so good or so hyper that other people thought you were not your normal self or you were so hyper that you got into trouble?		
	…you were so irritable that you shouted at people or started fights or arguments?		
	…you felt much more self-confident than usual?		
	…you got much less sleep than usual and found you didn't really miss it?		
	…you were much more talkative or spoke faster than usual?		
	…thoughts raced through your head or you couldn't slow your mind down?		
	…you were so easily distracted by things around you that you had trouble concentrating or staying on track?		
	…you had much more energy than usual?		
	…you were much more active or did many more things than usual?		
	…you were much more social or outgoing than usual; for example, you telephoned friends in the middle of the night?		
	…you were much more interested in sex than usual?		
	…you did things that were unusual for you or that other people might have thought were excessive, foolish, or risky?		
	…spending money got you or your family into trouble?		
2.	If you checked yes to more than one of the above, have several of these ever happened during the same period of time? **Yes** **No**		
3.	How much of a problem did any of these cause you—like being unable to work; having family, money, or legal troubles; getting into arguments or fights? *Please circle one response only.* **No problem** **Minor Problem** **Moderate Problem** **Serious Problem**		

The Mood Disorder Questionnaire consists of three main questions. The first question addresses the specific symptoms of mood disorder and is divided into a thirteen-part yes or no checklist. The second question concerns the co-occurrence of symptoms and is also in a yes or no format. The third question inquires about the severity of outcome, from "No Problem" to "Serious Problem."

In order to screen positively for bipolar disorder, a patient must:

1. Answer yes to at least 7 of the 13 parts in question 1

2. Answer yes to question 2 **and**

3. Have at least a moderate or serious degree of functional impairment on question 3

Patients who screen positively may benefit from a comprehensive diagnostic evaluation.

Hirschfeld R, J. B. Williams, R. L. Spitzer, et al. Mood Disorder Questionnaire, 2000: Jones and Bartlett Publishers, Sudbury, MA. www.jbpub.com. Reprinted with permission.

Now that you know whether or not you have some symptoms of bipolar disorder, let me tell you a bit about dialectical behavior therapy (DBT) and how this workbook is going to help you with the problems you are experiencing.

WHAT IS DIALECTICAL BEHAVIOR THERAPY?

Dialectical behavior therapy is a treatment that was created by Marsha Linehan (1993a, 1993b). Originally it was created to treat an illness called borderline personality disorder, but since then it has been found to be very effective in treating a range of other illnesses as well. One of the main reasons DBT will be effective in helping you with your symptoms of bipolar disorder is because it helps people learn to manage their overwhelming emotions in more effective ways. DBT is effective in helping people learn to handle distress in healthier ways and without losing control.

DBT Skills

One of the primary goals of dialectical behavior therapy is to teach you skills to help you to live your life more effectively. Throughout this workbook, the DBT skills you will learn fall into four categories, including *mindfulness*, which helps people to live more in the present moment rather than experiencing painful emotions that come from constantly thinking about the past or the future. I will be emphasizing mindfulness throughout this workbook, and you will learn to use it in many different ways to help with your symptoms of bipolar disorder, as well as to simply improve the quality of your life.

Distress tolerance skills will help you better cope with crisis situations (such as depressive or manic episodes) in healthier, less self-destructive ways.

One of the main problems people experience with bipolar disorder is difficulty regulating emotions. *Emotion regulation skills* help you to manage your emotions, as well as to tolerate your emotions when you can't change them or reduce their intensity.

The final set of skills you'll be learning relate to the relationships you have in your life. These are called *interpersonal effectiveness skills*. Relationships are a very important part of everyone's life. Unfortunately, having an illness such as bipolar disorder can make it more difficult for you to be able to act effectively in your relationships and keep them healthy. The interpersonal effectiveness skills you'll learn in this workbook will help you to maintain relationships through acting assertively and through taking good care of yourself.

WHO THIS BOOK IS FOR

In recent years, bipolar disorder has become more understood and the rate of diagnosis has increased. Often though, it can be difficult for professionals to make a diagnosis of bipolar disorder because the illness can present in very subtle ways. With this in mind, I wrote this book for those people who have a diagnosis of bipolar disorder and are being treated by a doctor for the illness, as well as for those people who have not necessarily been given the diagnosis.

If you screened positively on the Mood Disorder Questionnaire (MDQ) earlier in this section, and if you can relate to the symptoms of bipolar disorder you'll find outlined in chapter 1, you can benefit from the skills presented in this workbook. That being said, if you did screen positively on the MDQ, I want to emphasize that seeking professional help to either deny or confirm a diagnosis of bipolar disorder will be extremely helpful, since the majority of people with the illness do require medication.

HOW TO USE THIS BOOK

The most important thing you need to remember as you work your way through this book is that it's not just about reading; it's about doing the work to implement each of the skills into your life. In order to do this most effectively, I suggest you take your time working your way through the book, giving yourself time to really learn one set of skills before moving on to the next. Taking the time to do the written exercises will also help you to learn the skills presented.

This book is not meant to take the place of professional help. If you don't have a diagnosis but think you may have bipolar disorder, I urge you to seek medical help as soon as possible. If you have difficulties learning and using the skills in this book, or if you feel you do not currently have enough support in your life, I would encourage you to consult a professional psychotherapist.

Finally, before you start, it is very important that you take a moment to pat yourself on the back and congratulate yourself for having the courage to try to learn skills to change your life.

CHAPTER 1

What Is Bipolar Disorder?

Bipolar disorder is a biological illness that causes unusual shifts in your mood, level of energy, and ability to function in different aspects of your life (for example, working or going to school, taking care of yourself, and maintaining relationships). This illness used to be called *manic depression*, because it was thought that people with the illness would fluctuate only between episodes of highly elevated, euphoric moods and episodes of major depression. More recently, doctors have realized that the illness is not quite that black and white—that there are many moods that actually occur on a spectrum, some of which are included on the diagram below. Rather than just experiencing episodes of depression or mania, people with bipolar disorder can in fact experience various moods and symptoms that fall in between these two extremes, and this is why the illness was renamed *bipolar disorder*, implying that symptoms occur on a spectrum between the two poles of mania and depression.

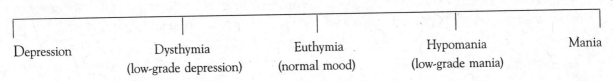

| Depression | Dysthymia (low-grade depression) | Euthymia (normal mood) | Hypomania (low-grade mania) | Mania |

We all have times in our lives when we feel sadness, we may have trouble coping, or we feel overwhelmed. The mood shifts that occur with bipolar disorder, however, are very different from the normal ups and downs that everyone experiences at times. The symptoms of bipolar disorder are much more severe and can result in damaged relationships, poor performance at school or in the workplace, and even suicide or other life-threatening behaviors.

For some people, the mood changes brought on by bipolar disorder can be dramatic. They can go very quickly from feeling euphoric or "high," or feeling extremely irritable, to feeling sad and hopeless. For others, however, the changes are not so severe or easily identified and can involve mild to moderate levels of mania, known as *hypomania*. For still others, both depression and mania can occur at the same time, leading to a tumultuous, chaotic experience of feeling extremely energetic but sad and hopeless at the same time. This is known as a *mixed episode*. I will describe these different forms of bipolar disorder in detail later in this chapter.

Usually, people experience periods of "normal" mood between these episodes (this is called *euthymia*), when they are neither manic nor depressed. While many people return to a fully functional level during these periods, many also continue to experience some symptoms, such as low mood (which, when lasting two years or more, is referred to as *dysthymia*), anxiety, or problems sleeping. This can continue to have an impact on relationships and on functioning in areas such as work and school.

Like diabetes, heart conditions, and many other physical conditions, bipolar disorder is a lifelong illness that requires careful and constant management with medication and other treatments, such as psychotherapy. When bipolar disorder is treated effectively, you can lead a healthy, productive life. The following sections will break down bipolar disorder into smaller parts so you can become more familiar with the illness and the specific symptoms you experience.

WHAT IS DEPRESSION?

As noted earlier, there are times in all of our lives when we experience feeling down, sad, or blue. Although we may sometimes say that we feel depressed, this is often not the case. Depression is an illness that encompasses all aspects of life. It impacts the way you behave, your mood, and your thoughts. It affects your eating habits, your patterns of sleep, the way you feel about yourself, and the way you see, think about, and perceive things.

The *Diagnostic and Statistical Manual of Mental Disorders* (American Psychiatric Association [APA] 2000), or *DSM*, is a book that provides criteria for diagnosing the various mental illnesses. It defines a *major depressive episode* as a period of at least two weeks of depressed mood or the loss of interest or pleasure in most activities. In addition, to meet criteria for a major depressive episode, a person must experience at least four other symptoms from a list that includes things such as changes in appetite or weight; changes in sleep; decreased energy; feelings of worthlessness or guilt; difficulty thinking, concentrating, or making decisions; recurrent thoughts of death; or suicidal thoughts, plans, or attempts. Major depression affects your ability to function in many aspects of your life.

■ *Patricia's Story*

Patricia had been having troubles sleeping for quite some time. She also wasn't enjoying things she used to and was feeling pretty irritable and not herself. She'd thought about it but couldn't figure out why she was feeling this way. She suddenly found that she was comparing herself to others, wondering what was wrong with her that she was no longer coping the way she used to and the way other people could. This, of course, made her feel worse about herself. Patricia continued to go through the motions, going to work every day and thinking that if she acted like everything was okay, maybe it would be. As time went on, however, her mood only worsened, and it became harder for her to keep pretending. Finally, beginning to feel guilty and hopeless that she would ever feel better, Patricia went to see her doctor, who told her she was experiencing a major depressive episode.

As you can see from this example, some people are able to continue functioning in at least some of their roles and can even sometimes mask their depression to such an extent that others don't realize that they're not feeling well. However, the longer you continue with this facade rather than seeking help, the more difficult things get and the more the depression will impact different areas of your life. Just because you can keep going like things are okay doesn't mean that things really *are* okay and you don't need help.

Sometimes you may find that you can get through an episode of depression without medications, while at other times you find that you just can't function well enough without them. If you've had recurrent bouts of depression, you may find that some are less severe, and you can get by without taking antidepressants, while at other times the episodes seem much worse. Remember that major depression is an illness, and taking medication for an illness is not a sign of weakness. You wouldn't question someone with high blood pressure taking blood pressure medications or someone with diabetes taking insulin. Instead of trying to tough it out, speak with your doctor to see if you need medications to help you through.

Depression Checklist

Take a moment to check off any of the symptoms below that you have had:

_____ Persistent low mood

_____ Increased appetite

_____ Difficulties falling asleep

_____ Feeling empty

_____ Social isolation

_____ Problems with memory

_____ Persistent anger

_____ Irritability

_____ Decrease in motivation

_____ Feelings of hopelessness

_____ Weight gain

_____ Waking early in the morning

_____ Restlessness

_____ Low self-esteem

_____ Tearfulness

_____ Loss of interest in things

_____ Aching limbs and muscles

_____ Decreased appetite

_____ Feelings of worthlessness

_____ Weight loss

_____ Loss of enjoyment in activities

_____ Poor concentration

_____ Thoughts of suicide

_____ Waking frequently during the night

_____ Decrease in energy

_____ Increased sleep

_____ Feelings of helplessness

_____ Feeling guilty

_____ Mental confusion

_____ Difficulty making decisions

_____ Inactivity

_____ Lethargy

_____ Dwelling on the past

_____ Persistent physical symptoms such as headaches, chronic pain, or stomach problems that do not respond well to treatment

Other symptoms of depression that you have experienced:

_____   _____

_____   _____

Remember that this is not a diagnostic tool—you may be having some of these symptoms and not be experiencing depression. If you are experiencing several of these symptoms and have not seen your doctor yet, I would encourage you to do so.

WHAT IS MANIA?

The *DSM* (APA 2000) defines a *manic episode* as a distinct period when there is an unusually and persistently high (or euphoric) or irritable mood that lasts for at least one week (unless the person is hospitalized, in which case it can last for less than one week). In addition, to meet criteria for a manic episode, the *DSM* specifies that at least three other symptoms must be experienced from a list that includes inflated self-esteem or grandiosity (a sense of being better or more important than others), decreased need for sleep, nonstop talking, distractibility, increased activity or agitation, and excessive involvement in pleasurable activities that are likely to result in negative or painful consequences (for example, using drugs or alcohol, engaging in risky behaviors such as gambling or sexual promiscuity, or overspending).

The experience of mania can be a double-edged sword: after you experience an episode of depression, it's natural to enjoy lifting out of this low mood and experiencing feeling happy and energetic. At its extreme, however, mania can be incredibly dangerous and destructive. Manic episodes can lead to behaviors such as those listed above, which cause problems with family, friends, the community, and the law. Making these problems even worse is the fact that, during a manic episode, you may be unable to understand that you are ill because you feel great; this could even lead you to refuse hospitalization or other means of support.

■ *Carla's Story*

Carla was nineteen years old and living at home with her parents, with whom she had always had a healthy relationship. Gradually, however, Carla's parents began to notice changes in her behavior. She started staying out much later at night, often coming home in the early morning. She became involved with a much older man who was a member of a well-known motorcycle club, and her parents could smell marijuana on her clothing when she returned home early in the morning. Carla stayed in her bedroom much of the time and had quit her job. She told her parents that she had started her own Internet business and was already earning thousands of dollars. When her parents voiced their concerns about her behavioral changes, Carla became extremely angry and aggressive toward her father. After that confrontation, their relationship continued to deteriorate, and Carla's mood became more and more unpredictable. Finally, not knowing what else to do, Carla's parents brought her to a hospital. The diagnosis was that Carla was experiencing a manic episode, and she was kept in the hospital involuntarily in order to be stabilized on medications.

Mania Checklist

Look at the following list of symptoms of mania and check off those you have experienced:

____	Elevated mood	____	Decreased need for sleep
____	Scattered thoughts	____	Increase in activity
____	Feelings of euphoria	____	Inflated self-esteem
____	Being overly friendly or outgoing	____	Irritability
____	Racing thoughts	____	Use of drugs or alcohol
____	Agitation	____	Gambling
____	Spending large amounts of money	____	Increased sexual drive
____	Driving fast or dangerously	____	Talking very fast
____	Inability to sit still	____	Inability to relax
____	Unsafe sexual practices	____	Physically aching all over
____	Rapid, unpredictable emotional changes	____	Thrill seeking
____	Socially unacceptable behavior	____	Lack of control
____	Ignoring responsibilities	____	Shoplifting
____	Feeling paranoid	____	Excessive energy
____	Little need for food	____	Poor judgment
____	Increased sociability	____	Confused thoughts
____	Verbal or physical aggression	____	Seeing, hearing, or otherwise sensing things that aren't there

Other symptoms of mania that you have experienced:

_____	_____
_____	_____
_____	_____

Again, this is not a tool with which to diagnose yourself. If you think you may be experiencing some of the symptoms of mania, you should see a medical professional as soon as possible.

WHAT IS HYPOMANIA?

Some people with bipolar disorder don't experience manic episodes but do have times when their mood is somewhat elevated. This is known as hypomania, and people tend to experience these episodes more often than manic episodes for two reasons: full-blown manic episodes tend to be less common, and hypomania often comes before full-blown mania in people who do experience the severe highs. The symptoms of hypomania are the same as those for a manic episode, but according to the *DSM* they are less severe, last only a minimum of four days rather than one week, and do not include the delusions or hallucinations that sometimes occur in mania. Unlike manic episodes, when you are hypomanic, you usually remain aware of the changes in yourself, and you are therefore more able to prevent yourself from acting on the urges and impulses you are experiencing.

According to the *DSM*, the best way to differentiate between a manic and hypomanic episode is the degree of impairment caused. Mania is diagnosed when symptoms are present to such an extent that hospitalization is required to keep you safe or when symptoms are at least severe enough to be causing significant problems in your life (for example, inability to work or go to school; legal problems due to reckless behaviors such as dangerous driving; or relationship problems due to impulsivity, such as sexual promiscuity or compulsive spending). During a hypomanic episode, on the other hand, you may have some of the symptoms of mania and may experience the urge to engage in these kinds of destructive behaviors, but you are able to remain in control of yourself and not act on these urges.

Here are some other ways to tell the difference between a manic and hypomanic episode (Benazzi 2007):

- A manic episode usually lasts longer than a hypomanic episode.

- Mania substantially impairs your functioning, where as hypomania often actually improves functioning (for example, you have more energy and so are able to get more things done in a day), or at worst causes only mild impairment.

- When manic, your thoughts become speedy and disconnected, and your speech becomes fast and nonstop. In a hypomanic episode, the thoughts might be described as racing or crowded, but not to the same extent as in mania, and these thoughts are often also described as creative.

- Mania is associated with aimless overactivity, such as starting many different projects and not really getting anything done, whereas hypomania often leads to an increase in goal-directed activities—in other words, you are able to achieve more.

As with a manic episode, you may welcome hypomania as a relief from depression or simply because of the increase in energy and good feelings that hypomania often brings with it. You may feel that in this state you can get more done and are more creative, so you may be reluctant to seek treatment to bring it to an end. This makes it especially important to be aware that, while not a full-blown manic episode, it is possible for hypomania to turn into one if left untreated. For people who never experience full-blown manias, a hypomanic episode left unchecked often leads to a crash into a depression.

Kevin's Story

Kevin was a successful account manager at a busy firm that required him to work long hours. He described his business as competitive and had aspirations to become the director of his department, which drove him to put in even longer hours. Kevin was also a father of three, and he prided himself on his ability to work long hours and still manage to attend his kids' soccer and baseball games. If this meant that he needed to regularly work from home into the early hours of the morning, Kevin was okay with that. He found that he needed little sleep, anyway.

When Kevin's wife, Kelly, finally grew tired of her husband's absence from the home and made the decision to move out with the children, Kevin crashed. He began drinking to fill the void left by his family, and one night, feeling depressed and hopeless, he attempted to kill himself.

Kevin was taken to the hospital in time to save his life and was subsequently diagnosed with bipolar disorder. Looking back armed with information about his diagnosis, Kevin was able to recognize that he had probably been in and out of hypomanic episodes for about three years.

WHAT IS A MIXED EPISODE?

The *DSM* defines a mixed episode as a period of at least one week during which the criteria for both a manic episode and a major depressive episode are met. Here, a person experiences rapidly changing moods such as sadness, anger, and extreme happiness, accompanied by the previously listed symptoms of a manic episode and a major depressive episode. The symptoms experienced in a mixed episode often include agitation, irregular appetite, insomnia, psychotic symptoms, and suicidal thoughts. Mixed episodes can be more difficult to identify because of the wide array of symptoms involved, but proper medical treatment is even more essential with these episodes, because the outcome for people experiencing them is poorer than for other forms of bipolar disorder (Strakowski et al. 2000).

WHAT IS PSYCHOSIS?

Sometimes, severe episodes of mania or depression can result in symptoms of psychosis. The term *psychosis* basically refers to a loss of touch with reality. Common psychotic symptoms include *hallucinations*, when people hear, see, or otherwise sense things that aren't actually there. Sometimes people are aware that these are hallucinations, depending on the degree of psychosis.

A second common symptom of psychosis is the presence of *delusions*, defined as false, strongly held beliefs that cannot be explained by the person's cultural or religious beliefs and that are not influenced by logical reasoning (APA 2000). When a person is in a delusional state, he is unable to recognize that his beliefs are false, even when presented with evidence that clearly contradicts those beliefs. In my early years as a mental health worker, someone explained to me that trying to convince someone he was delusional would be like someone trying to convince me that I had never gone to university. To that person, the delusion *is* reality.

Once you have entered a psychotic state, the delusions you experience often prevent you from recognizing that you are ill and in need of hospitalization in order to become stabilized on medication. One common delusion, for example, is the paranoid delusion: the belief that others are out to get you. This can lead to ideas related to medical treatment—for example, that people are trying to keep you medicated in order to control you; that your medications are actually poison; or that you are being kept in the hospital as part of some kind of conspiracy. As a result, you may become distrustful of family members, friends, and mental health professionals who are trying to help you.

In addition, the hallucinations sometimes experienced in these states can be very frightening, further alienating you from people who are trying to help. Sometimes this can result in you becoming involved in the criminal justice system or being admitted involuntarily to a hospital. For example, I once worked with someone who was stopped by the police for driving dangerously while he was trying to get away from "devils" that were chasing him. In his terrified and incoherent state, the police assumed he had been using drugs and he was taken to jail. He was subsequently hospitalized involuntarily.

It's important to remember that not everyone with bipolar disorder will experience psychosis. While this information can be frightening, I have included it because the sooner a psychotic episode is treated, the quicker it will be resolved. One of the most important aspects of treating bipolar disorder is arming yourself with information so that you and your loved ones will be more able to recognize what is happening and get treatment quickly.

DIFFERENT TYPES OF BIPOLAR DISORDER

In my work with people with bipolar disorder, I have found it quite common that they know very little about their illness. Often this is because receiving such a diagnosis can be overwhelming, and people frequently don't know what questions to ask to best help themselves. Have you tried to educate yourself about bipolar disorder? Are you someone who is still questioning whether or not you have been given the correct diagnosis? Having such an illness can be a very difficult thing to accept. Maybe, because symptoms can vary so much from the traditional conceptualization of the illness as consisting only of manic and depressive episodes, you can't relate to the diagnosis because you haven't had full-blown mania or depression. As I mentioned earlier, it is becoming more evident to professionals that bipolar disorder often consists of more than just the extreme highs and extreme lows in mood—that, in fact, there are many symptoms outside of these variations in mood that characterize different types of the illness. Some researchers have proposed that the diagnosis of bipolar disorder should be changed to "bipolar spectrum disorder" to fully capture the wide range of symptoms that can be experienced by different people with the illness (Ghaemi, Ko, and Goodwin 2002).

On the other hand, perhaps you are a person who accepts the diagnosis, but you don't have an accurate understanding of what it means. You might be unsure about what bipolar symptoms are, what might be symptoms of a separate, co-occurring disorder such as anxiety, and what is "normal" and completely unrelated to any disorder. This knowledge is extremely important in order for you to learn what you need to do to prevent *relapses* (the recurrence of symptoms) and to cope with manic, hypomanic, and depressive episodes. To help you understand what form of the illness you have, I have outlined the current categories of the illness below, as defined by the *DSM*.

Bipolar I

Bipolar I is the traditional, most widely recognized form of bipolar disorder, usually involving recurrent episodes of mania and depression, although about 10 percent of people with this diagnosis never suffer major depression (Frank and Thase 1999). In order to receive a diagnosis of bipolar I, you must have experienced one or more full-blown manic episodes that cannot be attributed to the use of alcohol or drugs (including antidepressants, which can sometimes cause someone to flip into a manic state), or to other general medical conditions. It is not uncommon for people with this form of bipolar to experience psychotic symptoms, as described above.

Bipolar II

Bipolar II involves periods of major depression and at least one period of hypomania. If you have had these severe changes in mood but have never experienced symptoms of a full-blown manic episode, you generally receive a diagnosis of bipolar II. People with this form of bipolar do not experience psychotic symptoms and do not require hospitalization for their symptoms when hypomanic. Over time, a small number of people with bipolar II shift to bipolar I due to the onset of mania.

Cyclothymia

According to the *DSM*, *cyclothymia* is when a person experiences long-term problems with fluctuating moods involving numerous periods of hypomania and periods of depressive symptoms. When they manifest, however, these symptoms are not severe enough to be diagnosed as a manic or major depressive episode. Cyclothymia can therefore be seen as a milder form of bipolar disorder, involving upswings that are similar to hypomania and downswings in mood that are fairly mild forms of depression. These episodes alternate throughout a person's life; but because a small number of such people develop full-blown bipolar disorder (either type I or II), this diagnosis is only given when a person experiences at least two years of these symptoms without the emergence of a manic or major depressive episode.

These are the current classifications of bipolar disorder. Because of the wide spectrum of symptoms that occur, the illness in its milder forms can be quite difficult to diagnose. In fact, more than two-thirds of the membership of a depression and bipolar support group in the United States reported that they had initially been misdiagnosed and treated for mental illnesses other than bipolar disorder, with the average time between the initial onset of symptoms and receiving a correct diagnosis of bipolar being approximately nine years (Thase 2006). In part, this can be attributed to the fact that the symptoms vary so widely from one person to the next, meaning that there really is no longer a standard presentation of bipolar disorder. Now let's look at how bipolar disorder develops.

CAUSES OF BIPOLAR DISORDER

The question of why some people develop bipolar disorder has yet to be fully answered, although scientists continue to generate new information and theories. Most mental health professionals believe that mental illness in general is caused by a combination of several factors working together. In bipolar disorder, these causal factors are usually divided into biological and psychological issues—in other words, the main reasons the illness develops are biological (including genetics and physical characteristics) and environmental (including how we deal with emotions and the way we think about things).

Biological Factors

Research has found a strong genetic component to bipolar disorder—that is, to some extent, bipolar is inherited. For example, depending on how you choose to define bipolar disorder, the concordance rates from studies of identical twins varies from 50 percent to almost 100 percent. In other words, if one twin has bipolar disorder, the other is 50 to 100 percent likely to also have it (Stoll et al. 2000). Thinking about this genetic component, consider the following questions.

1. Does anyone in your family have a diagnosis of bipolar disorder? If so, who?

_____

_____

2. Even if they have never been diagnosed, can you see symptoms in any of your family members (don't forget about grandparents, aunts, uncles, and cousins)? Consider these symptoms, which are often noticed by others:

    ■ Depressed mood

    ■ Drug or alcohol abuse

    ■ Risky behaviors

    ■ High energy

    ■ Little need for sleep

    ■ Variable mood

    ■ Cyclical moods

_____

_____

Genetics, however, is clearly not the only link. This point is clear when you consider the fact that even being an identical twin does not *guarantee* that both siblings will either have or not have bipolar disorder.

In recent years, technological developments (such as MRI scans) have allowed researchers to study the brains of people with bipolar disorder. While a single causal factor has not been found in people with the illness, abnormalities have been found in areas of the brain that are thought to be related to different aspects of emotional behavior (Vawter, Freed, and Kleinman 2000). In addition, it is strongly suspected that chemicals in a person's brain play a part in bipolar disorder. You may have heard reference to neurotransmitters. Although bipolar disorder is often referred to as an imbalance of these brain chemicals, doctors have been unable to pinpoint the exact role these chemicals play in the development and maintenance of the disorder. So while we still don't know exactly what the biological links are, it is widely accepted that they do play a part.

Stress Triggers

Among the psychological issues, stressful life events and the way a person copes with these stresses are thought to be the main elements that lead to the onset of symptoms in bipolar disorder. Examples of such triggers include a death in the family, loss of a job, and the birth of a child. These triggers obviously cannot be precisely defined, since what is stressful for one person may not be for another. Once the disorder is triggered, however, it progresses and develops a life of its own, so to speak. In other words, once the cycle begins, psychological and/or biological processes take over and keep the illness active.

Determining when and how your illness started can be very helpful. It gives you a starting point for life charting (which will be discussed in the next section) so that you can increase your awareness of the patterns of and triggers for your illness. Being more aware of these patterns and triggers will help you to be more prepared to deal with relapses.

For many people with bipolar I, the memory of their first manic episode is etched in their brain and they can recall in minute detail what happened and how they ended up in the hospital. For people with other forms of the illness, because symptoms of hypomania can be so subtle, it is often not so easy to figure out when and how the symptoms first began. Have a look at the following questions to see if you can determine when your illness first became part of your life.

1. How old were you when you first recall feeling really sad or extremely down and these feelings didn't seem connected to a specific situation?

_____

2. What was happening in your life? Were you in school? Were you working?

_____

_____

3. Where were you living at the time and with whom?

_____

_____

4. What stressors, if any, were happening in your life at that time (for instance, the birth of a new sibling or child, relationship problems with family or friends, difficulties at school or work, changes in residence, or the death of a family member, friend, or pet)?

_____

_____

_____

_____

5. How old were you when you had your first manic or hypomanic episode?

_____

6. Keep in mind that hypomania can be more difficult to recall, as the symptoms are more subtle. If you're not sure when your first hypomanic episode occurred, try to recall if there was a time in your life when:

   a. You needed much less sleep and had more energy than usual? (Age) _____

   b. Your mood was happier than usual? (Age) _____

   c. You had much more confidence in yourself and were more outgoing and sociable with others? (Age) _____

   d. You were using drugs or drinking alcohol excessively? (Age) _____

   e. You were engaging in risky behaviors like driving dangerously, gambling, or having unprotected sex? (Age) _____

   f. People commented that you didn't seem to be yourself, or called you arrogant or egotistical? (Age) _____

If you cannot recall the answer to these questions, try asking family members or friends who have known you for a long time. This information can help you to understand when the illness first presented itself, and the stressors that may have contributed to its development.

Putting It All Together: The Diathesis-Stress Model

When we look for the cause of bipolar disorder, it is clear that we can't put our finger on one simple factor. Instead, the best explanation according to the research available at this time is what is termed the diathesis-stress model (Frank and Thase 1999). The word "diathesis" means that a person has a physical condition (or a gene) that makes her more than usually susceptible to certain diseases. Just because this vulnerability is present, however, doesn't guarantee that the person will develop the illness. It must be triggered by something (a stressor) in order for the illness to manifest.

According to the diathesis-stress model, each person inherits certain physical vulnerabilities to problems that may or may not appear, depending on what stresses occur in her life. So, the bottom line according to today's thinking is that if you have bipolar disorder, you were born with the possibility of developing the disorder, and an event took place in your life to set it off.

LIFE CHARTING

It is essential to be as familiar with your illness and symptoms as possible. I hope the exercises above got you thinking about when your illness started. Life charting helps you to take a more in-depth historical look at how you have experienced your illness since its onset, as well as helping you to keep track of current episodes as they happen. This may allow you to see if patterns emerge that might help you better prepare for future episodes. Take a look at the following example, in which the straight line in the middle represents a stable or euthymic mood. Depressive episodes are therefore represented by curves below the baseline, and manic and hypomanic episodes are represented by a spike above the baseline. The more severe the depression or mania, the more pronounced the spike will be. The longer the episode lasts, the wider the curved line will be, providing a timeline that is as accurate as possible. If you experience mixed episodes, you can draw a squiggly line across the midline to represent this, or of course you can come up with your own way of depicting all of these events so that they are understandable to you.

Theresa's Life Chart

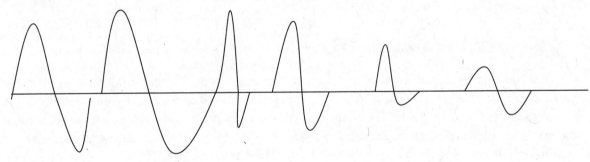

Spring 2004:	Spring 2004:	Summer 2004	Fall 2004	Spring 2005	Spring 2006
1st episode	Off meds	Drug use	Med change	Drug use	
Started school					

Theresa began life charting when she was twenty-four, three years after she'd been diagnosed with her first manic episode. Her illness had been quite tumultuous, worsened by her use of cocaine to try to improve her mood when she was feeling depressed. The first manic episode she charted (spring 2004) was related to the stressor of going to school and living away from home for the first time, which Theresa noted on her chart. Theresa had been hospitalized at that point, and the manic episode was quickly followed by depression, which she recovered from while she was still in the hospital. Upon discharge, however, Theresa decided she didn't want to stay on the medication that had been prescribed for her because she was experiencing side effects and felt overmedicated. This quickly led to Theresa's second hospitalization with a manic episode, again followed by depression that she was still recovering from when she was discharged. At this point, feeling quite low, Theresa used cocaine for the first time in an attempt to make herself feel better. This immediately resulted in a manic episode and her third hospitalization. Fortunately, because treatment began quickly, the manic episode didn't last long. Theresa recovered fairly quickly from the depression that followed and had a period of time when her mood was normal. However, a change in her medications in the fall of 2004 led to another manic episode, but again treatment began quickly, and it didn't take long for Theresa to recover. Since then, Theresa has experienced two more manic episodes (one related to drug use) and had to be hospitalized, but she was able to recover fairly quickly.

Over time, as Theresa continued to chart her episodes, she came to see some patterns. For example, she noted that whenever she used street drugs she experienced an episode of mania, which resulted in hospitalization. Also, a depressive episode always followed a manic episode for her, and her manic episodes (when not connected to drug use) seemed to occur in the spring. She also noted that episodes happened less frequently when she remained on her medication. Theresa continues to chart episodes as they occur in her life and finds this helpful.

Life charting can be incredibly useful to help detect patterns in your episodes (for example, some people notice they tend to experience manic or depressive episodes at certain times of the year); to connect the episodes to triggers (for example, drug use, or stressful life events such as relationship difficulties); and to help you and your care providers understand which medications and other treatments have been effective in helping to control your symptoms and prevent further episodes from occurring. For Theresa, life charting helped her to increase her awareness of her symptoms, which in turn actually helped to decrease the number of relapses she experienced. Because she became aware of her triggers and patterns, she stopped using illicit drugs and is more aware of symptoms as they begin, which allows her to seek treatment much earlier than before.

How to Do Your Own Life Chart

Your life chart is something you can tailor to suit your needs. It's important that it's clear and understandable so that you can use it to see patterns of your illness and to guide your treatment. The following steps are suggestions for how to create your own life chart and things you might want to include in the chart to make it most useful. They are based on guidelines set out by Monica Ramirez Basco in *The Bipolar Workbook: Tools for Controlling Your Mood Swings* (2006):

1. Taking a blank piece of paper, draw a straight, horizontal line across the middle of the page. This is your timeline, and the beginning of this line will indicate either the beginning of your illness or as far back as you can remember. Start with the very first episode you can recall, and plot it on the timeline (some people find it easier to start with the most recent episode they've experienced; do whatever works best for you). Indicate the date (or the season and year) the episode occurred, or if you can't recall dates, the age you were at that time.

As we saw demonstrated in Theresa's life chart, depressive episodes can be indicated by drawing a line that curves beneath the timeline, and a line above the timeline would indicate an elevated mood. For brief episodes, the line will be shorter; for longer episodes, it will stretch over a longer section of the timeline. Remember, if you experience mixed episodes, you can denote this on the chart with a squiggly line that goes back and forth over the timeline or in any other way that will be understandable to you.

2. Continue to chart all of the episodes you can recall in the same way.

3. Note on your timeline any periods of alcohol or drug use, as well as any major life events that occurred, such as any losses you experienced (Ramirez Basco 2006). Life events could include things such as deaths, change in jobs, having to quit school, financial losses, changes in family (births, deaths, marriages, and so on), physical problems (such as accidents or illness), other mental health problems that might have arisen (such as the development of an anxiety disorder), or any other events that you think had a strong negative or positive impact on your life.

4. Include any information you can recall about your treatment, including hospitalizations, medications (whether you started new ones or stopped taking your meds), courses of psychotherapy, and so on.

In order to make your life chart as comprehensive as possible, consider asking people you trust, such as your psychiatrist or family doctor, family, and friends to help you recall episodes and events that have occurred in your life.

MOOD CHARTING

We've already talked about the importance of increasing your awareness of symptoms as one way of helping to decrease the number of relapses you have. The more aware you are of how you feel, the more likely you will be to notice when you begin to experience symptoms of depression or mania. While life charting helps you to do this in the long term by looking at the bigger picture, keeping track of your mood on a daily basis is a way to help you increase awareness of your symptoms over a shorter period of time.

Many people walk around kind of oblivious to how they're feeling. They may be aware that they're having an off day or that they're feeling down, but they rarely give it much more thought than that. This lack of awareness is generally quite common and certainly unhelpful to those without bipolar disorder. But for people with the illness, this lack of awareness could land you in the hospital. A mood chart helps you to keep track of how you feel on a daily basis.

Following is a sample mood chart, but there are many different ones to choose from. If you don't particularly like the one I've included here, you can make your own or have a look online to find more choices.

Looking at the sample mood chart below, you'll see that the word "stable" is in the middle of the chart. This refers to the state you experience when your mood is neither depressed nor manic, but euthymic—your normal mood. If you find that your mood is elevated, you would chart accordingly, above stable for that day. If you're feeling down, you would likewise chart below stable to reflect your mood as accurately as possible. This mood chart also has a row to keep track of whether or not you have taken your medication as prescribed. It's extremely important to take your meds, and neglecting to do so will have obvious impacts on your mood. An additional row allows you to track the number of hours you slept the previous night. This can help you both to identify if there is any relation between your mood and the amount of sleep you're getting and help you identify sleep as a possible emerging symptom. For example, if you experience sleep difficulties when becoming manic or depressed, seeing your sleep patterns in relation to your mood could be an early-warning system for you if you notice that your sleep starts to become disrupted.

Keep in mind that while these types of exercises may seem cumbersome, they can prevent relapses, which could involve hospitalization and many other negative consequences. It's worthwhile to put in a little extra effort to keep yourself safe and healthy.

IMPACTS OF BIPOLAR DISORDER

If you have bipolar disorder, you are likely already aware of the multifaceted effects the illness can have on your life. This illness is not just a case of having greater variability in your mood than the average person. The effects that this variability causes are significant and can be life altering. Let's take a look at some examples.

School and Work

If you have experienced a depressive episode, you know the feeling of fatigue, being drained, and not having the energy or the motivation to do the things you need to do. Add this to the fact that depression can affect your ability to concentrate, solve problems, and make decisions, and it becomes quite obvious that going to school or work and performing up to your usual standards will be quite difficult when you're feeling depressed.

Going to work or school in a manic episode is just as problematic. The first challenge is making it to work, since you're feeling great and thinking about how much of your energy and creativity will be wasted on menial tasks. Next, you'll face difficulties concentrating, and chances are you'll be unable to slow your thoughts down enough to complete any goal-oriented activity. In addition to these problems, there are the conflicts that often arise. For example, you may be more irritable, or maybe you're feeling so good about yourself (to the point of feeling better than others) that you find yourself interacting with others in a negative way, damaging relationships. Or you may be using substances, further limiting your ability to function at school or work. This is often noticed by teachers or employers and could result in you being suspended from school or losing your job. It's a fact that people with bipolar disorder receive less education and lower wages than those without the diagnosis, and that they use more sick time and rely more on disability pensions, including worker's compensation (Leahy 2007).

Mood Chart

Month: _____

Year: _____

Day	1	2	3	4	5	6	7	8	9	10	11	12	13	14	15	16	17	18	19	20	21	22	23	24	25	26	27	28	29	30	31
Severely elevated																															
Moderately elevated																															
Mildly elevated																															
STABLE																															
Mildly depressed																															
Moderately depressed																															
Severely depressed																															
Took medication																															
Hours of sleep																															

Self-examination can be difficult, but it can also motivate you to try new things and work hard to make changes. So take a minute and think about the following questions in relation to work and school. Are these areas of your life suffering because of your illness? Below, write yes or no as appropriate.

_____ Has your performance at school or work suffered recently?

_____ Are you having trouble with concentration or memory, which may be impacting your work?

_____ Has your behavior caused problems in your relationships at school or work recently or in the past?

_____ Have you lost jobs or been kicked out of school because of these behaviors?

Relationships

People with bipolar disorder also have higher rates of divorce (Leahy 2007). Relationships are affected in all sorts of different ways when you have bipolar disorder. To begin with, most people who have not had prior experience with bipolar disorder don't understand the illness and the impact it has on your behavior. They may tend to attribute blame where symptoms have actually been at fault. This is not to say that when you have bipolar disorder all your behaviors are excused by your symptoms. But there is a point at which you become much less able to control yourself, or the desire to control yourself lessens and you become disinhibited because of the mania. So one impact on relationships can be that a lack of information results in a lack of understanding on the part of the person you're in the relationship with, so the person gets fed up with you and leaves.

A second problem arises from the behaviors themselves. For example, a spouse may have lived with his partner who has bipolar disorder for many years and has always been able to understand and cope with it. The breaking point may come, however, when the spouse with bipolar disorder begins engaging in behaviors such as sexual promiscuity, gambling, or substance abuse, that are unacceptable to the nonbipolar spouse, even though he is aware it is part of the illness. Understandably, when a person's life or quality of life is at risk, even if it's largely a result of the illness, he must take care of his own safety. What symptoms have you experienced that have been problematic and have led to relationships ending or being damaged?

_____

_____

_____

_____ Have you lost relationships because of how you have behaved?

_____ Do you communicate with the people you care about?

_____ Do you have a tendency to push those people away?

_____ Do you have healthy relationships in your life?

_____ Are you satisfied with the quality of the relationships in your life?

Substance Abuse

Do you use drugs or alcohol on a regular basis? If you do, you're not alone. It is a fact that people with bipolar disorder use substances at a higher rate than people without the illness. For example, Susan Altman and her colleagues (2006) reported that more than 60 percent of people with a diagnosis of bipolar I and 48 percent of those with bipolar II also met criteria for a diagnosis of substance abuse or dependence. Quite often, people use drugs (including prescription medications) and alcohol to help them deal with the symptoms of their bipolar disorder.

Is this you? To help you sort this out, I've provided some questions for you to consider. Mark each with a yes or a no.

Do you drink or use drugs:

_____ To help yourself feel less depressed?

_____ To help with problems sleeping?

_____ In an attempt to calm yourself down?

_____ To try to slow your thoughts so you can think more clearly?

_____ Because you're having difficulties in relationships and the substances help you feel better about the problems and yourself?

If you answered yes to one or more of these questions, you are probably using substances to help cope with your bipolar disorder.

On the other hand, some people with bipolar disorder drink or use drugs because it is a _symptom_ of the illness. Drinking and using drugs can be an example of the impulsive, risky behavior that sometimes occurs during a manic episode, when the illness tends to trigger urges to be involved in activities that are dangerous or exciting. Or substance use can occur when the illness prevents you from accessing the frame of mind that allows you to consider the consequences of your actions.

Is this you? Ask yourself the following questions and mark each with yes or no:

_____ Do you tend to have the urge to use drugs or alcohol more often when you're in a manic episode?

_____ Are you using drugs or alcohol because you want to live on the edge or have more excitement in your life?

_____ Are you drinking or using drugs because life seems dull and you're trying to spice it up?

_____ Are you drinking or using drugs because you want to hold on to the euphoric feelings that often accompany a manic episode?

If you said yes to one or more of these questions, it is likely that substance use is a *symptom* of your illness, rather than a way of coping with it. Of course, for some people substance use is both a coping behavior and a symptom. But awareness of how you're using substances will effect which skills you will use to deal with this additional problem. (We'll examine this issue more closely when you get to the sections of this workbook that focus on skills.)

Using drugs and alcohol can have obvious negative consequences even for people without a diagnosis of bipolar disorder. If you do have the disorder, the problems that substance use creates are much greater: use of drugs or alcohol can bring on an episode of mania or depression; it can prolong the duration of the episode once it has started; it can shorten the length of time of remission from bipolar disorder, when you're experiencing a euthymic or normal mood; it can cause symptoms to be more severe than they would be otherwise; and it can make the mania or depression more difficult to treat (Altman et al. 2006). If you have bipolar disorder and are also dealing with substance use, I highly recommend that you make reducing your use a priority in order to create the possibility of a better outcome for your bipolar disorder.

Suicidality

Unfortunately, suicide is a very real concern for people with a diagnosis of bipolar disorder. Rates of suicide attempts in people with bipolar disorder have been documented to be as high as 50 percent (Rizvi and Zaretsky 2007), and lifetime rates for completing suicide are reported to be 60 times higher than for the general population (Leahy 2007).

Thoughts of suicide can be related to a depressive episode, when things seem like they'll never get better and you're feeling hopeless about the future and helpless to make changes. According to Michael Thase (2005), 70 percent of suicides in bipolar patients occur during a depressive or mixed episode. But suicidal thoughts can also occur at other times; for example, coming out of a manic episode in which you've engaged in behaviors that have destroyed a relationship, triggering feelings of remorse and guilt that lead to despair and thoughts of death.

Do you have suicidal thoughts on a regular basis? If you do, have you told your doctor or psychiatrist? It's important to make people aware if this is a problem and to develop a crisis plan for yourself to prevent these thoughts from taking over. We'll look much more closely at this topic in the section of this workbook on crisis survival skills (chapter 5). If suicidal thoughts or behaviors are currently a problem for you, you may want to turn to that section now.

YOU ARE NOT YOUR ILLNESS

Now that you have a better idea of how your illness is affecting you, I have one more thing to share with you that is vitally important. Even though you *have* bipolar disorder, you are much more than that—*you are not your illness.* Many people with any type of mental health problem often begin to identify themselves as that illness; for example, people with depression who say, "I am depressed," as though depressed is all they are. Most people with bipolar disorder live their lives as though they are a walking disorder. Take a look at the following diagram (Velyvis 2007) to illustrate this point. The big circle is you; the smaller circles are different parts of you—for example, one circle would be bipolar disorder. You may also suffer from an anxiety disorder, which would be a second circle; and the third circle could be alcohol use. These are all *parts* of who you are, but they are not you.

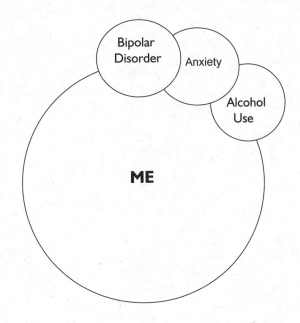

Family and friends can also contribute to this problem. When was the last time someone said to you, "Calm down, you're getting manic," when you thought you were simply excited about something? This can be frustrating, and you may find yourself starting to believe that all of your emotions are wrong and are caused by your illness. But that's not the case.

Bipolar disorder is like diabetes. Everyone experiences normal ups and downs in their blood sugar levels; people with diabetes need to get to know what the regular ups and downs are and what is actually being caused by their disorder (Velyvis 2007). Having a heart condition is also a good analogy. When we are exercising, or when we get excited, anxious, or angry, we all experience variations in our heart rate. People with a heart condition must get to know these variations so they can tell the difference between what is normal for them and what is due to their heart condition.

People with bipolar disorder do experience normal emotions. They become sad when someone they care about moves away, and this is not depression. They become excited when they are looking forward to attending an event, and this is not mania. What is important is for you to start to learn which emotions are normal for you and which are due to your illness. We'll discuss how you can start doing this later in the workbook.

For now, take a look at the following list to help you identify who else you are, in addition to being someone with bipolar disorder. Check off all that apply:

_____ Son or daughter	_____ Artist	_____ Worker
_____ Musician	_____ Pet owner	_____ Sibling
_____ Parent	_____ Teacher	_____ Listener
_____ Nature lover	_____ Athlete	_____ Friend
_____ Volunteer	_____ Grandchild	_____ Aunt or uncle
_____ Writer	_____ Poet	_____ Photographer
_____ Collector	_____ Advisor	_____ Scholar
_____ Reader	_____ Neighbor	_____ Grandparent
_____ Partner or spouse	_____ Caregiver	_____ Comedian
_____ Movie critic	_____ Theatre goer	_____ Traveler
_____ Employer	_____ Supervisor	_____ Speaker
_____ Niece or nephew	_____ Cousin	_____ Acquaintance

Who else are you?

_____   _____   _____

_____   _____   _____

_____   _____   _____

TREATMENT OPTIONS

Although you are not your illness, your illness definitely does have certain consequences for you. One of those consequences is that you do require treatment. For most people with bipolar, medication is required for the rest of their lives, although psychotherapy can also help to mediate the extent to which the illness will affect you. In this section I will explain what your options are for treatment, starting with a general note about medication.

Medication

If you have a diagnosis of bipolar disorder, you have probably been prescribed one or more medications to help control your symptoms. While there are many things you can do that will help decrease the likelihood of relapse and also help with the symptoms you continue to experience when you're not in a manic or depressive episode, it is important to understand that, because this illness has a biological component, medication is the cornerstone of treatment. Just like the person with diabetes or a heart condition, you *must* take medication to keep you as healthy as possible.

There is a very high chance that, should you stop taking your medication, you will experience a relapse. Many people experience relapses even when they have remained on their medications, because at times our bodies change and what was once the right medication or dosage may no longer work as effectively as it did before. Also, many people with the diagnosis of bipolar disorder experience breakthrough symptoms, which means that, even when you're not experiencing an episode of depression, mania, or hypomania, you may still be experiencing some symptoms of one or more of these states. So, while they're not diagnosable as an episode, the symptoms can still be bothersome and sometimes even impairing.

Having said that, I know that many people have a difficult time accepting the idea that taking medication is necessary. Many medications have unpleasant side effects. Some people simply have negative ideas about what it means to be dependent on such medications. Some people might find themselves pressured by others to not take their medications due to a lack of understanding of the diagnosis and the purpose of the medications. Whatever the reasons may be that deter you from taking your medications as prescribed, remember that when you *don't*, you are risking depression, mania, and all of the problematic behaviors that accompany these episodes. Think about how these things have affected you in the past. Are you really willing to risk having to experience these problems again? It is, of course, your choice—but it is a decision you must weigh carefully.

If you are having difficulties remembering to take your medications, if you don't like the side effects you are experiencing, or if you're simply wondering if you really need to be on all these medications, *please talk to your doctor or psychiatrist.* This decision is too important to make on your own; you need as much support and information as possible in order to act in your own best interests.

Psychotherapy

You read earlier in this chapter that there is a strong biological component, including genes and possibly brain structure, to bipolar disorder. So you may be wondering how a nonbiological therapy can help. Well, we know that stress plays a big part in bipolar, and there is considerable evidence that stressful life events, the way you cope with those events, and your family environment (including the way your family supports you with respect to stressful events) contribute to the development of manic and depressive episodes (Leahy 2007). In fact, bipolar disorder is not only worsened by those stressful life events, but it can also be the cause of them (for example, depression or mania can result in you losing your job or the breakup of a relationship). Since this is the case, if you tend to view these events from a negative perspective (the glass is half empty), if you don't have the ability to regulate your emotions or resolve conflicts in relationships, and if you don't have healthy coping skills, you are going to be more likely to experience bipolar episodes (Leahy 2007).

Although the research on the use of psychotherapy for bipolar disorder is fairly limited, there are some treatments that seem to be effective. I'll tell you about two that have been studied: cognitive behavioral therapy and interpersonal social rhythm therapy. Then I'll tell you why I think dialectical behavior therapy will be even more effective than these two treatments.

Cognitive Behavioral Therapy

Cognitive behavioral therapy (CBT) focuses on how you think and act and the connection between your thoughts, behaviors, and emotions. CBT is used to treat bipolar disorder because it has been proven effective in the treatment of unipolar depression and preventing relapse of unipolar depression; because it is also successfully used to treat other mental health problems such as anxiety disorders, substance abuse, and personality disorders (which often co-occur with bipolar disorder); and because it is a structured approach that focuses on teaching people skills (Zaretsky, Rizvi, and Parikh 2007).

In the studies that have been conducted on using CBT to treat bipolar disorder, there has been a significant reduction in relapse rate, fewer hospitalizations, fewer days spent in a bipolar episode, improved compliance with medications, and improved functioning in psychosocial roles (Zaretsky, Rizvi, and Parikh 2007). Although CBT has been demonstrated effective, its effectiveness in alleviating mania has not been established (Rizvi and Zaretsky 2007).

Interpersonal Social Rhythm Therapy

Interpersonal social rhythm therapy (IPSRT) was modified from *interpersonal therapy* (IPT), a type of psychotherapy that looks at how your mood is affected by relationships and changes in the roles that you play in your life (for example, getting married, the breakup of a relationship, getting a job promotion, or the death of a family member). IPT is known to be effective in the treatment of acute major depression (Gutierrez and Scott 2004), which is one reason therapists decided to modify it for use with bipolar disorder.

Interpersonal social rhythm therapy is IPT with the addition of educational elements regarding bipolar disorder, cognitive and behavioral interventions, and self-monitoring of social rhythms or your daily routines (Zaretsky, Rizvi, and Parikh 2007). IPSRT is based on the idea that a disruption in these daily routines leads to an instability in your circadian rhythms (your sleep-wake cycle) and can trigger bipolar episodes. Studies have shown that people with bipolar disorder receiving IPSRT while in an acute phase of bipolar disorder had a reduction in relapse rates (Rizvi and Zaretski 2007).

So, while both CBT and IPSRT include an emphasis on regular daily activities, enhancing medication compliance, and identifying and managing early stages of relapse (Gutierrez and Scott 2004), DBT as I outline it in this workbook does all of this and more.

Dialectical Behavior Therapy

Dialectical behavior therapy is a treatment that was created by Marsha Linehan in 1993 and was the first therapy that was proven to be effective in treating an illness called borderline personality disorder. This personality disorder shares many symptoms with bipolar disorder, including problems regulating emotions, impulsivity, unstable relationships, and unhealthy or self-destructive coping skills. In fact, these two illnesses can look so similar to each other that defining the boundary between them "has been particularly controversial, given the extent to which the symptoms of these two disorders overlap" (Magill 2004, 551). Some authors have proposed that the difference between the two illnesses is only a matter of degree, and that borderline personality disorder should actually be considered to be part of the bipolar spectrum (Magill 2004).

So if these illnesses are so much alike and DBT has been researched extensively and found to be helpful for the treatment of borderline personality disorder, it only makes sense that DBT will also be helpful in treating bipolar disorder. Even if the two illnesses are not one and the same, the many shared symptoms and the fact that there is a high rate of co-occurrence of the two disorders (Magill 2004) (meaning people diagnosed with one often also have the other) suggests that DBT is an effective treatment for bipolar.

Since its beginnings, DBT has also been successfully used to treat many other illnesses, such as other personality disorders, depression, substance abuse and dependence, eating disorders, and self-harming and suicidal behaviors (Dimeff, Koerner, and Linehan 2006). People with bipolar disorder can also face these problems, and DBT can help.

To date, there has been only one published study on the use of DBT for bipolar disorder (Goldstein et al. 2007). The authors of the study reported that the results were positive, with the participants exhibiting significant improvement in suicidality, self-harming behavior, regulation of emotions, and symptoms of depression. Hopefully this will lead to further studies that will provide evidence to support the presumed effectiveness of using DBT to treat bipolar disorder.

Those are the compelling arguments based on current research, and they suggest that DBT is the way to go with bipolar disorder. But let me tell you one last reason why I believe DBT will help you learn to live with your illness and minimize the negative consequences it can have: I see it every day in the clients I work with. I teach DBT to people with bipolar disorder on a daily basis, and these skills do help. So I hope that I've convinced you to at least give it a try.

Now let me tell you a little bit about what DBT is and what you can expect. DBT is broken down into four sections:

1. **Core mindfulness skills:** These skills help people to live more in the present moment, rather than getting stuck in thoughts about the past or future, which can trigger painful emotions. These are also skills that will help you get to know yourself better, because when you're focusing on the present moment, you're more aware of your own emotions, thoughts, and feelings.

2. **Distress tolerance skills:** This is a skill set meant to get you through a crisis situation without engaging in the old, self-destructive behaviors that likely would make the situation worse for you.

3. **Emotion regulation skills:** These help you to understand your emotional reactions and how to control them more effectively, as well as providing you with ways to reduce painful emotions so that they're less overwhelming.

4. **Interpersonal effectiveness skills:** These enable you to communicate more effectively so that you will be more likely to get your needs met. These skills also help you to achieve more of a balance in your relationships so that you're giving as well as taking, gaining more overall satisfaction from these connections.

Here is a summary of how each skill set will help you with symptoms of bipolar disorder.

	Increase...	Decrease...
Core Mindfulness Skills	• Your sense of who you are • Your awareness of symptoms • Your ability to concentrate • Your memory • Your ability to control your thoughts	• Confusion about who you are • Lack of awareness that can lead to depression or mania • Scattered, racing thoughts • Ruminating, which can trigger depression
Distress Tolerance Skills	• Use of healthy coping skills • Positive aspects of relationships • Sense of self-esteem	• Self-destructive behaviors • Burning out your loved ones • Anger toward yourself, which reduces self-respect
Emotion Regulation Skills	• Acceptance of emotions • Mood stability • Ability to control emotions	• Self-judgments for having emotions • Negative emotions from judging • Feelings of helplessness and of being overwhelmed • The emotional roller coaster
Interpersonal Effectiveness Skills	• Ability to get your needs met • Support from loved ones	• One-sided, unfulfilling relationships • Conflicted, unsupportive relationships

WRAPPING UP

This chapter has been devoted to helping you learn more about your illness and what it means to have bipolar disorder, as well as what your options are to live with it more comfortably. I hope that you will use the information provided in this chapter to help you to become more familiar with your illness and symptoms. Remember, greater awareness means a greater likelihood of preventing relapse. In the next chapter, I will introduce the first of the DBT-based skills presented in this book, a skill called mindfulness, which will help you to develop this awareness in different ways.

CHAPTER 2

Mindfulness Practice

Do you rely on others to tell you when you are becoming depressed or manic because you don't pay attention to yourself and so aren't aware of these symptoms? Or perhaps you purposely avoid noticing them in the hope that they'll go away. Do you lash out at people when you're feeling angry because you feel that you have no control over your emotions, and you react before you even know what's happening? Do you get caught up in thinking about how awful your life is, maybe remembering things you've done in the past that you regret or recalling awful things that have happened to you?

All of these things happen primarily because you spend a lot of your time in a state of unawareness of your emotions, thoughts, physical sensations, and behaviors. This chapter is all about increasing your awareness and specifically doing this through a skill called mindfulness.

MINDFULNESS AND BIPOLAR DISORDER

Mindfulness is a form of meditative practice that has been used for thousands of years in the Eastern world and is commonly a part of spiritual practices such as Zen Buddhism. It's taken us a while to catch up here in the West, but scientists have been studying mindfulness in recent years and are discovering all sorts of benefits from the practice. I will discuss these benefits in more depth later in this chapter. For now, there are two important things to note. The first is that, in spite of its roots, you do not have to be a religious or spiritual person in order to practice mindfulness. All you need is an open mind and a willingness to try something different. If you are spiritual and feel concerned that mindfulness will conflict with your own beliefs, I ask that you put those concerns on hold and read on while I explain what mindfulness is; a more thorough understanding should put your mind at ease.

The second important thing to emphasize here is that while mindfulness is a form of meditation, it is not the type of meditative practice that will have you sitting cross-legged on the floor and chanting mantras to yourself in an effort to clear your mind. While that type of meditation can be extremely useful, it is also very difficult, especially for someone just beginning to practice. My experience has been that people tend to get frightened away from mindfulness by thinking about it as meditation.

So, what is mindfulness? Mindfulness has been defined as purposely paying attention, in the present moment and without judgment (Kabat-Zinn 1994). Another way of saying this is that mindfulness is intentionally becoming more aware of the present moment and not judging whatever you find in that moment; observing the present moment without putting labels on it. Let's look at a couple of examples to help illustrate this.

How many times have you driven the same route in your car—for example, to work or somewhere else you go frequently—and when you reach your destination, you realize you have no memory of the last fifteen minutes of the drive? This is because you were on automatic pilot—you were engaged physically in a behavior (driving) while your mind was engaged in something else (for example, dwelling on an argument you had with your father or thinking about a deadline at work). We actually live much of our lives in this way.

Think about this: What did you have for lunch yesterday? You'll probably have to think about this long and hard, because you likely weren't *just* eating lunch. Maybe you were engrossed in watching the news as you ate; maybe you were at the office, sitting at your desk checking e-mails or doing other tasks; or maybe you went out for lunch with a friend and were so busy catching up with him that you barely noticed your food. While your body was engaged in the automatic behavior of eating, your mind was doing something else.

Okay, how about this one: Try to recall the most recent conversation you had with your partner, child, sibling, parent, or someone else close to you. Do you remember what you talked about? How much detail can you remember regarding that discussion? Perhaps, if it was something that was quite important or interesting to you, you will recall much of it. But consider these questions: What *else* were you doing while you were having that conversation? Were you really sitting down, paying attention only to what the conversation was about, or were you playing solitaire on the computer? Were you making your grocery list or getting dinner ready? Were you channel surfing, looking for something to watch on television? Chances are you missed at least some of that conversation because your mind was not fully participating in the discussion—it was busy thinking about other things.

Mindfulness is really about training your mind to pay more attention to the current moment without judging it, noticing when your mind wanders, and bringing your attention back to the moment. It is tuning in to what is happening now, either within yourself or in the environment, and doing so with an attitude of curiosity, acceptance, and openness toward the experience. For many of us, it is incredibly challenging to experience something without judging it or without adding our interpretation to it. For example, when we eat, we usually think of the food we are chewing in terms of whether it tastes good or bad, whether we like it or dislike it, and so on, rather than simply observing how the food tastes and feels without evaluating it.

Here's an exercise you can practice to help you get the idea of what mindfulness is all about: At your next meal or snack, slow yourself down and give the food your full attention. Sit down. Turn the television off. Put your book or the newspaper away. Experience the food with all of your senses. Look at it like you've never seen it before. Smell it. If you want, touch it and see what the different textures feel like. When you're ready, pick up your fork and slowly bring the food toward your mouth. Experience the sensations that occur in your body as you do this. Is your mouth watering? Is your stomach growling? Place the food on your tongue, but don't chew yet. Just notice for a moment how the food feels in your mouth. Is it warm or cool? Notice the different textures. If you notice your mind start to wander—perhaps you're becoming impatient and just want to swallow and move on to the next bite—simply observe this and bring your attention back to the food. Now you can chew. As you do so, notice how this feels. Notice the taste of the food, so much more intense now than when you don't eat mindfully. Is it sweet? Sour? Spicy? Try not to evaluate the food in terms of whether it tastes good or bad. Instead, just observe and describe your experience of it.

Now you can swallow. But as you do so, follow the path of the food as it slides down your throat and see if you can actually feel it land in your stomach. So? What did you think? Have you ever experienced food this way before? After eating mindfully for the first time, most people are surprised at how much they've been missing by not eating mindfully. They describe the taste of the food as more intense and the whole experience as simply more satisfying. Now just think, if you can experience a meal that way just by eating mindfully, what else is waiting out there for you?

I mentioned at the beginning of this chapter that researchers have been studying the effects of mindfulness and of meditation in general, and have found that it is extremely beneficial to us in all sorts of ways, including the following (Harvard Medical International 2004):

- It decreases medical symptoms, including chronic pain, fibromyalgia, psoriasis, and high blood pressure.

- It reduces anxiety and stress.

- It improves the functioning of your immune system.

- It improves sleep.

- It helps to prevent depression from returning.

- It fosters self-awareness.

- It improves your ability to tolerate upsetting thoughts.

- It activates a part of your brain that is connected to experiencing happiness and optimism—in other words, it helps you feel good.

There has been no research conducted on the use of mindfulness specifically for bipolar disorder to date. However, there has been one study conducted on the use of mindfulness-based cognitive therapy for bipolar disorder. This treatment, which incorporates mindfulness practice, was effective in decreasing symptoms of depression and anxiety in people with bipolar disorder who had been having suicidal thoughts or engaging in suicidal behavior (Williams et al. 2008).

There have also been studies showing the usefulness of mindfulness to treat severe mental health problems such as unipolar depression and depression relapse (Teasdale et al. 2000); generalized anxiety disorder (Kutz, Borysenko, and Benson 1985; Miller, Fletcher, and Kabat-Zinn 1995); and panic disorder (Kabat-Zinn et al. 1992). The fact that depression is a big part of bipolar disorder, and that anxiety often co-occurs with the illness (so much so that it warrants its own chapter, chapter 8), it only makes sense that mindfulness will also be helpful in treating bipolar disorder itself.

HOW TO PRACTICE MINDFULNESS

While the idea of mindfulness may seem simple—intentionally focusing on the present moment without judgment—putting it into practice can be extremely difficult. Keep in mind, this is pretty much the opposite of what we are taught as we grow up, that we shouldn't just be doing one thing, we should be multitasking! Western society, at least, has developed the faulty belief that it is more efficient for us to be doing three things at once, rather than only one. So this is learning a new way of doing things, which can often prove challenging.

Many of my clients come back after first learning about mindfulness and tell me that they weren't very good at it, or they couldn't do it very well. What they mean by this, of course, is that their attention kept wandering and they found it very difficult to stay focused. You can think of mindfulness as *returning to* the present moment. Yes, you are human, and so your attention *is* going to wander. This is inevitable. Being mindful isn't about staying focused on something; rather, it is noticing that your attention has gone astray, and without judging yourself, returning your attention to whatever is happening in this moment. Mark Williams and his colleagues (2007) refer to this coming and going of our attention as "mind waves." And just as waves in the ocean are perfectly natural, so are the waves of attention in your mind. The going away and coming back again of our attention is just what the mind does and is therefore the heart of mindfulness practice, not a failure to practice correctly.

It's also important to remember that the only goal in mindfulness is to be more aware of the present moment. After first starting to practice, many people also return and tell me that it isn't working. Keep in mind that the point of mindfulness isn't to help you relax or calm yourself. It's not to help you sleep; it's not to help you concentrate better. All of these can be pleasant side effects of mindfulness, but none of them is the goal of mindfulness. So if you find yourself becoming frustrated with the exercises and thinking, "It's not working," remind yourself that the only goal of the exercise is to be in the present moment more often. When looked at from this perspective, mindfulness always works. It may not be easy, but if you are being mindful, you're spending more time in the present than if you were to continue living on automatic pilot.

When you're first beginning to practice, it is sometimes helpful to start with activities that you find easily hold your attention. This tactic can help to ease the frustration that often arises when you have difficulties staying focused on the moment. If you start out by being intentionally mindful in situations in which you are more able to stay focused, these experiences will provide you with evidence that you *can* do this and will allow you to move on to the exercises in which it's more difficult for you to remain focused.

■ Jim's Story

Jim was having trouble staying in the moment while practicing a breathing mindfulness exercise. He would get frustrated and judge himself each time he noticed that his attention had again gone to a stressful situation he was dealing with, rather than remaining on his breathing. Jim was ready to give up on mindfulness because he said the frustration and anger he was experiencing were making him feel even worse than he did before. I asked Jim to put aside the breathing mindfulness exercises for

INSTRUCTIONS FOR MINDFULNESS PRACTICE

Okay, so here we go. Here are the steps to follow when doing any kind of mindfulness exercise:

1. Choose something to focus on. This can be anything; the number of ways to practice mindfulness is literally infinite. For beginners, it is often easiest to start with something concrete: listening to music, for example, or choosing an object to look at.

2. Bring your attention to the object—start focusing on it. If you've chosen music, press play and start to listen. If you've chosen an object, start examining it as though you've never seen it before, using all of your senses.

3. Notice when your attention wanders. Remember that this is expected; the key is, at some point, to realize that it has happened. It may take only a second, or you may find a few minutes have passed before you notice. Regardless of how long it takes, just notice that it has occurred.

4. Gently bring your attention back to your focus. In other words, without judging yourself for not staying focused, simply redirect your attention back to the music, the object, or whatever your focus is. This can also be difficult, because you may have a tendency to be hard on yourself for not doing it "right." Instead of falling back into this old pattern, see if you can just accept this as an opportunity to come back to the exercise.

    Repeat steps 3 and 4 over and over and over again. You may notice fifty times in just one minute that your attention has wandered. Mindfulness is when you continue to notice these events, and your gently bring your awareness back to the present moment.

now, and I had him think about what kinds of things he was doing already that really engaged him and held his attention easily. He came up with playing the guitar, which he does on a weekly basis with a friend. So Jim's homework was to start playing the guitar mindfully.

The next time I met with Jim, he reported that he had been "successful" in mindfully playing the instrument; in other words, he was finding that his attention was not wandering nearly as much as it had been, and he was more able to stay in the present moment. This gave Jim a new understanding of and appreciation for mindfulness. He saw how much more he enjoyed playing his guitar when that was all he was doing with his body and his mind. The fact that he had been able to do this activity mindfully gave Jim the confidence to keep practicing mindfulness. He then thought of another activity that he was already able to focus on well—driving—and he began driving mindfully. From there he worked his way back to breathing exercises. He still found that his attention was much more likely to wander, but with a better understanding of mindfulness and a new confidence that he could do such exercises, he kept practicing and his frustration decreased.

Take a moment to consider what kinds of activities you do currently that you are able to be completely engaged in, with your body and your mind. The following are some examples that clients have told me are moments when mindfulness tends to come more naturally. Which of these activities do you already do with a lot of focus? Which do you find easily hold your attention without you having to make an effort to stay in the present moment?

_____ Watching the sun rise or set   _____ Playing with a pet

_____ Hiking   _____ Playing a musical instrument

_____ Playing a sport   _____ Walking

_____ Reading a good book   _____ Dancing

_____ Having a discussion with someone about a topic you find very interesting

_____ Watching an engrossing movie or television show

_____ Spending time with children, grandchildren, nieces, or nephews

Other activities you find you are able to engage in without your attention wandering much:

_____   _____

_____   _____

_____   _____

     Keep in mind that, while you may be very focused on doing these sorts of activities, you're not actually practicing mindfulness unless you intend to do so. It does not come naturally for us to notice when our attention wanders and to bring it back. If you can start with something that you do with a lot of focus already, it can help you work your way up to other exercises that may be more difficult, like Jim's experience with the breathing exercises. The important thing is to remember that you *do* have to work your way up. The goal is to be able to live life more mindfully, so you can't just stick to what's easy for you. Use those activities as evidence for yourself that you *can* be mindful, and then incorporate other exercises that will challenge you more.

     There is no such thing as failing at mindfulness or doing it wrong, as long as you notice and are aware of whatever you are experiencing. So to notice that you're finding a certain exercise difficult *is* mindfulness. To be aware that you're becoming frustrated with a practice *is* mindfulness. Often peoples' expectations of themselves and the practice are too high, and they will report that it's not working. If these thoughts come to you, remind yourself to just notice these thoughts and any emotions that accompany them. Mindfulness is an ongoing process and requires a lot of practice, but it will be well worth the effort in the long run.

Informal vs. Formal Mindfulness Exercises

     There are two types of mindfulness practices, both of which are extremely important. Informal exercises include any kind of practice that you can do as you're going about your normal day—for example, doing the dishes, brushing your teeth, walking, or driving mindfully. Informal exercises are incorporated into day-to-day life and do not require you to set aside time in your day. Some practices, such as breathing exercises, can be both formal and informal, depending on how and where you choose to practice them.

The formal practices are those exercises that require us to set aside a certain amount of time so that we can sit or lie down in a quiet place in order to be mindful. Examples of these formal practices are observing thoughts exercises and progressive muscle relaxation, both of which I will outline later on in this chapter.

I say that both informal and formal practices are important because while it is essential to live life more mindfully and to practice as you go about your daily routines, the formal exercises give you a deeper understanding of your experiences and provide opportunities for you to be mindful of your thoughts and emotions. This distinction should become clearer as you read through the formal exercises provided throughout this chapter and put them into practice. For the time being, keep in mind that in order to benefit as much as possible from practicing mindfulness, you will need to use both forms.

How Long Should You Practice Mindfulness?

This is a difficult question with many answers. Some authors and clinicians believe that practices as long as forty-five minutes a day are necessary in order to fully incorporate mindfulness into your life and to get the most out of the experience. To my knowledge, there have been no studies conducted comparing the benefits of longer and shorter practice times, but even if this is true, practices as long as forty-five minutes are often not realistic or feasible for many people. Keeping in mind that the longer you're able to practice, the more quickly you will benefit from mindfulness, you first need to look at your lifestyle and figure out what is realistic and what you're willing to do.

If you have never practiced mindfulness or any other type of meditation before, I recommend that you start out with briefer exercises and work your way up to longer ones. When I first introduce mindfulness to a group, we start off doing exercises for only about one and a half minutes. I encourage people to practice daily in between group sessions, and I increase the time by thirty seconds each week until we get to five minutes. In my experience, five minutes is not too long, even if you are having difficulties concentrating due to hypomania, depression, or other problems such as attention deficit disorder. But five minutes is long enough to experience different emotions and thoughts that can be distracting.

In terms of the length of your own practice, remember that just because something is uncomfortable doesn't mean that you have to stop. You can simply notice that discomfort has arisen in you. Or just because the urge to stop the exercise has come up, it doesn't mean you have to act on the urge—just notice it. I suggest that you experiment with shorter and longer exercises to see what generally works best for you. Remember that this will vary at times as well. For example, when life is more stressful and you have more painful emotions in your life, it is usually much more difficult to stay in the moment. At these times you may find you are unable to tolerate longer exercises until you have been practicing for a while. Whatever you decide on for yourself, remember that in order to live life more mindfully you need to practice exercises regularly—at least once a day. And because you can practice mindfulness informally, you can actually do multiple exercises in a day without having to find extra time in your busy schedule to do so.

The Question of Eyes: Open or Closed?

People tend to want to close their eyes when they sit down to do a formal mindfulness exercise. There are some differences of opinion about whether eyes should be kept open or closed when practicing mindfulness. I suggest that you keep your eyes open. It's much easier to become distracted by thoughts, memories, and images when your eyes are closed. In addition, some people experience periods of time when they space out, lose time, or (to use the medical term) dissociate. If this is you, it is even more important for you to keep your eyes open to help keep you grounded in the moment.

Keeping your eyes open, however, is not a hard and fast rule. For some of the formal practices, especially if they involve imagining certain things, you may find it necessary to close your eyes in order to accurately picture those things. And if you're just starting to practice and find it very difficult to do the exercises with your eyes open, feel free to close them. But set a goal for yourself of working toward doing mindfulness with your eyes open.

HOW MINDFULNESS CAN HELP RELIEVE BIPOLAR SYMPTOMS

Mindfulness is a skill that, although difficult, will be helpful for anyone who practices it. In this section, I'm going to explain why this skill will be especially helpful for people with bipolar disorder.

Controlling Your Thoughts

We often dwell on or ruminate about things that have happened in the past and about how things might turn out in the future, both of which usually trigger painful emotions for us. For example, do you find your thoughts going to the last depressive episode you had and how awful it felt? Or to that mania you experienced that led to you gambling away thousands of dollars? And how often do you catch yourself worrying about the next time you have one of these episodes?

Dwelling can also turn into *catastrophizing*, or imagining the very worst consequences of an event. For example, you might dwell on the argument you had yesterday with a loved one in which you said some hurtful things you now regret. In this instance you might start thinking about what you could have done differently, other things you might have said that wouldn't have been so hurtful, and so on. This could actually be helpful if you stopped there, but you probably won't. Instead, you'll likely start to make assumptions about how the other person feels about you and make predictions about how your relationship with the person will be affected. You may even start to worry that there won't be a family get-together at Christmas this year because this relationship has ended so badly, when the fact is that you don't know the relationship has ended at all.

Granted, not all of the events that people ruminate about are turned into terrible events because they catastrophize about them; many people really have lived through horrendous experiences such as suicide attempts that occurred when they were depressed, or being victims of crimes such as assault or sexual abuse. If this is you, though, think about this for a moment: When you get stuck in this mode of thinking—dwelling on what happened, wishing it hadn't—is it helping you in any way? Does it help you let go of the memories by thinking about the event again and again and wondering, for example, what would have happened if you had done something differently or what your life would have been like if that thing hadn't happened to you? I bet you'd agree that ruminating does nothing for you but cause suffering; I will discuss this in much further detail in chapter 9, when I introduce the skill of radical acceptance.

By allowing yourself to get caught up in this kind of thinking, you can actually trigger many painful emotions that wouldn't be there if you weren't ruminating. In the above example, you may still feel angry at the person for the hurtful things he or she said, and you may feel guilty if you've said something hurtful to this person you love. But by ruminating about the situation, you create additional emotions such as anxiety and sadness, because you've created an imaginary future (Williams et al. 2007) in which the relationship is over and there will be no more family celebrations at holidays. If you weren't so caught up in catastrophizing about this situation and creating an imaginary future in which the relationship is over, all you would feel is the original guilt and anger about the interaction.

Most people engage in this kind of thinking at times. Ruminating preoccupies you, uses a lot of energy, and interferes with your ability to live life fully. This type of thinking also has a great impact on your mood and can actually trigger depressive episodes. Imagine if you were thinking like this on a regular basis, about the many painful events that happen in your life. You would be constantly triggering more and more painful emotions about things that may or may not have happened in the past and about what might happen in the future, rather than experiencing life as it unfolds around you.

Let's continue with this example and how your emotions snowball as a result of dwelling or ruminating. As I mentioned above, people have a tendency to create imaginary futures for themselves that they then begin to live in as though what they have imagined is real. For example, thinking about how difficult Christmas is going to be this year because it will be the first Christmas without the whole family together would trigger intense sadness, perhaps fear that you'll be blamed, and maybe guilt because you blame yourself. You may get so caught up in these thoughts and emotions that you forget that this hasn't happened yet and that you don't in fact know how the situation will turn out. And yet you're experiencing all sorts of painful emotions as though these events have already occurred.

Most of us have had some kind of experience like this; for example, you have an argument with your sister on the telephone, she ends up hanging up on you, and then you don't talk to her for five days. You're angry with her for the things she said, but you start to worry that she's no longer speaking to you, and you think about how you can resolve this. The more time passes, the more anxious you become about talking to her and trying to resolve the situation. Finally, you call her and quickly realize she's forgotten all about the phone call and has been sick with the flu. What was the point of feeling all that uncomfortable anxiety?

So where does mindfulness come in? First of all, if you're focusing on being more aware of the present moment, you won't be living in the past and reliving the argument you had last week or the trauma that occurred three years ago. And you won't be living in the future and anticipating what's going to happen. Mindfulness helps to prevent the painful emotions from coming up by helping you to be aware of when you're living in the past and the future. This increased awareness means you'll be quicker to catch this type of thinking when it starts, so you can do something to prevent yourself from getting caught up in it. Essentially, mindfulness in this respect helps you to gain control over your mind instead of allowing your mind to control you.

Here are some mindfulness exercises you can practice that will help you in gaining control over your thoughts. They involve oberving your thoughts, which is extremely helpful in increasing your awareness of your thoughts and emotions.

In Clouds

Pretend you are lying in a field of grass, looking up at the clouds. Whenever a thought enters your mind, imagine that it rests on a cloud that's floating by. Don't judge the thought, and don't label them; simply observe them as they float through your mind. Don't grab onto them or get caught up in thinking about them—just notice them. When you notice your attention straying from the exercise, gently bring it back to observing and labeling the thoughts.

On Falling Leaves

In your mind's eye, visualize yourself standing in a forest, enjoying the sights and sounds of nature. As you stand there, you see leaves start to fall from the trees. Whenever a thought enters your mind, imagine that it rests on a leaf that's drifting down. As you watch each leaf fall and as the thought becomes visible, see if you can pick up the leaf and place it in a pile according to what the thought is about. For example, when the thought "I'm not having any thoughts" drifts down on its leaf, you might put this in the "worry thought" or "observing thought" pile. When the thought "This is a stupid exercise" appears on its leaf, you might label it and put it in the "anger thought" or "judgment thought" pile, and so on. As best you can, don't judge yourself for how you're labeling certain thoughts. Just continue placing the leaves in piles. There is no right or wrong answer!

Standing in a River

In your mind, picture yourself standing in a shallow river. The water comes up to just above your knees, and there is a gentle current pushing against your legs. As you stand there, picture your thoughts coming past you on the current, floating down the river. You don't grab onto them and you don't get caught up in them; you simply watch them as they float past you in the water. When you notice yourself thinking about a thought instead of just watching it, bring your attention back to the exercise and focus on just observing. As best you can, don't judge the thoughts that go by. Just become aware of what those thoughts are.

Relaxation

I mentioned earlier that in mindfulness the only goal, if there is one, is to intentionally continue to be aware and accepting of the present moment. When you notice your attention has wandered from this moment, bring it back to the present. Relaxation is not a goal of mindfulness; however, it is often a beneficial side effect.

People often report that doing a mindfulness exercise helps to calm them down. This can be attributed to a variety of factors; for example, being mindful of thoughts can lead to an awareness that you were becoming anxious thinking about that argument you had with your family member. Once you become aware of the emotion and its trigger, you can do something to reduce your level of anxiety, which in turn will lead to you feeling calmer or more relaxed.

Some people with bipolar disorder say that practicing mindfulness regularly improves their ability to focus. This can also have a calming effect. If your thoughts are less scattered and aren't racing or crowded, you may experience an overall feeling of calmness. Paying attention to certain things when practicing mindfulness might also induce relaxation. Listening to the sounds of birds chirping or waves on a beach, for example, will likely help you to feel calmer.

Of course, there is a wealth of information about how to do relaxation exercises, and if you engage in these exercises mindfully, you will usually have even more success in achieving a relaxed state. Here is a classic mindfulness exercise for relaxation.

Progressive Muscle Relaxation

Sitting or lying down in a comfortable position, focus on each group of muscles one by one. Beginning with your toes, tense and release each group of muscles, concentrating only on that feeling of tension and the release of tension as you let your muscles relax. Slowly work your way up through the front and back of your lower legs and then your upper legs; your buttocks; your lower, middle, and upper back; your stomach and chest; your hands, arms, shoulders, and neck; and then, into your face, including your jaw, brow, and eyes. Focus all of your attention on the action of tensing and releasing these muscles. When you notice your mind has gone to other things, don't judge yourself. Simply bring your attention back to the sensations.

This is a practice that is meant to help people become more relaxed. When you purposely tense up your muscles and then let them go, they are actually more relaxed then they were before you tensed them.

Keep in mind that relaxation can be extremely helpful when you're hypomanic or manic, as it decreases stimulation and can help to calm you. I've had feedback from people that when they're in a hypomanic state, these kinds of exercises do help to slow their thoughts down and therefore help them to feel calmer. Of course, when manic, many people are too disorganized to even think of this. But if you can, try it. Regularly practicing relaxation and any other type of mindfulness exercise, though, may help you to prevent a manic or hypomanic episode from occurring. So think of these exercises more as preventative, rather than something that will help to bring you down once your mood is high.

Improving Concentration and Memory

When you're feeling depressed, are you one of those people who have a really hard time concentrating? Do you find you can't possibly read a book, and even having a conversation with someone or watching television is just too demanding? This is a common problem for people with both bipolar and unipolar depression, and it's actually one of the criteria set out for the diagnosis of major depressive disorder. Some research indicates that people who are depressed have a reduction in the size of the part of their brain called the hippocampus, which causes cognitive impairment such as memory problems and difficulties concentrating (O'Brien et al. 2004). Practicing mindfulness is a way of exercising your brain in order to regain strength in the areas that depression has weakened.

Practicing mindfulness exercises regularly can also help with the difficulties in concentration that arise when you are in a hypomanic state. As I mentioned earlier, racing or crowded thoughts that go along with hypomania can be slowed down with mindfulness. One person I worked with was having problems reading because of difficulties concentrating, and this was distressing to her because she enjoyed reading immensely. By reading mindfully—noticing without judgment when her attention wandered and then bringing it back to the passage she was reading—she found that, over time, reading took much less effort and her concentration improved.

Another client was having difficulties with excess energy due to hypomania and found herself starting all sorts of projects and not actually accomplishing anything. She felt disorganized, like she was rushing around in circles. So she began practicing being mindful of whatever activity she was doing in that moment and found immediately that this helped her to slow herself down and really focus on just doing that one thing.

Because of difficulties with concentration, many people with bipolar disorder report problems remembering things. Gin Malhi and colleagues (2007) have done research that has shown this problem to be present during depression and hypomania, as well as outside of these affective episodes when your mood is stable. (The term *affective episode* is used as a short form for depressive, manic, or hypomanic episodes.)

Remember the earlier example of having no memory of driving a certain route you take on a regular basis? As noted earlier, this happens when your body is engaged in an activity you do so regularly you don't have to think about it, freeing your mind up to think about other things. This is especially problematic in mania and hypomania, when the excess energy has you doing many things at once and it's impossible to focus your mind on all of them. But it also happens in depression, when your mind is so busy dwelling on things that you're not able to fully focus on what you're doing in the present. Other typical examples of activities you may do mindlessly include walking, brushing your teeth, doing the dishes...the list is endless. People tend to do these activities on automatic pilot. Your body goes through the motions while your mind wanders off and does other things, like dwelling on the past or worrying about the future. It's no wonder, then, that you can't recall if you brushed your teeth or took your medication, because your mind wasn't engaged in the activity. This is where mindfulness comes in.

When you are in the present moment, you are fully engaged in whatever activity you are doing in that moment. Because you are bringing your mind with you, you retain much more detail about the experience than you would otherwise. Think about some experiences in your life that you can recall in vivid detail. They might be big events, like graduating from high school or college, and you might be able to recall small details like what you were wearing or what the weather was like that day. Or they may be less significant things, like the first time you took your child to the park, and you may recall her playing on the swings or falling and scraping her knee. Whatever the event was, the reason you recall it in so much detail is because it was an important event to you, and so you participated in that activity with your mind and body—you were being mindful of the experience.

Here are some exercises that will specifically help you to increase your ability to concentrate and remember.

Observing an Object

Choose an object to focus your attention on. This could be an everyday item like a pen or pencil, or it could be something that you don't often pay attention to—for example, a snow globe you've had since you were a child that sits on a shelf. It's something that's always there, but you've never really looked closely at it. Using all of your senses, begin examining the object. Look at it closely, like you've never seen it before. Touch it. What does it feel like? Are there different textures to it? Is it smooth, rough, or ridged? Just observe the object without judging it. See if it makes noise you can listen to or if it has an odor you can smell. If it's food, taste it. As best you can, experience the object as though you've never seen it before, and when you notice that your attention wanders from the object, gently bring your attention back.

We often get involved in stories of things, as well, so be aware if this starts to happen. You may still be thinking about the object, but instead of observing it you begin to think about where it came from, where it was made, the person who made it, and how it ended up in your possession. This is no longer mindfulness, because you are no longer in the present moment with the object but are caught up in thinking about its past. If this happens, just notice and bring your attention back to observing.

Observing Sounds

Sitting quietly, focus your attention on any sounds that you hear—the sound of your breathing, the sound of people talking in the next room, the sound of the refrigerator running in the kitchen, the sound of air coming through the vents, and so on. Don't reach for sounds, but let them come to you, thinking of your ears not as actively searching, but simply as receptors for sounds. As best you can, don't label what you're hearing, just observe it. For example, instead of saying to yourself "dog barking" when you hear this sound, see if you can observe it without putting any words on it. Just let yourself hear it without labeling it. When you notice your mind wandering, wondering perhaps what a certain sound is or where it's coming from, just notice this without judgment and come back to the exercise.

Counting Breaths

This is an exercise that you can do formally or informally. You can set aside a specific amount of time out of your day to count breaths, or you can do it as you drive to an appointment or sit in a meeting. When counting breaths, start by sitting quietly and noticing your breath. Don't try to change your breath—simply begin to observe it. Next, as you draw a breath in, count the number one to yourself; as you slowly breathe out, count the number two. Count your breaths this way until you reach the number ten, and then start over. When you find that your mind has wandered from your breath and from counting, simply notice this without judgment and return your focus to the exercise.

You may suddenly notice that you've reached the number twenty-three, or you may find that you are a multitasker and can count your breaths while you also think about other things, such as what you'll have for dinner tonight or planning for your next day at work. If this is you, just notice this has happened and return your attention to just counting your breaths, starting at the number one. If you are distracted frequently, see if you can actually visualize the numbers in your head as you count them to yourself, as this takes even more concentration. This exercise can be very helpful if you're having problems falling asleep at night, but you can practice it anywhere, at any time.

Increasing Positive Emotions

I've just mentioned that it is very difficult to really be engaged in an activity when you're doing one thing and thinking about another. Another positive effect that occurs when you're doing an activity mindfully is that you're more able to enjoy it. For example, I could play with my dog and at the same time be distracted by worrying about all the work I have to catch up on. Or, if I'm being mindful of playing with my dog, all that is in the present moment is the love I have for my dog and the happiness I get from playing with her. In this moment, there is nothing for me to have anxiety about, but there is a lot for me to feel happiness and love for.

Looking at mindfulness from this perspective, you will find that when you live more in the present moment there is less pain. If, in this moment, you are mindfully reading these pages, what painful emotions come up? Likely, very few or none at all. It's when you're reading this book and your mind starts to take you into the past or the future that the painful emotions start to arise. For example, in reading the section about depression, you start to think about the time you were depressed and you acted on the urge to use cocaine to try to make yourself feel better. Maybe this resulted in the end of your relationship with your partner, and you recall how painful that ending was and how much you regret it.

Or you might be reading the section on mania and start to worry about when the next manic episode might start. Then you think about what you might do while you're manic that you'll regret later. You might become anxious, thinking about how long you might be hospitalized this time and whether or not this might result in your losing your job again. These kinds of thoughts will undoubtedly lead to fear, perhaps anger, and maybe other uncomfortable feelings.

Allowing your mind to control you in this way often results in these painful emotions. Being more aware of the present moment decreases your pain. Ask yourself right now: In this one moment, what emotional pain do you have? In this one moment, sitting at your desk or on the couch or wherever you happen to be reading this book, what is there for you to feel sad, angry, hurt, ashamed, or anxious about? Reading this book may not induce feelings of happiness, but is it really a painful experience? (I certainly hope not!) In chapter 7, when we look at emotions, I'll go into more detail about how mindfulness can increase positive emotions.

For now, practice these exercises to help increase your awareness of your emotions.

Be the Gatekeeper to Your Mind

This is an exercise that helps you to be mindful of your emotions and thoughts. Pretend that you are standing at the "gate" of your mind, watching the feelings and thoughts that are coming through, just as a gatekeeper stands at the gate to watch people coming and going. Don't judge these feelings and thoughts; just observe what they are so that you can become aware of what is in your mind, as a gatekeeper must be aware of who is coming through the gate. Welcome the emotions and thoughts as they come through rather than trying to block them. When your mind wanders or you feel yourself trying to stop the feelings and thoughts from entering, simply observe these things and go back to watching the feelings and thoughts enter. If you find that feelings and thoughts are coming through the gate too quickly, you can slow them down by having each one knock before entering so that you can open the gate, acknowledge them, and then let them through.

Controlling Behaviors

Everyone experiences urges at one time or another. It could be an urge to hurt or kill yourself, to use drugs or alcohol, to overeat or undereat, or even just to lash out at loved ones when you're feeling angry or sad. Some people have already learned ways to control their behavior and not act on these urges. For others, these urges often become habits. You may come to relate certain thoughts and emotions to this harmful behavior and engage in this habitual behavior without awareness, mindlessly. When you aren't aware of what you're thinking or feeling, you are much more likely to act on these urges and automatically engage in behaviors that you will likely regret later on. This is an idea that I will be expanding on in later chapters, but take a moment here to consider what urges you often act on mindlessly:

_____ Using drugs   _____ Drinking

_____ Overeating   _____ Gambling

_____ Yelling   _____ Hitting people

_____ Driving dangerously   _____ Oversleeping

____ Overspending   ____ Self-harming

____ Breaking things   ____ Avoiding problems

____ Lashing out at people

Other urges you experience or have acted on:

_____   _____

_____   _____

_____   _____

Now think about what emotions and thoughts are connected to these urges. For example, the urge to hurt yourself may often come when you're feeling depressed, when a relationship has ended, or when you're feeling like you've failed at something (for instance, not doing well at school). If you can become more aware of these emotions of sadness or shame when they first present themselves, and of the thoughts of self-harm when they first arise in you, you can better prepare yourself for the urges and consciously choose other, healthier ways of coping.

How do you increase your awareness? Well, through mindfulness, of course. The first step to changing any behavior is to increase awareness of it. Mindfulness helps you to be more aware of what you're doing so you can then choose how to act in that situation, rather than reacting automatically. Being more mindful of your thoughts and your emotions means you will be aware of them as they arise. This will give you time to engage in problem-solving behavior and will increase your chances of resisting the urge.

Here is a mindfulness exercise that can help you to increase your awareness of different aspects of yourself in a given moment so that you will have more control when urges do arise.

Breathing Space

The breathing space exercise provides a connection with your breath that can be used in times of stress, when you are most vulnerable to being controlled by your emotions. It is a quick exercise that helps you to refocus and be able to access your wise mind more often.

Start by increasing your general awareness of what you are feeling, physically and emotionally. Observe any sensations without judging them, simply paying attention to what's going on in your body and mind.

Next, bring your attention to your breathing. Without trying to change your breathing, simply focus on the physical sensations of the air flowing in through your nostrils and down into your lungs to expand your diaphragm. Then notice how it feels as the air comes back out from your lungs and you expel the air out through your nostrils. Whenever your attention wanders from your breathing, just notice this has happened and gently bring your attention back to your breath.

From here, expand your awareness from your breath to include a sense of your whole body. Notice any physical sensations that might be occurring within your body, observe any emotions that might be present, and note any thoughts that are going through your mind. When your mind wanders and gets caught up in these thoughts, just notice that this has happened and welcome yourself back to the moment, bringing your attention back to the exercise.

Getting to Know Yourself

Hopefully by now you understand that mindfulness is about living in the present moment. Another benefit of living in the here and now is that you become more aware of yourself—any emotions, physical sensations, and thoughts you're experiencing. This helps you to get to know yourself better.

Have you ever had the sense that you don't know who you really are? Many people feel unsure of what they truly like or dislike and are so unaware of their own opinions, thoughts, and beliefs that it feels as though they don't have their own identity. Many of us have experienced this to some degree; for others, this is an ongoing problem that leaves them feeling empty and without direction. Especially if you have a mental illness such as bipolar disorder, you may experience low self-esteem that can cause these kinds of problems. By increasing awareness of your internal experience, you can come to know yourself better as you observe your thoughts, emotions, and physical sensations.

Here is a mindfulness exercise that will increase your awareness of your own internal experience and help you get to know yourself better.

Be in Your Body

Sitting quietly, focus on the different sensations you are experiencing in your body. Notice, for example, the feel of your buttocks on the chair or the feel of your arms against the armrests. Notice any tension you may have in your muscles. Notice that you feel cool or that you are flushed. Notice any emotions you may be experiencing—for example, anger about a situation that happened before you left for work this morning or perhaps frustration because you're finding it difficult to do this exercise. When your mind takes you away from noticing these sensations, simply bring your attention back to the exercise and let the other thoughts go. Notice if you're trying to avoid feeling any sensations and instead accept them and observe them without judgment. Just acknowledge that this is what is present in you at this moment in time.

You may find that you are often not aware of physical sensations you're experiencing. Instead, you frequently ignore these and cut yourself off from them for one reason or another. For example, if you have pain, you don't want to feel it because it's unpleasant. But being aware of your body, even painful aspects of this awareness, is extremely important in many different ways. Exercises like this one assist you in observing your physical self, which is very helpful in increasing your awareness of your body and your emotions.

Focus on One Sensation

Another way of focusing on your body is to take a fingernail and run it sharply (not so hard that it hurts) across your upper lip, just between your lip and your nose. Then sit quietly and try to focus on that sensation for as long as possible. See how long you can feel it. Again, when your mind wanders to other things, tell yourself that this is okay and bring your attention back to the sensation.

Awareness of Symptoms

Last, but far from least, mindfulness can help you to increase your awareness of any symptoms you may be experiencing in the present moment. This can actually reduce your chances of relapse. Let's go back to our earlier analogies of physical illness. A person with diabetes experiences feelings of light-headedness and weakness and notices her hands are trembling. If she is tuned in to her body, she will quickly notice these symptoms for what they are and will eat a candy bar to increase her blood sugar level. If she isn't so in tune, she might not notice these symptoms or recognize them as symptoms of her diabetes. As a result of her lack of awareness, she could slip into diabetic shock and experience severe medical complications. She could even die.

Bipolar disorder is exactly the same: If you are living in the present moment, you can be aware of when symptoms first start to arise, which means you can seek help sooner. This can, in fact, prevent a full-blown episode of depression or mania from occurring. If you're practicing mindfulness on a regular basis, you will gradually develop this increased awareness. Here is an exercise that will help you to increase your awareness of your internal experiences.

The Body Scan

Similar to the progressive muscle relaxation exercise you learned in the section on relaxation, the body scan has you focusing on different groups of muscles with the intention of only observing any sensations you find there.

Sitting or lying down, get into a comfortable position that you will be able to remain in for the duration of this exercise. Start by taking a deep breath, and then bring your attention to your toes. Notice any sensations that are present. You may observe a tingling sensation, you may suddenly have an itch in that area, or you may feel nothing at all. The only objective is to sense whatever is present in the area. From your toes, expand your attention to the rest of your feet, and notice what sensations are there. You may have some pain or tenderness, or again, you may not notice anything specific. Whatever is there, just notice it as best you can without judgment.

Work your way from your feet to your legs—your shins and calves, your quadriceps and hamstrings (the front and back of your upper legs). As you pause at each group of muscles, just notice whatever sensations are present. Again, don't judge your experience, even if what you observe is not what you would like it to be. When you notice your thoughts starting to wander, gently bring yourself back to focusing on whatever muscle group you're working on.

Next bring your attention to your buttocks. This is one area where we often hold tension, so again, notice whatever is present. You may find that you're tensing these muscles or that they are relaxed. Just observe this. From here, come up into your lower back, your middle back, and your upper back, again pausing at each of these locations and taking the time to observe whatever sensations may be present. Coming up into your shoulder and neck area, you may find that you're crunching your shoulders up to your ears. This is another place we tend to hold tension. Whatever is there, simply notice it.

Now focus on your arms—from your upper arms to your biceps, your wrists, and into your hands. Are you clenching your hands into fists? Do you have pain or tension in any of these areas? Just welcome the experience, whatever it is, and accept it without judging it.

The abdominal muscles are another place we often hold tension. Focus on these now, and just sense whatever is present in this moment. Are you tensing your stomach, or are you relaxed in that area? Just observe. Working your way upward, notice any sensations in your chest. You may notice you're breathing shallowly. Whatever the experience is, it's already there. Just let it come to your awareness.

Now focus on your neck and gradually work your way upward, noting any sensations that may be present in your jaw and then in the rest of your face. Are you clenching your jaw or is it relaxed? Are you squinting your eyes, are you frowning, or is your brow furrowed? Just observe whatever is present.

Finally, observe any sensations present in your head. Is there any pain or discomfort? Or perhaps you feel nothing at all in this area. Whatever is there, just observe or sense it. Bringing your attention to your breathing to finish off this exercise, try to maintain this awareness and bring it with you into whatever you do or wherever you go from here.

This exercise not only increases your awareness of any physical sensations you may be experiencing, it can also draw your attention to emotions that may be present. For example, when you're feeling angry, you may notice that your heart beats more quickly or you clench your fists or your jaw. When you're feeling anxious, you may experience sensations in your stomach or you may tighten up in certain areas of your body. So use this exercise not only to get to know your body sensations better, but to improve your knowledge of how your body reacts to emotions.

Practicing the mindfulness exercises from the above sections that will help you observe your thoughts, emotions, and physical sensations will also help you to increase your awareness of your bipolar symptoms.

■ Kathleen's Story

Kathleen was a fifty-nine-year-old married woman who had been diagnosed with bipolar disorder about twenty years earlier. She came to my bipolar disorder group wanting to learn more about this illness. She had lived with bipolar for a long time, but she still didn't fully understand or know how to cope with the disorder.

Kathleen and her husband had a good relationship. He was very supportive of her, and together they had developed a good understanding of her symptoms of depression and mania. Unfortunately, this understanding had not prevented Kathleen from needing to be hospitalized every two to three years when she would experience a severe manic episode.

Upon joining the bipolar disorder group, Kathleen began practicing mindfulness exercises daily. She not only did informal practices in an attempt to live her life more mindfully, but she would also do formal practices a few times a week, lasting anywhere from five to twenty-five minutes each. As a result, Kathleen developed a new awareness of her emotions and discovered that she was often feeling angry and was lashing out at her husband and her children as a result. To help her reduce these feelings of anger, Kathleen began working with her therapist to discover its source. But in the meantime she found that the awareness mindfulness brought helped her stop taking her emotions out on the people she loved. The result was an improved relationship with her family.

Kathleen also developed a new awareness of symptoms that she hadn't recognized before, because they weren't quite as obvious as the other symptoms that she and her husband had always relied on as indicators of relapse. These symptoms included things like feeling jumpier or more agitated than usual and experiencing racing thoughts. While Kathleen's husband might be able to point out the results of these symptoms over time, Kathleen's new awareness allowed her to catch these symptoms before they led to any major behavioral changes. As a result, she could speak with her psychiatrist, who could adjust her medications so she wouldn't get to the point where she needed to be hospitalized for stabilization.

WRAPPING UP

In this chapter you've learned about how mindfulness is going to help you with your bipolar symptoms, as well as many different ways to practice mindfulness. The mindfulness exercises provided here are only starting points for your practice. As you begin to work with them, remember that it's perfectly acceptable to start with the ones that come more easily for you, in which your attention is drawn away less often. Gradually work your way to the exercises that are more difficult for you so that you can expand your practice and be able to use mindfulness in a variety of settings and in a variety of different ways. Although it is challenging when you first begin, the benefits of mindfulness as you practice over time are well worth the effort.

I would encourage you to *not* read any further in this workbook over the next week. Instead, begin practicing mindfulness exercises for at least five minutes a day, every day. You can break these five minutes into five one-minute practices if you'd like, or just do one five-minute exercise. You can do formal or informal practices. It doesn't matter how you do it, as long as you do it. Use the following worksheet to help you keep track of your mindfulness practice. Some examples have been provided for you.

In the next chapter, I will introduce skills to help you further your mindfulness practice, with a long-term goal of helping you to live your life more mindfully.

My Mindfulness Practice: Example

Date	How I practiced	How long I practiced	What I noticed about my attention
8/21/07	Counting breaths exercise	5 minutes	Wandered a lot, stressed out due to work; was eventually able to calm myself with this
8/22/07	Progressive muscle relaxation	20 minutes	Fell asleep
8/22/07	Brushing my teeth	1.5 minutes	Very distracted; not used to thinking about my teeth when I brush them
8/23/07	Body scan	15 minutes	Extremely relaxing; also helped me notice some emotions I didn't realize I was still feeling

Date	How I practiced	How long I practiced	What I noticed about my attention

CHAPTER 3

Continuing to Increase
Your Awareness

The next skills taught in DBT are skills that will help you to continue increasing your awareness, of both yourself and your environment. In other words, these skills will help you to become more comfortable practicing mindfulness and will help you to act from your emotions less often so you can make healthier choices for yourself. The first skill, mindfulness to your present experience, highlights the benefits of practicing mindfulness during everyday tasks. For example, by being mindful of your present experience, you will find that your concentration and memory improve, and you get to know yourself better because you're spending more time in the present moment. The second skill, mental noting, will help you to increase your practice by breaking mindfulness down into smaller parts. The third skill, living life mindfully, is really the goal of mindfulness. This final skill will help you to see how bringing mindfulness to your life more frequently allows you to be more actively and fully involved in your life.

I'll start with a description of the skills that help you to increase your awareness through practicing mindfulness. Remember that, especially when you have bipolar disorder, increasing your awareness of your internal experience (thoughts, emotions, and physical sensations) is key to identifying and possibly preventing future depressive, manic, or hypomanic episodes.

MINDFULNESS TO YOUR PRESENT EXPERIENCE

Mindfulness is all about living more in the present moment and accepting whatever you find in that moment. One way to practice this is to bring your full attention to whatever you find yourself doing, feeling, or thinking—being mindful of your present experience.

Especially when you have bipolar disorder and are manic or hypomanic, the tendency is to do many things at once. Often people report starting many different projects and not actually finishing any of them because their mind is racing so quickly that it becomes nearly impossible for them to keep their attention on just one thing for any length of time. The idea behind being mindful of your present experience, like mindfulness in general, is that you do one thing at a time with your full attention. For example, if you're talking to a friend on the phone, that's all you're doing, and you're completely focused on the conversation. If you're eating, you are only eating, and that's all you're paying attention to. Remember that it's natural for your attention to wander from whatever task you're focusing on. The idea isn't to keep your attention from wandering, but rather to gently (in other words, without judging yourself) bring your attention back when you do wander.

I've had clients with bipolar disorder tell me that this is one of the most helpful skills they've learned with regard to hypomania because it helps them to slow down. Instead of doing many things at once, which often leads to feelings of being overwhelmed, deliberately doing one thing at a time with your full attention helps you to get things done without becoming overwhelmed or anxious.

On the other hand, some people have described frustration with this skill because they feel it slows them down and makes them less effective when they are hypomanic and can get many things done by multitasking. Marsha Linehan describes a study in which people were separated into two groups (2003c). Each group was given the same set of tasks to accomplish, but one group was told to get everything done as quickly as they could by multitasking. The other group was told to do one thing at a time with their full attention.

According to Linehan, the more efficient group in this study was the group who did things mindfully. This doesn't mean that you can't do more than one thing at a time, but you need to bring your focus with you rather than splitting your attention. So when you're at work writing an e-mail and the phone rings, you can answer the telephone. But doing so mindfully means you need to stop writing your e-mail and give the phone call your full attention.

Granted, it may very well be the case that when you're hypomanic you have the ability to do many things at once and be effective. Doing things in this way, however, will keep you speeded up and can feed into the hypomania. Remember that this state is the double-edged sword that might feel great but can also escalate into full-blown mania or end in a depressive crash, either of which could require hospitalization or lead to other negative consequences.

Being mindful of your present experience also keeps you in the present moment. From the previous chapter, you'll recall that living in the present is helpful because so many people tend to dwell on the past, which triggers painful emotions such as regret, sadness, guilt, shame, and anger; or they spend a lot of time worrying about the future, which increases anxiety. When you are doing activities mindfully, your attention may wander to the past or the future, but you immediately bring your attention back to the present, reducing those unnecessary painful emotions and the likelihood that you'll get caught up in them.

Peter, for example, was experiencing anxiety in crowded places or when he was in a place where he perceived he wouldn't be able to leave easily if he became anxious and felt the need to escape. This anxiety had gradually developed over the last two years, and it had escalated to the point that he was now avoiding situations such as going to church and other events that would require him to be seated in a place where he would not be able to leave easily. In addition, he was no longer able to take the train to work every morning as he used to because of this anxiety.

In our first session, Peter was able to see how he was spending much of his time living in the future, which was causing him a lot of anxiety triggered by what-ifs: "What if I have to leave in a hurry and I can't get out?" "What if I start to feel sick, and I have to leave in the middle of the church service?" "What if I have a panic attack and I can't escape?" Peter and I discussed ways that he could practice being mindful of whatever experience he was having, and in the very next session, he reported a decrease in his anxiety. He had attended his daughter's soccer game and mindfully watched the game rather than creating imaginary futures for himself. He got back on the commuter train and read the newspaper mindfully to keep his mind off his anxiety about not being able to escape. When the anxiety got a little worse on the train, he did some abdominal breathing, which helped to calm him. Although we did more work to assist with his anxiety, Peter was able to decrease the amount of time he was spending in the future by focusing on the present moment. This reduced his anxiety substantially and made it much more tolerable.

So you can probably see that being mindful of your present experience can be quite helpful in a variety of ways. Next I'm going to tell you about a skill that will help you practice being more mindful of your present experience. This mindfulness skill, called *mental noting*, will help you continue to hone your mindfulness practice so that you can reach the point of living your life mindfully.

MENTAL NOTING

This mindfulness skill has you simply using your senses to notice and then label whatever comes to your attention about your present experience. For example, stop right now and focus only on the sensations occurring in your left hand. Try to simply sense your left hand and note whatever sensations come to your awareness. The trick here is to just notice your experience with acceptance and then to describe it, rather than judge it in some way. For example, mentally noting the experience in your left hand may have you describing it as hot or cold; these are just descriptive terms. There is no interpretation or judgment involved; you're simply describing what you notice.

Judging your experience could include a thought such as "This is stupid. I don't feel anything in my left hand right now." If this is what your experience was like, this kind of judgment is completely natural; judging our experience is an automatic behavior. (I'll tell you about the problems that can arise from this in the next chapter.) For now, just be aware that the practice of mental noting is simply sensing whatever experience you are having in the moment, accepting whatever you find in that moment, and describing it factually, without judgment. For most of us this takes a lot of practice.

The other thing to remember when you're trying to practice mental noting is that we all have a tendency to experience multiple things at once. For example, you may look around a room and notice all of the things in the room. This may be observing, but it's not mental noting. The mindfulness skill of mental noting means that you are noticing and labeling one thing at a time, with your full attention. So you might pick one thing out of that room and focus all of your attention on mentally noting just that one thing. This can be a great skill to help you reduce stimulation when you're feeling manic or hypomanic. By focusing your full attention on just one thing at a time, you can help to calm yourself and slow yourself down.

Mental noting can also be used to help you to put some distance between yourself and your emotions about an experience, so that your emotions don't control your behaviors. Let's look at some examples:

- Noticing that your thoughts are racing and you're experiencing urges to go out and spend a lot of money, start a large project, or throw a last-minute dinner party for thirty friends, you mentally note your experience—including the urges, emotions, thoughts, and any physical sensations—and you realize you are becoming hypomanic. (Now you can do something about it.)

- Feeling anxious about a social event, you mentally note this experience to yourself: "I have a knot in my stomach. My palms are sweaty. My legs are trembling. I'm having thoughts about looking foolish because I don't know many people there." Rather than getting caught up in the emotion, mentally note your experience to help you keep some distance from it, preventing the emotion from taking over.

- Imagining yourself doing something you dislike, such as cooking, and as you do this activity you focus on mentally noting your actions. As you do so, the negative feelings of dislike, boredom, or whatever else may be associated with the activity will be less likely to emerge because you're engaged in the activity and accepting of it, rather than doing it while thinking about how much you dislike doing it.

You may be thinking that you already notice what you're doing and experiencing all the time, so how is this acting skillfully? The thing is, we often neglect to notice things. For example, our thoughts, physical sensations, and emotions often sail by under our radar. And instead of factually labeling things, we often make interpretations. The problem with this, of course, is that our interpretation is often incorrect, but we act as though it's a fact rather than an assumption.

Let's look at another example: You're walking down the street on a sunny day. Coming toward you, quite a distance away, is your next-door neighbor. You recognize her by the bright red jacket she's wearing. As she gets closer to you, you watch her suddenly cross to the other side of the road without looking up or acknowledging you in any way. After watching this behavior, you may decide that she was being rude or snobbish, and you might feel angry or hurt as a result. If you look more closely, however, you'll see why this is an interpretation rather than a description of your neighbor's behavior. If you were to accurately label what you saw, all you could say is this:

- My neighbor was walking quickly toward me.

- Her head was down.

- Her hands were in her pockets.

- About fifty feet from me, she crossed the street.

Based on this description of what you noticed, you can make many interpretations: she doesn't like me, she's avoiding me, she thinks I'm crazy, and on and on. But if your goal is to practice the mindfulness skill of mental noting, you need to stick to the facts and describe only what your senses tell you. If you do this, there will be no hurt or angry feelings because you haven't interpreted. Of course, this isn't easy. We are so used to making interpretations and assumptions that we're often not even aware that this is what we are doing—to the point that we actually mistake these interpretations and assumptions for facts. It does take practice, but over time you'll be able to distinguish thoughts (including judgments, interpretations, and assumptions) from facts.

The above is an example of mentally noting something externally; it is also important to mentally note internal experiences. I mentioned earlier that we often neglect to notice things. Some people tend to focus more on what's happening outside of them and ignore their own internal experience, while others are very focused on themselves and don't notice what's going on around them. Which are you? The trick, as with most things in DBT, is to find a balance. You need to be aware of both internal and external events. Here are some exercises to help.

Mental Noting with External Experiences

- Look around the room you're sitting in. Pick an object and practice mental noting by labeling exactly what you see. (For example, I am looking at an azalea bush on my living room floor. It has some green leaves sprouting from the bottom of it, has lots of white flowers on it, is about two feet tall, and so on.)

- Look at a picture hanging on a wall and notice the colors in it. Don't judge the colors and don't compare them to others; simply describe what you see.

- Go for a walk and mentally note your environment using your senses. (For example, I hear a dog barking; I see a squirrel running; I feel the wind against my face; I smell freshly cut grass; and so on.)

Mental Noting with Internal Experiences

- Notice any physical sensations you may be experiencing and label them without judging them, interpreting them, or trying to figure out what they mean. (For instance, I have a knot in my stomach. I'm holding my breath, and my jaw is clenched.)

- Practice any of the observing thoughts exercises from the mindfulness chapter (chapter 2) to help you use mental noting with your thoughts and emotions.

- Practice noticing when you are interpreting rather than describing things by paying attention to your thoughts and simply saying to yourself "interpretation" or "description" as you notice these things happening. (By the way, this type of exercise will help you to be more aware of when you're making interpretations and assumptions so that you can decrease this habit.)

For people with bipolar disorder, mentally noting internal experiences is extremely important to help identify symptoms of depression, mania, and hypomania. The more you can pay attention to your internal experience, the sooner you'll become aware of symptoms as they arise. For example, mentally noting to yourself that your thoughts are coming more quickly, that you've been feeling much more energetic for the past few days, and that you are feeling much more confident right now could be a clue that you are entering a high. This may not always be the case, of course, so you want to assess the situation by using the skill of mental noting. This will allow you to simply notice and describe your experience rather than jumping to the conclusion that you are becoming manic. The fact that you are mentally noting your symptoms—noticing them with acceptance—also means that you're less likely to generate more emotions for yourself by judging them and worrying about what they mean. Instead, you're simply sensing whatever is present within you at that moment and describing it nonjudgmentally.

■ Shawn's Story

Shawn was a man I worked with in a group who explained how he had used mental noting to help him deal with hallucinations he was experiencing. Hallucinations can obviously be a frightening experience, and when he began to have them, he would typically work himself up into a panic because he knew this meant he was becoming manic. The panic would then get in the way of him being able to act effectively to get help before the mania became full-blown. After learning this skill, however, Shawn was able to simply note what his experience was with acceptance. Thus, he didn't trigger extra emotions in himself that blocked his ability to act in a way that would be helpful to him. As a result, he was able to contact his doctor and explain what was going on, his meds were changed, and he was able to stave off a full-blown manic episode.

Mental noting is about allowing yourself to simply experience something in the present moment without your emotions and thoughts (assumptions, interpretations, and judgments) getting in the way. In this way, you will be able to open yourself to each experience more fully, rather than allowing your thoughts and emotions to shut you off from it. When you make assumptions, interpretations, or judgments about something, you come to believe that you know what that something is. In reality, you don't know what it is; you've simply "covered up the mystery with a label" (Tolle 2006, 25), and the label prevents you from exploring.

LIVING LIFE MINDFULLY

The overarching goal of mindfulness is to live your life with more awareness. As you practice the skills of being more mindful of your present experience and mental noting, over time these practices will begin to flow naturally from you. The result will be that you are living a more mindful life. When you get to this point, you will notice that you are more able to engage in whatever you are doing and emotions such as anxiety and sadness will interfere less and less.

You may be thinking right now that these skills are very difficult, that you have to really work hard to use them and even just to remember them, and that it takes a lot of energy to practice mindfulness. As you keep practicing, however, you will find that these skills start to flow more naturally. Think back to your experience of learning how to ride a bike or do another difficult task. At first you really had to focus your attention and concentrate on what you were doing. But gradually, as time went on, you were able to get into the activity and just enjoy it without worrying that you were going to fall and hurt yourself.

More than likely, there are certain aspects of your life in which you are already fully engaged and during which you slip into a kind of mindfulness automatically. These are the activities in which you look up and suddenly an hour has passed without your really being aware of the time. Some examples include playing a sport, doing certain aspects of your job, or being in a relationship with a certain person. What are some activities in your life that you are easily able to be mindful of?

_____   _____

_____   _____

_____   _____

For people with bipolar disorder, achieving this level of mindfulness—being fully engaged in an activity and throwing yourself into your experiences—might actually seem kind of frightening. You are told continuously that you need to regularly monitor you mood and behavior to ensure you don't lose control and become manic or hypomanic. As we'll explore later in this book, you've probably had many experiences of having your emotions invalidated. For example, when you're feeling excited about something, you're told to calm down because you seem to others as if you might be becoming manic. So you may be wondering how you can fully engage in an experience when you have to continuously monitor and keep yourself in check.

The answer to this question is through mindfulness and with practice. Think about the activities you are already able to mindfully engage in. Do these end in catastrophe each time you do them? Of course not! Mindfully living your life does not mean losing control. In fact, mindfulness leads to the opposite—gaining *more* control because your emotions aren't getting in the way of your ability to experience your life. We'll talk more about this in the next chapter when we look at how our thinking styles can get in the way of our ability to make healthy choices about our lives.

For now, remember that the more you practice all of the skills in this workbook, the more natural they will become for you. Right now it may be extremely difficult for you to distinguish between your symptoms of bipolar disorder and the characteristics of your personality. The more you get to know yourself through practicing these skills, the clearer this distinction will become. And gradually, when you begin to experience emotions and physical sensations or engage in behaviors that are out of character for you, this will come to your attention fairly quickly because you are regularly being mindful of your experience. In other words, you will be using skills to effectively manage your illness.

WRAPPING UP

Hopefully these DBT skills have helped to deepen your understanding of mindfulness so that you can continue to increase your awareness of yourself and your environment through regular practice. You may want to take a break between this and the next chapter of the book to give yourself an opportunity to practice mental noting of both internal and external experiences. If you are aware that you already tend to focus on one or the other, practice the one that is harder for you. In other words, if you know you tend to avoid your internal experience, work on noticing emotions, thoughts, and sensations. If you're aware that you tend to focus on your internal experience, practice mindfully paying attention to things that are external to you.

Also, don't forget about being mindful of your present experience and living life mindfully. Try to be aware of activities that you are already able to be mindful of, and notice how it feels to be able to do this. The skills in this chapter will help you to further your understanding of mindfulness and become more comfortable in developing your own practice.

In the next chapter, I'll be teaching you about the three different ways we think about things and how each of these modes of thinking can impact us. We'll look at how you can think about things in ways that will help you to choose how to act in situations, rather than reacting from your emotions. Remember though, that the mindfulness skills you've learned so far are the building blocks for the rest of the skills I have to teach you. Please keep practicing them as you continue working your way through this book.

CHAPTER 4

Choosing How to Act vs. Reacting

Have you ever been so caught up in your emotions that you felt like you couldn't even think straight? When you have bipolar disorder, it can often feel like you are at the mercy of your emotional states—like you're the passenger in the car, just along for the ride. Believe it or not, this doesn't have to be the case. This next subject, looking at the three different thinking styles, is one of the primary DBT skills, and it is a skill that people are often able to begin using immediately. The goal here is to gain more control over your emotions and your behaviors.

UNDERSTANDING THREE DIFFERENT WAYS OF THINKING

We all have three different ways of thinking that guide our actions: emotion mind, reasoning mind, and wise mind (Linehan 1993b). Many of the skills you'll be learning in this book will help you learn how to make healthy choices for yourself based on what you think and feel about a situation; this is wise mind. While this may sound fairly straightforward, you may be surprised at how difficult it can be to get there. Let's look at some examples of how the way we think about things can get in the way of our ability to make choices or decisions that are in our best interests.

■ Louise's Story

Louise recently started a relationship with a woman. It was her first lesbian relationship, and she was anxious about how her family and friends would respond. Her new partner, Diane, had always been open with her family and friends about her sexuality, and so it was difficult for her to understand Louise's fears. But she tried to be supportive until Louise was ready to introduce her to her loved ones. After three months, however, Diane was becoming impatient and concerned about Louise's reluctance, and she would try to speak with Louise about how this was impacting their relationship. But Louise's anxiety about the reactions of her friends was too high. She worried that they wouldn't accept her. Even though she was happier with Diane than she had ever been in her relationships with men, she broke off the relationship and continued to hide her real identity.

Here we can see how Louise's emotions controlled her choices. She reacted from her emotions, rather than taking the time to weigh both her feelings and her thoughts to help her come to a healthier decision for herself. Let's look at one more example.

■ Rob's Story

Rob had been working at his job for about two years and was quite happy there. Rob worried, though, that his bipolar disorder was going to get in the way of his being able to keep his job. He had been let go from his last job because he had suffered depression that had impacted his concentration and memory to the point that his performance at work had suffered.

Rob met with his manager for his scheduled performance appraisal and was given some constructive feedback about his performance, including the fact that he seemed unfocused and lacking in attention at times. This was something the management team wanted him to work on in order to be able to advance within the organization. Rather than hearing the message that his managers wanted him to advance, however, Rob took this as a sign that he was eventually going to be fired again due to his difficulties with concentration and memory. Angry with this feedback and anxious about how it would look if he was fired from another job, Rob went and found a new job and quit the one he liked so well.

In these examples, we can see how both Louise and Rob were overcome by what DBT refers to as *emotion mind* (Linehan 1993b). Emotion mind is essentially the style of thinking that takes over and causes you to react from your emotions, to the point that it feels like your emotions are controlling you.

Emotion mind is the thinking style that often gets you into trouble. The key to recognizing emotion mind is that when you are there, your behavior is dependent on how you feel. In other words, your way of thinking becomes dominated by your emotions, which then control your behaviors. For example, you feel angry and you lash out at someone; you feel anxious and you avoid the situation causing this anxiety; or you feel depressed and you withdraw and isolate yourself.

Emotion mind is not a bad thing, however; it also encompasses positive emotions such as love, joy, and excitement. So the goal is not to get rid of emotion mind, because we want to feel these positive emotions. And, as uncomfortable as it can be, we need to feel painful emotions such as grief and anger. As I will discuss in chapter 6, emotions often motivate us to do things, and the ability to feel emotions is part of what makes us human. We would be unable to empathize with others if we didn't feel these things ourselves.

Take a moment to look at some examples of emotion mind, then see if you can think of times when you have acted solely from your emotions:

- Drinking or using drugs to avoid or escape from feelings

- Feeling highly energized and on top of the world, then calling friends in the middle of the night to tell them how much you care about them

- Yelling at your boss because you're feeling hurt and angry after receiving some constructive criticism

Consider times in the past you may have been acting from emotion mind, and write down one or two instances here:

_____

_____

_____

The balancing counterpart to emotion mind is *reasonable mind* (Linehan 2003a), also known as reasoning mind. Reasoning mind is the part of your mind you use to do logical, thinking kinds of activities, where there is very little or no emotion involved. You can think of reasoning mind as the cool, logical, matter-of-fact part of yourself that emerges when you are just attending to facts and are able to think rationally. Examples of reasoning mind would include writing out a grocery list, following directions to get to a place you've never been before, or balancing your checkbook (unless, of course, this triggers anxiety or other painful emotions). Computer programmers, mathematicians, and architects are examples of people who would likely be in reasoning mind frequently in order to do their jobs.

Reasoning mind is obviously very important, and you need to be able to access this thinking style to help you do all sorts of things. However, some people spend much of their time in reasoning mind and are thrown out of balance because they are out of touch with their emotions. This can lead to avoidance of feelings and an inability to manage and express emotions when they do arise.

Below are some additional examples of reasoning mind. Have a look, and then see if you can think of some times when you've acted from this way of thinking:

- Pushing away or avoiding your feelings, rather than allowing yourself to experience them; for example, by telling yourself those feelings aren't logical or rational

- Making a decision solely based on logic, rather than taking into consideration how you feel about the possible outcomes

Times when you have acted from reasoning mind:

_____

_____

_____

Wise mind results when you are able to think from both emotion mind and reasoning mind together (Linehan 1993b). It is finding the balance between your emotions and your logic so that you can act in ways that fit with your morals and values and make healthy choices that are in your best interest. When you are in wise mind, you still feel your emotions (emotion mind), but you are also able to think straight (reasoning mind). Putting these two elements together helps you to get to a point of knowing what the most effective thing is for you to do in a situation. When you're in wise mind, you will feel stable and unwavering, while the other two ways of thinking have you in a state of unbalance and uncertainty. Let's look at an example to further your understanding of how you are impacted by each of these thinking styles.

Let's say that you have a doctor's appointment scheduled for 9:00 A.M. You wake up in the morning, and you feel awful. You're tired, you feel depressed, and you may be anxious about having to go. Emotion mind in this situation would have you say, "Forget it! I'm not going. I feel lousy." You might pull the blankets over your head and try to go back to sleep. Here your emotions are controlling your behavior.

Reasoning mind would have you consider the pros and cons of the situation; for example, "If I don't go to this appointment, I'll have to pay a twenty-five-dollar fee for not canceling, and the doctor is usually so busy I may not get another appointment for a week or so."

In wise mind, you would combine these first two lines of thinking: "I really feel lousy and I don't want to go. But if I don't go, I'll have to pay the cancellation fee and will have to wait for another appointment." Wise mind would have you make a decision that takes into consideration both how you feel and what you think about the situation, rather than relying on just one or the other. In this way, you are more able to act in your own best interest and make a decision that will be healthy and wise: "I can't afford to pay the cancellation fee, and I need to see the doctor quickly, so *it's in my best interest* to go, even though I don't feel up to it." Wise mind helps you to determine what is truly best for you, which in this case is to get out of bed and get to your appointment in spite of your fatigue, depression, and anxiety.

Sometimes when you've been in emotion mind a lot, it's hard to reach wise mind. Some people think they don't even have a wise mind (Linehan 1993b), or that they've never used it. Every single one of us has a wise mind, and we use it on a regular basis. But because it often doesn't have a huge impact on our lives, it's sometimes harder to recognize. Take a moment now to look at the following examples of wise mind. Then see if you can think of some examples of when you have acted from this balanced way of thinking, and write them in the blanks below:

- Getting out of bed in the morning when you're feeling depressed

- Going to work or school even though you're anxious

- Choosing to cook nutritious food for yourself instead of eating junk food, even when you have little energy to do this for yourself

- Going for a walk instead of watching another hour of television, even though you feel like isolating yourself

Times when you have acted from wise mind:

_____

_____

_____

Distinguishing Wise Mind from Emotion Mind

Sometimes it's difficult to tell the difference between emotion mind and wise mind, because there are emotions present in both of these thinking styles. Here are a couple of tips to help you differentiate between these two modes (Linehan 1993b):

- Assess how strong the emotion feels. If it seems intense, then you are likely in emotion mind. On the other hand, if the emotion is present but does not seem really strong or doesn't feel overwhelming, this is probably wise mind.

- If you're trying to make a decision from wise mind, sit with your decision for some time before acting on it. If you find that your decision remains constant and you have a sense of peace or calm about it, you are likely in wise mind. If you find that you keep alternating back and forth between different options, you are likely still in emotion mind, being controlled by your fluctuating emotions. In this case, you need to give yourself more time to come to a wise decision.

What's Your Habitual Way of Thinking?

Now that you have an understanding of the three different ways of thinking, it's time to practice some awareness. Looking over the examples of times you have been in reasoning mind, emotion mind, and wise mind, can you pinpoint where you spend the majority of your time? Are you a person who is most often in reasoning mind, avoiding feelings by just thinking logically? Are you a person who is frequently in emotion mind, allowing your emotions to control your behavior? Do you feel you are usually able to strike a balance between these two, so that you're acting in your own best interest from wise mind? Or maybe you find you tend to alternate between all three of these states, depending on circumstances. At this point, is doesn't really matter where you find yourself; the important part is developing an awareness of what your habitual way of thinking is. This way you'll be able to employ the skills you learn in this book to help you get to wise mind more often. For most people with bipolar and other mental health problems, it is emotion mind that causes most of the difficulties, so I'll be discussing the consequences of being stuck in this way of thinking fairly often.

As you read in the last chapter, one of the first steps to changing a behavior is to become aware of when the behavior is occurring. Most people aren't normally aware of how they think about things—they just act. This can cause difficulties if you're spending too much time in reasoning mind or emotion mind. Remember, the key here is balance. But before you can work on balance, you need to develop self-awareness. So from this point forward, your job is to try to increase your awareness of what thinking style you're in. To do this, you need to actually start asking yourself the question "What thinking style am I using?" You need to do this on a regular basis—and by this I mean multiple times each day.

For most people, the difficulty isn't identifying what is most influencing their thinking once they've stopped to consider it, but just remembering to ask the question. To help incorporate this practice into your daily life, I suggest that you try pairing it with something else you do multiple times each day. Some examples include eating (as long as you eat at least three times daily), drinking liquids, and using the washroom. All of us engage in these behaviors at least three times per day, so if you can ask yourself the question "What thinking style am I using?" whenever you engage in one of these activities, you will be asking yourself the question at least three times daily. This will also help you make this part of your daily routine, so that the skill of bringing your awareness to your current way of thinking will become more natural for you.

Keep in mind, the more often you can remember to ask yourself that question, the more quickly you will develop awareness. Once you become aware of what is influencing your thinking, you'll find that you have more control over your behavior. You'll be taking yourself off of automatic pilot and will be consciously *choosing* how to act from wise mind, rather than reacting from emotion mind.

How Wise Mind Will Help You Be More Effective in Life

Many people are habitually unaware of their emotions and thoughts, and their goals in different situations. This makes it very difficult to interact with others in a way that is successful—that is, in a way that helps you to meet your goals and to feel good about yourself. Using mindfulness to increase your awareness can help you to be more effective, or healthy, in many different ways.

Have you ever found yourself in a situation where you may have known that engaging in a specific behavior might do you more harm than good, but you went ahead and did it anyway because, on some level, it felt good? For example, you're unhappy with how you're treated at work, so you quit your job suddenly without giving notice and with a few choice words for your boss. This might have felt good at the time, but you know that now you can't ask your boss for a reference letter due to your behavior. This is an example of being unhelpful to yourself.

Let's look at another example: You've started taking a new medication that's supposed to help stabilize your mood, but you notice you've started gaining weight and have been experiencing some other unpleasant side effects, so you stop taking the new medication without telling your psychiatrist. Again, this may feel better in the short term, as the weight gain and other side effects stop, but two weeks later you end up in the hospital with a manic episode. This was unhelpful (and unhealthy) behavior.

Can you think of examples of when you've acted in a way that may have been satisfying in the short term, but in the long run may have been harmful, or at the very least not beneficial to you?

_____

_____

_____

_____

Essentially, being effective in DBT refers to doing what it takes in a situation to get your needs met (Linehan 1993b). Often what gets in the way of doing what works is your thoughts about the situation. For example, you think that the way you've been treated at work isn't fair, so why should you give two weeks notice and be civil to the boss? Or you think that it's not fair that you have to take medication every day when most other people don't, so why should you have to put up with annoying side effects? In other words, you're often responding not to the reality of the situation itself, but to the way you *wish* the situation was (Linehan 1993b).

Another factor that often interferes with acting in a healthy way or in a way that will be helpful to you is that you don't know what you want in a situation. It's very difficult to figure out how to meet your goal if you're not even sure what your goal is. Slow yourself down and give this some thought before acting—in other words, be mindful. In many situations we have more than one goal. In the example of quitting your job, your goals may be to let off some steam and get "justice" by telling your boss what you really think of her. But you may also have the longer-term goal of having a reference to get your next job. When this is the case, use wise mind to help you decide which is the most important goal, especially if one likely precludes the other.

The third stumbling block, related to the second, is that you may focus on your needs or wants only in the short term, rather than thinking about what will be most helpful for you in the long run (Linehan 1993b). While you might get some satisfaction out of yelling at an employer whom you feel didn't treat you with respect, in the long run you must remember that you need that person to say good things about you to help you get the next job.

In order to be effective in a situation, therefore, you must be able to access wise mind. It makes sense that you would be frustrated with the side effects from the new medication, but rather than letting this frustration control your actions by stopping the medication, you need to access the other thinking styles. Reasoning mind, for example, would have you think about the likelihood of a manic or depressive episode and the other dangers of stopping the medication without letting your psychiatrist know. By balancing reasoning mind with emotion mind, you will be able to use wise mind to determine what your goal is and how you can act in your own best interest; for example, "I'm frustrated with the side effects and have decided the weight gain is not acceptable. I need to book an appointment with my psychiatrist to inform her of this and request that she prescribe a different mood stabilizer."

I should add here that, although the focus of this skill is to meet your long-term goals, that doesn't give you license to do so at the expense of others. You still need to act within the parameters of your own morals and values. So if you're competing with a coworker for a promotion, it's not helpful for you to start a rumor that the person has been stealing from your employer. Such a decision would not have come from wise mind, because it isn't in your best interests. Acting in ways that don't match your principles decreases your self-respect and will not serve you in the end.

Take a moment now to think of a situation in which you could practice being healthy or helpful to yourself. Consider the questions below to help you practice mindfulness in order to determine what will be most helpful for you in this situation:

1. Describe the situation:

_____

_____

2. What are the emotions you are experiencing about this situation?

_____

_____

3. What is your urge in this situation? (What is emotion mind telling you to do?)

_____

_____

4. What is your long-term goal in this situation?

_____

_____

5. What would be a helpful action for you to take in this situation? (In other words, what can you do that would make it most likely for you to meet your long-term goal?)

_____

_____

Keep in mind that acting in a healthy, helpful way to yourself, as with using any other type of skill, is not a guarantee that you will get your needs met. But it will increase your chances of doing so.

REDUCING REACTIVITY THROUGH HEALTHY LIFESTYLE CHOICES

There are often things that we do that make us more likely to react from our emotions. Developing a new awareness is only part of the solution to stopping yourself from being controlled by your emotions. Many of the skills that I'll be introducing in this book will help you to learn to access wise mind. The first thing to look at is your lifestyle—things you may be doing right now that increase the likelihood that you will act from emotion mind.

In the following section, you will read about some concrete lifestyle changes you can begin to work on immediately that will help to balance your way of thinking and decrease the extent to which you react from emotion mind. Many of these strategies are adapted from the work of Marsha Linehan (1993b).

Improve Your Sleep Habits

Do you notice that not getting enough sleep or getting too much sleep can impact your mood? Not enough sleep can cause you to feel irritable; too much sleep can also cause irritability, as well as a lack of energy and motivation. Especially if you have bipolar disorder, balancing sleep is probably the most important and most easily controlled factor that can help reduce the extent to which you react from emotion mind.

Sleep is important in maintaining good health in general, but it is even more important if you have bipolar disorder, since unbalanced sleep can actually trigger a manic or hypomanic episode. Marguerite, for example, only experienced manic episodes whenever she traveled long distances, because her sleep schedule became so disrupted. And when she did have these episodes, she inevitably required hospitalization, which illustrates the importance of self-care in this area.

You may have heard that we all need to sleep a certain number of hours. At various times, I've heard that the average person needs seven and a half, eight and a half, and even nine and three quarters hours of sleep a night, numbers that have come out of various studies done over the years. Experience has taught me, however, that we all have our own magic number. One person, for example, may feel rested after a mere six hours of sleep, while others are unable to function optimally unless they get eight and a half. The trick here is to find your own magic number, and this isn't always easy. Here are some guidelines to help you figure this out, if you don't already know your own magic number:

1. If you aren't already, start filling out a mood chart (from chapter 1). This chart allows you to track the number of hours you are sleeping.

2. Choose a time when you feel your mood is relatively stable (in other words, you are experiencing a mood that is relatively normal for you). This may mean you need to wait for a while, but it's important in order to get an accurate understanding of yourself.

3. Start by allowing yourself seven and a half hours of sleep. This usually means you'll need to set an alarm clock to wake you. Monitor your mood at this number of hours for a few days and see what you notice. If you're regularly feeling tired and sleepy, then increase your sleep by fifteen minutes and monitor there for a few days. Continue in this way until you find yourself feeling rested or you notice an improvement in your mood.

4. If you're someone who is currently sleeping a lot (for example, over ten hours per night), you'll likely want to work your way down instead, so start decreasing by fifteen minutes and follow the guidelines above to get to your magic number.

You shouldn't need more than ten hours of sleep per night, and if you're requiring less than six this is probably not enough (unless this has been a long-term pattern for you and is not an indication of hypomania or other mental or physical health problems). Once you find your magic number, it is extremely important to stay there, even when your mood starts to become depressed and all you want to do is sleep or when you become manic or hypomanic and don't want to sleep at all (in this case you may not sleep, but you should still try to rest).

It's also important to try to make sure you are regularly going to bed and getting up at the same time every day, give or take about half an hour. Even if this means you occasionally need a nap during the day, this is easier on your body than an irregular sleep pattern. That being said, of course napping should be kept to a minimum or it will disrupt your sleep schedule.

The following are some additional tips for those people who have a hard time falling asleep. Keeping in mind how dangerous it can be for people with bipolar disorder to not get enough sleep, you should make every effort to develop healthy sleep habits.

-   Reduce caffeine and nicotine intake, as these are both stimulants that will cause wakefulness. If you have to have coffee or tea, try to switch to decaffeinated or drink your caffeinated beverages only earlier in the day. Note that some teas that look like herbal teas may actually contain caffeinated tea, so be sure to read labels. Caffeine is also contained in many sodas and in chocolate and some other foods. It's also helpful to avoid going to bed after ingesting a large meal, as well as on an empty stomach.

-   Develop a routine that includes calming or soothing activities that will help you to wind down at bedtime. For example, taking a hot bath, reading a book, doing a relaxation or mindfulness exercise, or saying your prayers can all help to wind you down.

- Use your bed only for sleep. Don't engage in non-sleep-related activities in bed, like reading, watching television, talking on the phone, or working on your computer.

- Make sure your bed is as comfortable as possible, with your room at a comfortable temperature. Reduce the noise level in the house as much as possible, or use earplugs if necessary. If you share a bed with a partner who snores or disrupts your sleep in other ways (for example, tossing and turning or talking while asleep), have separate beds or make other arrangements that are agreeable to you both.

- Help slow or stop racing thoughts with mindfulness exercises, or help yourself relax with relaxation techniques.

- If you are unable to fall asleep after a moderate amount of time (around thirty minutes), get out of bed and do something calming such as having a warm glass of milk or a cup of caffeine-free tea (but don't drink so much that you'll be up again to use the bathroom in a short while!). You can also read a relaxing book or watch something calming on television. Avoid stimulating activities at this time, and return to bed when you're feeling tired.

- If you are wakeful throughout the night, turn your clock around so you can't see what time it is. Often we start to get anxious when we see we only have two more hours before we have to get up, and this makes it harder to fall back to sleep. Try not to put pressure on yourself to fall back to sleep—simply accept that right now you are awake, and concentrate on a mindfulness exercise to help slow your thoughts (counting breaths, an exercise mentioned in chapter 2, is a helpful one for sleep).

- Both depressive and manic or hypomanic episodes, as well as anxiety, can cause sleeplessness. Try practicing mindfulness or relaxation exercises, as noted above. If you have been prescribed medications to help you sleep, take them as prescribed. Also, expressing your feelings can often help with sleep, so if you think emotional stress may be contributing to your sleep problems, talk to your doctor or seek professional help from a psychotherapist.

Assess Your Sleep

Think about these questions to see if you could be doing more to improve your sleep habits. Are you currently making sure you get enough sleep, but not too much?

_____

_____

What could you do to be more effective in this (for example, reducing caffeine or going to bed earlier)?

_____

_____

What is one small goal you can set for yourself to start working toward being more effective in this area?

_____

_____

Avoid Substance Use

Substance use is another area that is extremely important in reducing your reacting from emotion mind, especially when you have bipolar disorder. Mood-altering drugs will make you more vulnerable to emotion mind. Alcohol is a depressant, so if you're already feeling depressed, drinking alcohol isn't a great idea. In addition to making it more likely that you will be controlled by your emotions while you're drinking, alcohol continues to impact your mood as it leaves your body. The physical effects of a hangover, for example, usually leave you vulnerable to your emotions, as you may experience nausea and fatigue as well as emotions such as increased irritability, depression, and anxiety (Salloum and Thase 2000). In addition, alcohol impacts your sleep due to what is called a rebound effect (Roehrs and Roth 2001). Many people aren't aware of this and drink alcohol to help them sleep. However, four to five hours after you've ingested the alcohol, the rebound effect kicks in and you will find that your sleep is disrupted.

Research has also suggested that people with both bipolar disorder and alcohol dependence tend to experience more frequent bipolar episodes with shorter periods of euthymic mood between episodes (Salloum and Thase 2000). In other words, if you have bipolar disorder and are dependent on alcohol, you will be depressed and manic more often, with fewer and shorter times of stable mood.

Street drugs can be dangerous for anyone. Cocaine and other stimulants, for example, can trigger a "substance-induced psychotic disorder" (APA 2000, 338) in people without bipolar disorder, so imagine what they might do to you. Even marijuana can cause complications. Over the years, marijuana has become a much more accepted drug, in spite of the fact that it remains illegal. Society's perception of marijuana has caused a certain complacence about the drug, and it is often seen as harmless. For people choosing to use marijuana, however, it is important to know that it can induce psychotic symptoms in people without a mental health problem (Van Laar et al. 2007). It also increases the risk of depression and anxiety, and in people with bipolar disorder, it increases the risk for manic symptoms (Henquet et al. 2006).

Substance abuse is, unfortunately, quite common in people with bipolar disorder. It's estimated to be a problem in at least one-third of hospitalized patients with the diagnosis (Goldberg et al. 1999). The consequences of using drugs and alcohol for people with bipolar disorder can be quite serious. Studies have shown, for example, that alcohol or drug use in people with bipolar disorder is associated with a poorer response to medications, poorer recovery from bipolar symptoms, and less improvement in functioning after experiencing an affective episode (Strakowski et al. 2000). In other words, if you have bipolar disorder and you use drugs or alcohol, you are less likely to recover and reach your previous level of functioning than someone who does not use substances.

Another study found that people with bipolar disorder who had a history of substance abuse or dependence were significantly more likely to experience thoughts of suicide, to have lower rates of remission from manic episodes while hospitalized, and to experience mixed episodes rather than pure manic episodes (Goldberg et al. 1999). The importance of this, as you may remember from chapter 1, is that mixed episodes are associated with poorer outcomes than other forms of bipolar disorder (Strakowski et al. 2000).

Assessing Your Management of Substance Use

Is substance use an area you need to work on? Answer the following questions to help you determine how you might decrease emotion mind activity by decreasing substance use.

How are you currently managing your use of drugs and alcohol (for example, trying to limit consumption or attending AA meetings)?

_____

_____

What could you do to be more effective in this (for example, start to reduce use or speak to your doctor about your problem)?

_____

_____

What is one small goal you can set for yourself to start working toward being more effective in this area?

_____

_____

Taking Care of Your Mental and Physical Health

There are a variety of ways you can take care of your mental and physical health, which in turn will help you to decrease your emotional reactivity. We'll examine each of these in turn.

TAKE CARE OF PHYSICAL ILLNESS AND PAIN

Do you remember the last time you had the stomach flu or a cold? Or maybe you're someone who, in addition to bipolar disorder, is also dealing with diabetes, fibromyalgia, a previous injury, or migraine headaches. Do you notice how pain or physical illnesses tend to make you feel more irritable or maybe cause you to sink into self-pitying thoughts? This is an example of how physical illness and pain can make you more emotional. The lesson here is that if you are experiencing some type of physical illness, you need to take care of yourself or your emotions will take over. See a doctor for treatment and take medications if they are prescribed, and if neither of these are necessary, take care of yourself by resting and delegating some of your responsibilities so you're not doing too much. Unfortunately, this isn't always possible, especially if you're dealing with long-term illness or pain. If this is the case, you need to acknowledge that you're dealing with an additional challenge and try to be as aware as possible of when this is impacting you in order to separate your mood from your behavior.

■ Dean's Story

Dean was a forty-nine-year-old man who had been struggling with bipolar disorder since the age of twenty-three. For the last ten years, he was also dealing with a severe back injury sustained at work, which resulted in him being on a disability pension. Dean's pain was constantly with him, and when he came to treatment he talked about how his anger was impacting his third marriage and his relationship with his stepchildren. After learning about the three different ways of thinking and how his pain could increase his susceptibility to emotion mind, Dean was able to be more aware of when his pain was making him more vulnerable to emotion mind. This allowed him to react less often and communicate with his family more effectively about when he wasn't feeling well enough to do things, which had a positive impact on his relationships.

Taking care of your health also includes taking medications as prescribed. This can be a problem if you have to take medications for the rest of your life, like most people with bipolar disorder. But bipolar disorder is an illness, and it does require treatment with medication and frequently with other methods, such as psychotherapy, as well. Taking care of your health, therefore, includes managing your bipolar disorder as effectively as possible.

IMPROVE YOUR EATING HABITS

Eating a healthy, balanced diet is an important part of taking care of your physical and mental health and can help to reduce the likelihood of emotion mind taking over. Have you ever noticed how you feel if you skip lunch? You may become irritable and possibly even anxious because the symptoms of low blood sugar (the result of skipping meals) can include shakiness, dizziness, light-headedness, and nausea, all of which are also symptoms of anxiety. Therefore, undereating increases the extent to which we are controlled by emotion mind.

Overeating can also be problematic in this way. Many people overeat during depressive episodes. Food can be comforting when you're feeling sad and lonely, and it can also alleviate boredom. For some people, it is simply an automatic behavior they engage in while doing another activity like watching television. If you are someone who overeats, think about how you feel after you've eaten that extra serving for dinner or that bag of chips. Usually there is guilt, shame, anger, and other emotions toward yourself—in other words, emotion mind has once again taken over. By eating in a balanced way—neither undereating nor overeating—you reduce your emotional reactivity. Overeating or disordered eating (such as fasting, bingeing, or purging) is not uncommon in people dealing with mental health problems. Distress tolerance skills, discussed in chapter 5, can help you stop acting on these urges.

For now, here are a few suggestions you may want to consider when it comes to eating a balanced diet.

CUT DOWN ON CAFFEINE

This includes coffee, tea, soda, chocolate, and anything else you ingest that contains caffeine. Caffeine is a stimulant, so it speeds you up, giving you a temporary increase in energy. It can cause mood changes, such as a high feeling, irritability, and hyperactivity. It can cause insomnia and symptoms of anxiety such as restlessness, racing heart, and nervousness, as well as other, more intense symptoms, all of which increase the likelihood that your behaviors will be controlled by your emotions. If you examine the above symptoms a bit more closely, you may notice that all of these symptoms of caffeine intake can also be used to describe a hypomanic episode. So consider this: when you are already coping with these kinds of symptoms on a regular basis, do you really want to add to your discomfort by ingesting caffeine?

I once worked with a woman who, when we first began meeting, was drinking about six large cups of coffee per day. She managed over time to cut this down to about two cups of coffee a day and reported an improvement in her sleep and a decrease in her feelings of anger and irritability, which had a positive impact on relationships in her life. While the effects may not be this dramatic for everyone, most people notice some kind of positive changes when they decrease their caffeine intake.

DISCOVER WHETHER FOODS AFFECT YOUR MOOD

There are certain foods that can reportedly aggravate mood changes in some people. In a very small study that Mary Ellen Copeland (2001) refers to in her book about depression and manic depression, people reported that certain foods had a negative impact on their mood. These included the following:

- Fermented foods (some examples include yogurt, bread, wine, cheese, pickled foods, vinegar, olives, chocolate, vanilla, Tabasco sauce, beer)

- Eggs and dairy products

- Meat

- Tomatoes

Keep in mind that this is not a list of foods to cut out of your diet. Rather, if you would like to try alternative ways of cutting down on the mood changes caused by bipolar disorder and reducing your reacting from emotion mind, you may want to experiment by removing these foods from your diet, one at a time, for a trial period. The idea here is that by discontinuing a food for approximately two weeks and monitoring your mood during that time, you will be able to determine if this food may have been impacting your mood. Or perhaps there are other foods that you know affect your moods. Experiment with cutting out those foods, one by one, for a trial period. Of course, if you are concerned about your diet and need assistance in either getting to a balanced weight or eating in a more nutritious way, consult your doctor or a dietician for help.

EXERCISE

Exercise is another factor to consider when looking at how we care for our physical and mental health. We all know exercise is good for us, but sometimes it's just so hard to do it, especially when your mood is low. However, exercise is known to be a natural antidepressant; it makes you feel good, and it can also help improve sleep. In other words, exercising will help in a variety of ways to decrease the extent to which you are controlled by your emotions. Remember, if you haven't exercised for a long time, it's a good idea to get checked out by your doctor before you begin engaging in physical activity. Here are a few suggestions to help you get out and exercise:

- Set small goals for yourself. For example, instead of deciding to go out and join a gym when you haven't really exercised in two years, try going for a walk three times a week. Also, make sure your goals are achievable. If you decide to start walking, for example, set a goal of at least ten minutes, three times per week, instead of one hour each day.

- If you can find a partner to exercise with, you will be more likely to do it.

- Don't wait for motivation to come. Usually people don't feel motivated to do something until they've actually started doing it.

- Don't overdo it. If you start to feel highly energetic and see symptoms of hypomania returning, slow yourself down. You can still exercise, but the goal is moderation. Otherwise you could be feeding into an oncoming manic or hypomanic episode.

- Make exercise part of your routine. This makes it more likely that you'll continue to exercise even when your mood starts to become depressed again.

- Remember, anything more than what you're doing now is going to help, so instead of getting down on yourself for what you're *not* doing, how about a pat on the back for what you are accomplishing!

Assess Your Mental and Physical Health

Answer the following questions to help you assess if there are things you can do with respect to your physical health that would decrease your vulnerability to emotion mind.

How are you currently taking care of yourself physically and mentally? For example, are you taking medication regularly, attending appointments with doctors or other specialists such as physiotherapists, eating nutritious meals, exercising regularly, and so on?

_____

_____

_____

What could you do to be more effective in this? For example, do you take your medications for bipolar disorder? Are you working on increasing physical activity?

_____

_____

_____

What is one small goal you can set for yourself to start working toward being more effective in this area?

_____

Striving for Healthy Relationships

Relationships are an extremely important part of our lives, and we will be looking at them in much more detail later in this workbook, so I'll only say a few words about them here. Trying to have healthy relationships in your life is helpful in reducing emotional reactivity. Surrounding yourself with supportive people gives you a feeling of stability in your life, and having positive influences around you can help you to live your life in a more healthy way. Having people to talk to who are not as influenced by their emotions as you are can help you practice accessing wise mind more often as well.

Ending relationships that are unhealthy in some way (for example, because the person is verbally abusive, has a drug or alcohol problem, or consistently takes a negative attitude toward life that affects your mood) can also have an impact on the degree to which you get caught up in emotion mind. You will have an opportunity to evaluate yourself in this area in chapter 10.

Increasing Your Sense of Mastery

When was the last time you felt good about yourself for something you achieved? It may have been something that seemed small, like making a phone call you had been avoiding, or it may have been something as monumental as applying for a job. Can you think of a time? We should all be doing something like this that makes us feel good about ourselves, ideally once a day. This skill is called *building mastery* (Linehan 1993b), and it's not about what you do, it's about the feeling you get when you do it. Building mastery is about improving how you feel about yourself or building your self-esteem. It's about doing something and then thinking to yourself, "Hey, look what I did!" and feeling good about it. Doing this on a regular basis helps to improve your self-esteem and self-respect, which in the long term helps to decrease how much you react from emotion mind.

Mastery is a very personal skill. What might give a sense of mastery to one person doesn't necessarily have the same effect for the next. Following are some examples of activities that might give you a sense of mastery. Have a look at the list and try to think of things you are currently doing that build mastery for you:

- Going for a walk

- Going to work or school

- Getting out of bed in the morning

- Not acting on an urge

- Washing the dishes

- Taking your medications

- Joining a gym

- Attending a social event

- Taking lessons in a foreign language

- Doing something you've been avoiding (for example, calling someone, answering the telephone, or opening a bill)

Assessing Activities That Give You a Sense of Mastery

Look at the following questions to help you assess where you're at with mastery. Is it something you're already doing regularly? Or is not doing these kinds of activities regularly causing you to judge yourself, triggering more painful emotions?

What are you currently doing that gives you a sense of mastery?

_____

_____

What could you do to be more effective in this?

_____

_____

What is one small goal you can set for yourself to start working toward being more effective in this area?

HOW BEING MINDFUL OF JUDGMENTS CAN DECREASE EMOTION MIND

How often do you hear yourself judging other people, either out loud or thinking judgmental thoughts? Or maybe you're someone who is much harder on yourself than on others.

The skill of being mindful of your judgments is one of the most difficult DBT skills to comprehend and to put into practice, but it is extremely important because of the huge impact the judgments have on making you more vulnerable to your emotions.

Judgments are so commonplace in our society that we often don't even realize when we are judging. For example, we grow up hearing statements like "What a good girl you are," "That was bad," or "You're right." So from a very young age, we hear judgmental messages so frequently that we usually can't help but use this same language ourselves. In addition to the fact that we regularly hear judgments, many people also have a hard time with this skill because there are times when judgments are absolutely necessary, so the goal is not the elimination of all judgments. There are times, for example, when we need to judge if a situation is safe for us to stay in or not. Going through a performance appraisal at work or being graded at school are also necessary judgments. The judgments we want to work on reducing with this skill, therefore, are only the unnecessary judgments that trigger emotion mind. Let's look at an example.

■ Rinty's Story

Rinty lives north of the city, and on his route to and from work, he must take a two-lane highway with lots of traffic and sometimes farm equipment. The speed limit on that road is sixty miles per hour, but often Rinty finds himself behind slower-moving traffic. This causes him frustration, and when he first moved to this area and was in this situation, he had a tendency to make things harder for himself by judging the slow driver in front of him. He would start off saying things like "Come on you idiot, go faster!" (knowing that the driver obviously couldn't hear him). This, however, would trigger more anger, which in turn would cause Rinty to judge more: "Speed it up you moron!" His adrenaline would start pumping, his face would become flushed, and all Rinty could think about was how angry he was at the person blocking him from his goal of getting to work on time.

This is a great example of the vicious cycle that judging creates. Usually, you start off with a small amount of a painful emotion—for example, anger or hurt. From this emotion comes a judgment, either of yourself, another person, or a situation. This inevitably triggers more emotion, which triggers more judgments...and on and on, until you are completely engulfed in emotion mind.

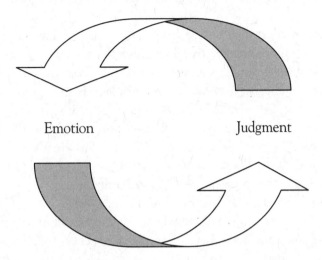

Emotion   Judgment

Does this sound familiar to you? When was the last time you were caught in this cycle? Was it helpful? In other words, were you effective in getting your needs met? How did you feel about yourself and the situation afterward?

The Impact of Judgments

You've just seen how, in general, judgments tend to fuel your emotions and keep you stuck in emotion mind. But that's not where the consequences of judging end. Let's look at self-judgments for a moment. Do you notice that you often say things to yourself like "There must be something wrong with me"? Or do you call yourself a jerk or an idiot when you've made a mistake? Most people say these kinds of things without realizing that they really do have an impact on how you feel about yourself. Over time they lower your self-esteem and can add to feelings of depression and anxiety. You've probably heard about how people who are being verbally abused by another person will, over time, internalize these messages; in other words, when you hear that you're stupid, worthless, or unlovable over a long period of time, you come to believe it. Think of your self-judgments as you verbally abusing yourself. Over time, the result is the same, and you come to believe these things.

Taking judgments as facts in this way also influences how you act toward people and in situations. If you think of a situation as wrong, for example, and take this judgment as a fact rather than acknowledging that it is simply your opinion, you might act in a self-righteous way, and you might refuse to listen to the opinions of others since you already think they're wrong. Through judging, you shut yourself off from seeing any other possibilities or points of view.

Judgments can also impair your ability to be effective in interpersonal situations. If you have a problem with someone and are unable to express yourself in a nonjudgmental way to that person, how do you think they'll react? Usually, some painful emotions will be triggered for them—again, often hurt or anger—and they will shut down or maybe become defensive and argumentative. Either way, you will likely not get your need met, and you may have done some lasting damage to the relationship. Both of these consequences can increase the amount of time you are spending in emotion mind.

In addition, judgments don't give people information about what you want them to do differently. For example, if you tell a coworker that her presentation was bad, you're not providing feedback about what she might have done differently to make it good. You might have judged it as bad because you thought she could have used more audiovisual aids to make it more interesting, or you may have identified things she presented as facts that you knew were false. But in your statement "The presentation was bad," there is no way for your coworker to know what you really mean.

Another example is saying someone is a loser. What do you really mean by this? Is it that you don't approve of the fact that she doesn't have a job? Or is it that you just had an argument with her and she said some things that were hurtful? Negative judgments don't impart information that can help to solve problems; they are only hurtful and damaging.

Often, when I first introduce this skill, people are skeptical and have a hard time believing that judgments they use regularly really have that much of an impact on them. If you don't believe there's a benefit from making a change, it's going to be very difficult for you to change that behavior. So if you have any doubt about the negative emotions triggered by judgments, I suggest you take the time over the next few days to use the Monitoring Judgments Worksheet.

In the first column of this worksheet, you'll want to provide as much detail as you can about the situation that triggered the original emotions for you. (Remember, when you judge, it's usually because something just happened to trigger negative emotions in you, such as anger.) The more details you can provide, the more insight you might be able to achieve regarding where the emotions came from. Once you've identified the situation, turn to the second column and try to see if you can tell what the original emotion was. There may have been more than one, so think hard.

The third column on this worksheet asks you to see if you can identify what the judgment was that you made in the situation. This can be tough, because it may have happened so quickly that you weren't aware of it. Once you've identified your judgment, see if you can figure out which extra emotions were triggered because of the judgment, and put these into column four. With the first example provided in the chart, you're arguing with your friend, you feel misunderstood and angry to begin with, and then you judge her as a bad friend. This judgment leads you to feel more anger on top of the anger you were feeling already. This is the extra emotion.

The last step in the worksheet is to try to increase your awareness of what the consequences were of judging. In this example, you became so angry with your friend that you haven't spoken to her since the fight happened. Examples of consequences are nearly endless and could include you engaging in some sort of unhealthy or self-destructive behavior, assaulting someone, criminal charges, or loss of relationships. In other words, the consequences are usually due to you reacting in some way to the negative emotions triggered by judgments.

If this worksheet helps to convince you that judgments really do increase your emotion mind behaviors and have painful consequences for you, you'll want to move on to working to change your judging behaviors. If you're still not convinced, then you'll want to move on to the next chapter and perhaps come back to judgments at a later date.

MONITORING JUDGMENTS WORKSHEET: EXAMPLE

Situation	Emotions	Judgment	Extra Emotion	Outcome
Arguing with my friend because she wouldn't give me a ride to work	Misunderstood, angry	She's a bad friend.	More anger	No resolution to argument; I haven't talked to her for over one week.
Sitting on the couch, watching TV by myself	Depressed, lonely	There must be something wrong with me. I shouldn't feel like this	Anger toward myself, even more sadness	Feel worse than before; end up drinking to avoid my feelings.

MONITORING JUDGMENTS WORKSHEET

Situation	Emotions	Judgment	Extra Emotion	Outcome

Reducing Judgments to Decrease Emotion Mind Behavior

As with any behavior, the first step in trying to reduce your judgments is to start noticing them. You can do this in a number of ways. First, mindfulness can be extremely helpful in this situation, because we are generally not used to being aware of our thoughts. Start practicing the observing thoughts exercises from chapter 2 on a daily basis to increase your awareness of judgments.

Sometimes you may not be aware that you're judging, but you become aware of a sudden painful emotion such as anger. This can be a clue that you're judging, so try to look at your mind when this happens and see what thoughts are present that are triggering the anger. Being aware of your thinking style can also be helpful, since being in emotion mind can be a clue that there are judgments going on.

Keep in mind that self-judgments are often much more difficult to notice because they are usually habitual and you may not say them out loud, which makes them less noticeable. So if you're a person who judges yourself and others, I suggest that you work on your self-judgments after you've had some practice noticing your judgments of others. Also, if you're aware that you have a tendency to judge more in certain situations than in others (for example, many people can relate to the earlier scenario of judging while driving), you may want to focus on practicing the skill specifically in that situation.

So once you become aware of the judgment, what do you do with it? You turn it into a nonjudgmental statement. Keep in mind that this means that you're trying to craft neutral statements. You're not trying to turn a negative into a positive, first of all because you likely wouldn't believe it. For example, if you call yourself stupid, it really won't be believable or helpful to you if you change that into a statement in which you call yourself smart.

Also be aware that if you label someone as good, she can then do something that will earn her the title of bad. So the trick is to get rid of the label altogether (Linehan 2003c) and stick to the facts. Remember, descriptions, not interpretations.

When turning a judgment into a nonjudgmental statement, try to remember to look at these two things:

1. **What are you really trying to say with this judgment?** Judgments are usually a shorthand way of saying something much longer (Linehan 1993b), so what is it that you're really trying to say? Quite often we're trying to express consequences or our opinion of something. Here's an example: Paulette and her friend Janine have an argument that they are unable to resolve. Afterward, Paulette thinks to herself that Janine is a bad friend. What does Paulette really mean by this? Perhaps she's trying to say that she didn't like the way Janine spoke to her (opinion) and that she's feeling hurt by Janine's behavior (consequences). Or Paulette may mean that she disagrees with Janine's opinion (opinion), and this may be something that prevents them from remaining friends (consequences). So when you're trying to be nonjudgmental, first take out the shorthand judgment and then try to express the long version of what you really mean.

2. **What is the emotion you're trying to express?** As noted earlier, we most often judge because of an emotion. So what is the emotion you're trying to express? Being nonjudgmental is not about stuffing your emotions, being passive, or not stating your opinions about something. On the contrary, it's about learning how to assert yourself more effectively. Remember also that this

skill is not going to make your emotion go away, but it will reduce the unnecessary or extra emotions you are experiencing, which will make it easier for you to access wise mind.

When learning to be mindful of judgments and to be nonjudgmental, some people get stuck in the trap of making excuses. For example, when you're stuck driving behind a truck doing ten miles per hour under the speed limit, you might try to be nonjudgmental by saying, "Maybe the person is a new driver." But statements like this don't really get you to a nonjudgmental stance. The implication of making these kinds of excuses is "Maybe the person is a new driver, so I *shouldn't* be angry that he's driving slowly." (Shoulds and shouldn'ts tend to be judgmental.) This just turned the judgment onto yourself, which is still going to increase your anger and lead to emotion mind.

Remember, we're looking at rephrasing the judgment, not excusing behavior. So rather than trying to think of excuses for why the person might be driving slowly, what could you say instead? Remember the two things to consider: what are you really trying to say, and how do you feel? One way you could rephrase this is "This person is driving too slowly and I'm feeling frustrated because I'm stuck behind her."

In order to help further your understanding of this skill, I've provided some examples of judgments and a nonjudgmental statement for each of them.

1. **Situation (facts only):** You have just recovered from a manic episode in which you used cocaine after being clean for nearly two years.

   Judgment: "I'm such a loser. I've messed everything up."

   Emotion: Anger and disappointment at yourself; hopelessness

   Nonjudgment: "I fell off the wagon while I was manic, and now I'm angry and disappointed in myself. I feel like I have to start all over."

2. **Situation (facts only):** You are having a discussion with a friend about an argument you had with her last week.

   Judgment: "I can't believe you said those things. You were awful to me!"

   Emotion: Pain, anger

   Nonjudgment: "I was very surprised and hurt by some of the things you said, and I'm still feeling angry about it."

3. **Situation (facts only):** You're in the mall and you see a child throwing a temper tantrum. You watch as the parent tells the child he can have the toy he wants if he stops crying.

   Judgment: "That person is a bad parent."

   Emotion: Surprise, disapproval

   Nonjudgment: "I disagree with the way the parent handled that situation."

4. **Situation (facts only):** You look at yourself in the mirror.

   Judgment: "I'm fat."

Emotion: Sadness, worthlessness, anger at yourself

Nonjudgment: "I'm unhappy with my weight and with the way I look right now."

Now let's examine some of your own judgments. Most of us have judgments we use on a regular basis, or situations in which we tend to judge. In the worksheet below, see if you can create nonjudgmental statements for challenging situations. I've broken each down in the categories we looked at above. First, describe the situation with facts only. Next, identify the judgment you've made. Third, state any emotions you have about the situation. And finally, try to combine the description and your emotions to come up with a nonjudgmental statement. Remember, this is a difficult skill to learn, so you may want to enlist the help of a support person to review these statements for you and ensure that they are, in fact, nonjudgmental.

1. **Situation (facts only):** _____

   Judgment: _____

   _____

   Emotion: _____

   Nonjudgment: _____

   _____

2. **Situation (facts only):** _____

   Judgment: _____

   _____

   Emotion: _____

   Nonjudgment: _____

   _____

3. **Situation (facts only):** _____

   Judgment: _____

   _____

   Emotion: _____

   Nonjudgment: _____

   _____

4. **Situation (facts only):** _____

   Judgment: _____

Emotion: _____

Nonjudgment: _____

_____

5.   Situation (facts only): _____

Judgment: _____

_____

Emotion: _____

Nonjudgment: _____

_____

Quite often people have a hard time thinking of nonjudgmental words to replace their judgments with. Rather than thinking of things as good or bad, or right or wrong, here are a few words that often encompass what we're really trying to say:

- Helpful or hurtful

- Effective or ineffective

- Healthy or unhealthy

- Comfortable or uncomfortable

- Necessary or unnecessary

- Appropriate or inappropriate

A few final words about judgments: First, I hope you understand after reading this section that practicing mindfulness to judgments can reduce the amount of time you spend in emotion mind. So by reducing judgments, you will be reducing your emotional pain, which will make it easier for you to access wise mind.

Second, I can't emphasize enough how pervasive judgments are in our society, which can make this skill extremely difficult to practice. Many clients return to see me after learning about judgments and tell me how awful they are because they are judging constantly. They conclude almost immediately that they're obviously no good at this skill. Be careful that you don't judge yourself like this for judging (Linehan 1993b). These kinds of self-judgments will just make you feel worse about yourself.

In addition, now that you have learned this skill, you may begin to notice how much the people around you are judging. When this happens, remind yourself to try not to judge them for this habit. I always encourage people to share these skills with others, so you can certainly teach your loved ones about being more mindful of their judgments as long as you keep in mind that they might not be open to making the changes you're working on yourself. If they're not prepared to take a look at their own behavior, remind yourself that you can't change others, then refocus on you.

Now we've covered all of the core mindfulness skills. These techniques allow you to practice mindfulness in ways that will help you to be more successful in living your life. Make sure you don't just read about these skills, but that as you go along you are also putting them into practice. As much as you can, try to notice your judgments and try to change them to nonjudgments whenever possible. And try to be effective in situations by knowing what your goal is and doing what you need to do to meet it.

WRAPPING UP

A lot of information has been covered in this chapter, including the three different ways we think about things and how using wise mind can help you to be more effective in life. You've also learned some important skills that will help you reduce reactivity from emotion mind. Hopefully you're thinking about lifestyle changes that will help you gain some control over your emotions and increase your ability to access wise mind. Make sure you're using the worksheets provided. These will help you identify the areas you need to work on and think about how you can set small goals to help you work toward making those changes. As time goes on, you will want to come back to those worksheets to check your progress. They can also help you set new goals once you've reached the original ones.

In the next chapter, I'll introduce the DBT crisis survival skills, which will help you to get through crisis situations without making things worse for yourself (Linehan 1993b). Practicing any of these skills requires the use of wise mind, so I strongly encourage you to continue being aware of what thinking style you're using and to assess how you can get to wise mind more often using the skills you've learned so far.

Please remember that the way to get the most out of this book is to go through it slowly, taking the time to do the written exercises and making the effort to practice the skills you've just learned before moving on. Also, while it's very important to practice the new skills, please don't forget to keep working on the ones you've learned in past chapters.

CHAPTER 5

How to Survive a Crisis Without Making It Worse

We all have times in our lives when we encounter emotional crises, when our emotions about a situation are so strong they just overwhelm us and make it difficult to think straight. In these times, some of us instinctively engage in activities that help to reduce the intensity of the emotions and make them somewhat more tolerable. Many of us, however, learned instead to engage in behaviors that actually make the situation worse. We don't do this on purpose, of course. We act in a way that we know is going to help us cope in the short term, but often these coping skills have unhealthy and even self-destructive consequences.

IDENTIFYING SELF-DESTRUCTIVE BEHAVIORS

Think about some times in your life when you've encountered these kinds of situations. They may happen frequently, especially if you are regularly experiencing depression, mania, and mixed episodes. However, the urge to act self-destructively when painful emotions emerge can also occur outside of these mood-related episodes; for example, when a friend or family member dies, a relationship ends, or you're simply experiencing a lot of stress at work. Are you aware of how you generally cope with these situations? Following are some examples of typical behaviors people engage in that may help them cope in the short term, but in the long term make the situation worse. Check the ones that apply to you:

_____ Drinking alcohol

_____ Overeating

_____ Cutting yourself

_____ Verbally lashing out at someone

_____ Avoiding other people or isolating yourself

_____ Using drugs

_____ Engaging in disordered eating (for example, fasting or purging)

_____ Gambling

_____ Throwing things

_____ Engaging in dangerous sexual practices (for instance, having unprotected sex or having sex with someone you just met)

_____ Using sleep to escape

_____ Threatening suicide

_____ Becoming violent toward others

_____ Threatening others

_____ Banging your head against a wall

_____ Pulling out your hair

_____ Attempting suicide

Other ways you cope using self-destructive behaviors:

_____ _____

_____ _____

_____ _____

_____ _____

_____ _____

These are just a few examples of behaviors you may engage in to make yourself feel better in the short term. For example, cutting often makes you feel emotionally better for a short period due to a physiological process that takes place in your body. Self-harming behavior can also provide physical pain that distracts you from your emotional pain. Likewise, using drugs or drinking alcohol numbs emotions and may make you feel better for a short while. But all of these behaviors have long-term consequences that outweigh any short-term benefit they may provide.

Cutting leaves scars, may require medical attention, may be life threatening, and often leads to feelings of guilt, shame, and anger toward yourself. The high from substance use is inevitably followed by the sobering up or crash, which often comes with physical repercussions (for example a hangover), as well as emotional consequences—again, in guilt, shame, and anger toward yourself. These types of unhealthy behaviors also usually have negative impacts on your relationships, as your ways of dealing with crises can tax the people you love.

DISTRESS TOLERENCE SKILLS: HOW TO SURVIVE A CRISIS WITHOUT MAKING IT WORSE

The purpose of this chapter is to help you to learn new coping skills that won't have unhealthy, self-destructive consequences. These skills will not get rid of your emotions, nor will they solve the problems you're currently dealing with. They will simply help you to survive the crisis without making things worse (Linehan 1993b).

Hopefully you are still practicing the mindfulness exercises from the previous chapters, which will help you to notice when painful emotions are coming up for you and when you begin to experience an urge to engage in harmful behavior. The sooner you notice these things, the more ability you will have to choose how to act in the situation using wise mind, rather than simply reacting from emotion mind. It's also important to remember that you won't always be able to do something to make the pain decrease or disappear. But by practicing mindfulness to help you accept the pain, you can make it more bearable (this will be discussed more in chapters 7 and 9). The following are skills to help you not act on those intense emotions and urges so that you are acting in your own best interests in the long run.

Costs and Benefits of Self-Destructive Behaviors

Sometimes people are ambivalent about giving up coping strategies that they know have worked for them in the past, even if they also know those coping behaviors aren't healthy. Change can be extremely uncomfortable, and it takes a lot of energy and effort to replace those old, comfortable skills with new, healthier ones. Even if you're not on the fence about this decision now and you've made up your mind that you want to change, sticking to this decision in the face of the next crisis can be extremely difficult.

This is where doing a cost-benefit analysis can be very helpful. In DBT, this skill is known as looking at the pros and cons of a behavior (Linehan 1993b). Reminding yourself of the positive and negative consequences of coping both in a healthy and in an unhealthy way can help you to act from wise mind and stick to your decision, even in the midst of a crisis.

The cost-benefit analysis helps you to identify the positive and negative consequences of engaging in the problem behavior you're considering. Take a moment to review the following sample cost-benefit analysis, which looks at the unhealthy coping skill of smoking marijuana. Notice that this analysis gets you thinking about your problem behavior from as many different perspectives as possible and helps you to see the bigger picture. It also has you score each positive and negative consequence on a scale from 1 to 5 so that you can actually compare the numerical value of stopping the behavior versus not stopping.

EXAMPLE: COST-BENEFIT ANALYSIS OF SMOKING MARIJUANA

Benefits of Self-Destructive Coping Behavior: Smoking

_4_ Helps relax and calm me   _3_ Helps avoid/escape emotions

_1_ Feels good   _2_ Distracting

_4_ Don't have to face problems

Total: _14_

Costs of Self-Destructive Coping Behavior: Smoking

_5_ Feel guilty afterward   _4_ Get the munchies; gain weight

_2_ Bad for my health   _3_ It's an avoidance technique

_5_ Putting myself at risk for bipolar symptoms

_4_ My spouse doesn't like it; causes relationship problems

Total: _23_

Benefits of Healthy Coping: Not Smoking

_4_ Makes me deal with things   _4_ No weight gain

_4_ Feel better about myself   _2_ I have to learn other ways to cope

_4_ Relationship is better   _2_ Not engaging in illegal behavior

_3_ Not risking my physical and/or mental health

Total: _23_

Costs of Healthy Coping: Not Smoking

_5_ Don't sleep as well   _4_ Harder to relax

_3_ Have to find other ways to cope   _3_ No quick escape

_4_ Have to face problems and emotions

Total: _19_

You can then compare the numerical costs and benefits of each behavior. As you see in this example, the benefits of coping in a healthy way outweigh the benefits of coping in a self-destructive way. Most often, this is what happens when you complete the cost-benefit analysis, but you may find there are times when you can't think of reasons to learn new ways of coping. Your old, unhealthy patterns are just too comfortable and too hard to give up. When this happens, don't forget to ask the people you care about for help. More than likely, they'll be able to help you think of additional reasons to try to stop the problem behavior.

Now complete the following cost-benefit analysis to look at one of your own problem behaviors. You can copy the blank form so you can use it as many times as you like for each of the target behaviors you'd like to work on.

It is usually most effective if you do this kind of analysis over a period of a few days, to ensure you're giving it a lot of thought and carefully considering the costs and benefits. It's also important to make sure you complete this exercise while you are in wise mind and not while you're experiencing an urge to engage in the problem behavior. If you do the analysis while you're having the urge, it's likely to come out in favor of you acting on it (Linehan 2003b). Later in this chapter we'll focus on skills that will help you to not act on the urge.

As I'll discuss shortly, having these completed cost-benefit analyses to review will help you the next time you're experiencing an urge. If you have a hard time doing the cost-benefit analysis on your own (thinking of reasons to change a behavior you're attached to can be tough), ask a support person for help.

Once you've decided on the behaviors you want to change, you'll want to practice the distress tolerance skills outlined in the rest of this chapter to help you manage your urge.

HOW TO MANAGE YOUR URGE

Urges can occur because of bipolar disorder. For example, you may experience urges related to depression (such as wanting to isolate yourself), mania (such as wanting to smoke or drink), or mixed episodes (such as having the urge to cut yourself). But they also happen outside of this illness. For example, if you're feeling bored, you may have an urge to eat or to do something else to ease the boredom. My point here is that it doesn't matter whether an urge is connected to your illness or not—there are things you can do about urges when they arise.

When you first notice an urge, rate its intensity on a scale from 0 to 10 (where 0 means you aren't experiencing an urge and 10 means the urge is highly intense). After rating your urge, remember that the key is not simply to avoid acting on the urge, but to try to put some time between when you notice the urge and engaging in any behavior. The idea here is not to simply say, "I will never again give in to this urge." If this is a behavior that's been with you for a while and has helped you cope in the past, saying you're just done with it will likely feel overwhelming and probably won't be effective for very long. Instead, promise yourself that you will not act on the urge for just fifteen minutes. That is, for the next fifteen minutes you will act as skillfully as you can to prevent yourself from falling back into that old behavior. This will hopefully seem much more doable, since you're not saying forever, but instead you're putting some time between the urge and your action. This waiting period gives you a chance to use skills instead of automatically acting on the urge. It can be useful if

COST-BENEFIT ANALYSIS OF: _____

Benefits of Self-Destructive Coping Behavior: _____

_____ _____   _____ _____

_____ _____   _____ _____

_____ _____   _____ _____

Total: _____

Costs of Self-Destructive Coping Behavior: _____

_____ _____   _____ _____

_____ _____   _____ _____

_____ _____   _____ _____

Total: _____

Benefits of Healthy Coping: Not _____

_____ _____   _____ _____

_____ _____   _____ _____

_____ _____   _____ _____

Total: _____

Costs of Healthy Coping: Not _____

_____ _____   _____ _____

_____ _____   _____ _____

_____ _____   _____ _____

Total: _____

you set an alarm clock or timer of some sort, as time can do funny things when your emotions and urges are intense. It's important to wait a full fifteen minutes before making any further decisions.

During those fifteen minutes, you'll want to use the following distress tolerance skills (Linehan 1993b) to help you not act on the urge. We've already looked at one coping skill: the cost-benefit analysis. It can be helpful if you pull out the analysis you've already completed for the urge you're experiencing and review it to remind you of the reasons why you don't want to engage in this behavior. This can help you access wise mind and prevent you from reacting primarily from your emotions.

Distracting Skills

The next set of distress tolerance skills in DBT is the distracting skills (Linehan 1993b). Have you ever tried to just stop thinking a thought, to push a certain thought, memory, or image out of your mind so it will stop upsetting you? Have you noticed that this usually doesn't work very well? Generally, the harder you try to stop thinking about something, the more you think about it. Try an experiment with me right now to help illustrate this point. As soon as you've finished reading these instructions, for the next sixty seconds, no matter the circumstances, I want you to *not* think about pink elephants. No matter what happens or how much you want to, do *not* think about pink elephants—and certainly don't picture them in your mind. Try very, very hard to get any images of pink elephants out of your mind. Start now.

Have sixty seconds passed? What are you thinking about? Most people will be thinking about pink elephants. You may succeed at pushing those thoughts or images out of your mind for brief periods, but they tend to come back into your thoughts quite quickly. So, one trick to help you get rid of unwanted thoughts is not to push them away, but instead to mentally note their presence and then gently turn your mind away from them by distracting yourself. This is where distracting skills will be helpful.

There are many ways to distract yourself from distressing thoughts and emotions without making things worse, and you probably use some of these techniques already. You can remember these skills by the acronym RESISTT:

Reframe

Mindfully Engage in an activity

Do something for Someone else

Intense sensations

Shut it out

Think neutral Thoughts

Take a break

I strongly suggest that you keep a pen and paper handy to make a list of the distress tolerance skills that are most effective for you as we review each of these sets of distracting skills.

DISTRACT YOURSELF BY REFRAMING

Reframing basically means seeing something in a different way or in a different context. Sometimes you can decrease painful emotions by thinking about your situation in a different way, by putting a positive spin on it. For example, thinking about a person you know who is also having problems in his life but isn't coping as well as you are can make you feel a little bit better about how you're doing (Linehan 1993b). The goal of this skill is not to think badly of other people or to put them down in any way, but rather to help yourself feel just a little bit better about how you are coping.

A different way to reframe is to compare your problems to the magnitude of problems other people are facing. For example, someone once told me about a time when she was feeling suicidal and was trying to distract herself by watching television. As she was flipping through the channels, she came to a news broadcast on the war in Iraq, and the thought suddenly occurred to her that the people in Iraq were dealing with a whole lot more than she was. It struck her that surely she could cope with her problems if they were surviving suicide bombers on a daily basis. By acknowledging her problem (not invalidating or minimizing it), and also acknowledging that there were other people with problems even worse than hers, she was actually able to make herself feel a little bit better. The point is not to get down on yourself and judge yourself harshly for feeling down, but simply to allow that others are dealing with issues that are objectively more difficult than yours and to take comfort in the perspective you gain.

Another way to use this skill of reframing is to think of a time in your life when you faced a crisis situation but didn't cope as well as you are now (Linehan 2003a). For example, you might think to yourself, "Yes, I am having difficulties coping with my bipolar symptoms, and sometimes this makes me want to hurt myself. But this time last year, as well as dealing with bipolar disorder, I was also drinking daily. Now I'm no longer drinking." In other words, comparing yourself in the present to a time when you weren't doing so well, even when it feels like you're not doing so great right now, can remind you that things could be worse and that you're really not doing so bad.

The things we say to ourselves about a situation can also have a big impact on how we're able to cope with the crisis. We often focus on how painful things are, picturing the worse-case scenario, and this can get us thinking that the pain will never end. We can focus on thoughts like "This will never get better," and we may start to wonder how we're ever going to get through the crisis. If you notice yourself involved in thoughts like these, think about things you can say to yourself that might help you to think differently about the crisis (reframe it), rather than thoughts that make it even tougher to cope. Take a moment now and write out some examples of things you could say to yourself to help you get through a crisis. I've provided some examples to start you off:

■ *I can do this!*

■ *It seems hard right now, but I know it won't last forever.*

■ *This pain will end.*

■ *I can make it through.*

- _____
- _____
- _____
- _____

While these types of countering thoughts can be very helpful, sometimes it can be more powerful to reframe in order to find meaning in the crisis (Linehan 1993b). For example, as a young man, Jonathan had been diagnosed not only with bipolar disorder but with a heart condition as well. He struggled with taking his heart medication on a regular basis and had a difficult time accepting the changes his illness meant for him, even years after his initial diagnosis. At times, when things got tough, he would stop taking his heart medication and end up in the hospital. When he was eighteen years old, he befriended a twelve-year-old girl who had just been diagnosed with a very similar heart problem, and she too was struggling with the illness and the changes it meant for her life. Jonathan was able to find meaning in his own illness because he realized that his experience would allow him to help this girl come to terms with her diagnosis. Now when Jonathan has a crisis, stopping his medication isn't an option because he wants to set a good example. This helps him use other coping skills to get through the crisis situation without making things worse.

Like Jonathan, you can also use reframing to help you see the situation in a more positive light, finding the silver lining in a tough situation. Sometimes finding a higher purpose to the problem you're experiencing helps the crisis you're facing become a little bit more bearable.

Consider Isabella. She was diagnosed with bipolar disorder at age twenty-four. She had experienced an extremely difficult childhood, growing up with a mother who also had bipolar disorder. When her mother was ill, Isabella would often be neglected because her mother was unable to care for herself properly. For years Isabella struggled with her memories of her mother not being there when she needed her, which would lead to feelings of unworthiness, sadness, and loneliness. These emotional states often led to Isabella engaging in self-harming behaviors as an attempt to cope. When she was diagnosed with bipolar disorder, Isabella found the diagnosis very difficult to take. But she also found meaning in it, because it helped her to finally understand a little bit about what her mother had gone through. Isabella was better able to see that her mother had done the best that she could. This meaning didn't make Isabella's illness any easier to live with, but it did help her to accept it. Now when she finds herself dwelling on memories from her childhood and having urges to self-harm, she focuses on the meaning she has found and looks for other, nonharmful ways of coping.

Have you been able to find meaning in your illness or in the crises you've experienced?

_____

_____

_____

Can you think of other ways of reframing your situation that may help you feel better when you're in a crisis?

_____

_____

_____

DISTRACT YOURSELF BY MINDFULLY ENGAGING IN AN ACTIVITY

Distracting yourself from painful thoughts and feelings can be quite helpful, especially if the thoughts and feelings are about a problem that can't be solved right now. Mindfully engaging in activities that will distract you can help you to take a break from the pain and rest from those emotions for a while so that you may be able to access wise mind. Mindfully engaging in an activity means reminding yourself to focus on just this one moment instead of experiencing the current crisis, as well as all the other crises you've ever experienced, all at the same time. You likely have enough pain right now with whatever you are dealing with. It isn't helpful to also have to experience pain from the past. Remember, when you're practicing mindfulness, even if you have a hard time staying focused on the present, you are spending more time in the present moment than you would be without mindfulness. This reduces the painful emotions you're dealing with now.

Distracting yourself by mindfully engaging in an activity is most helpful if the activity is something at least somewhat enjoyable to you, and it must be something that engages your mind (in other words, it will provide a distraction from the thoughts and emotions you're experiencing). Examples include mindfully going for a walk, reading a book, organizing your closet, or visiting a friend.

Keep in mind that the goal of whatever activity you choose is to distract yourself from your urge and the emotions and thoughts triggering the urge. So when you go for a walk, make sure you don't continue to dwell on these things as you walk. Rather, focus on the walk and the environment around you. If you visit a friend, make sure you talk about things other than your problem. The following is a list of activities that may help you to distract yourself from crisis situations. There is space at the end for you to add your own ideas.

- Go for a walk
- Play with your pet
- Play solitaire on the computer
- Surf the Internet
- Watch a comedy on television
- Read an engaging book
- Look at photographs
- Look at your old school yearbooks
- Start a scrapbook
- Sit in the sun

- Put a hot water bottle on your neck
- Write a letter to an old friend
- Watch the birds outside
- Get in touch with an old friend
- Garden
- Knit
- Try to learn a new language
- Play video games
- Sign up on Facebook and see what old friends you can find

- Go to the park
- Watch children play
- Fly a kite
- Write a poem
- Water your plants
- Window-shop
- Rollerblade
- Play an instrument
- Play a sport
- Remember a fun time you've had in the past
- Plan a vacation
- Organize a closet or an area in your house
- Pay your bills
- Go hiking
- Ride your bike
- Go for a drive
- Bake a cake
- Take a hot bubble bath
- Cut the grass
- Do a Sudoku puzzle
- Paint your nails
- _____
- _____
- _____
- _____
- _____
- _____
- _____

- Go to the nearest pet store and play with the animals
- Go to a museum or art gallery
- Go to a place where you'll be around other people, like the mall or a church
- Go to a movie
- Dance
- Mindfully observe a favorite object
- Write a letter to yourself like you would to your best friend in a crisis
- Take up pottery
- Invite a friend to your house
- Clean
- Go swimming
- Go to the gym
- Go to the zoo
- Do some yoga
- Go outside and observe nature
- Cook your favorite meal
- Light a candle and stare at the flame
- Listen to relaxing or fun music
- Take a nap
- Chat online
- _____
- _____
- _____
- _____
- _____
- _____

Sometimes you can do an activity that may actually change the emotion you're feeling, which will help you to not act on urges. If you're feeling angry, for example, you could try watching something funny on television, or you could read a book that might make you feel happy. Music can also be very helpful in this way. If you're feeling sad, try putting on some upbeat music that might cheer you a bit. Keep in mind, though, that these kinds of activities can also backfire, so you don't want to watch a sad movie when you're already sad or a scary movie when you're feeling anxious. In other words, try to be mindful of any emotions these activities may be generating, and make sure they're not adding to your emotional distress. Can you think of ways that you may be able to change the emotion you're feeling when in a crisis?

_____   _____

_____   _____

_____   _____

While these activities can provide distraction when you're experiencing a crisis, many of these activities can also be incorporated into your life on a regular basis as a way of caring for yourself and helping to reduce your overall stress level. As a result, these activities can actually reduce the number of crisis situations you encounter. Think about activities you may be doing now or that you could begin to incorporate into your life that will help you to feel calmer and more peaceful (for example, taking a hot bath to relax, spending time with your pets, baking yourself a favorite treat, spending more time with family or friends, or listening to soothing music).

_____   _____

_____   _____

_____   _____

See if you can start doing these activities for yourself on a regular basis. You may notice that you experience feelings of guilt whenever you take time to do something like this for yourself (Linehan 1993b). If this is the case, you need to make an extra effort to start engaging in these kinds of calming activities regularly. Over time, the guilt will go away and you'll learn to use these skills to help you care for yourself.

On the other hand, you may notice that you tend to spend too much time engaging in these kinds of self-care activities (Linehan 2003a), which may result in you putting off responsibilities or obligations. If you find yourself in this situation, you need to practice moderation. Yes, self-care is important, but so is fulfilling responsibilities. Make sure you work on creating more of a balance in your life.

DISTRACT YOURSELF BY DOING SOMETHING FOR SOMEONE ELSE

Sometimes what is most helpful to get your mind off your own problems is to focus your attention on doing something for someone else (Linehan 1993b). Some people do volunteer work, which can be a helpful distracting activity. If you don't, you could look into places you could volunteer. Or if you're not looking for this kind of commitment, you could do something nice for a friend or family member. For example, bake some cookies and surprise someone with a visit; ask your elderly next-door neighbor if you can take him to the grocery store; ask your friend if you can babysit for a while so he can have some time to himself. Of course, you also need to consider what you can *safely* do in your current situation. If you are trying to stave off feelings of sadness, babysitting your friends' kids can be safe and enjoyable. But if you're feeling suicidal or are experiencing hallucinations, you'll want to use skills that will be more helpful in keeping yourself (and others) safe.

The idea here, don't forget, is to distract yourself from your crisis by focusing your attention on someone else. So again, use your mindfulness skills to keep your attention off your own problems and directed on the activity you're doing. Write down some ways you could do things for others to help you distract yourself when in a crisis:

_____

_____

_____

DISTRACT YOURSELF WITH INTENSE SENSATIONS

Physical sensations can also provide a good distraction from intense emotions and urges. For example, if you're having an urge to cut yourself, you could squeeze an ice cube in your hand instead (Linehan 1993b). This creates an intense physical sensation that can distract you from the emotional pain you're feeling. Here are some other examples of how you can distract with physical sensations. Make sure you add your own examples to the list:

- *Taking a hot or cold shower or bath*

- *Lying in the hot sun*

- *Going for a walk in cold weather*

- *Snapping a rubber band on your wrist*

- *Chewing on ice or frozen fruit*

- _____

- _____

- _____

- _____

- _____

DISTRACT YOURSELF BY SHUTTING OUT THE SITUATION, PHYSICALLY AND MENTALLY

Sometimes the environment you are in contributes to the overwhelming emotions you are experiencing. When this is the case, it is often extremely difficult to get to wise mind while you remain in that situation. In these instances, it is to your benefit if you can leave the situation physically and go somewhere calm and quiet. A new environment can give you the space to practice some skills that might help you shut the situation out and regain control of your emotions.

But what happens if you leave the situation physically and you're still not able to get the emotions to come down because your mind continues to go over and over the problem? This is when you need to shut the situation out mentally with a DBT skill known as *pushing away* (Linehan 1993b). This is a skill in which you use your imagination with the goal of convincing your mind that this is not a problem that can be worked on in the present moment. To practice this skill, follow these steps (Linehan 2003a):

1. Make a list of the problems that are triggering painful emotions.

2. For each of the items on your list, ask yourself the following question: "Is this a problem that can be solved right now?" (In other words, "Do I have the skills to work on this? Is there a solution to this problem that I can begin to work on implementing? Is now a good time for me to try to work on this problem?")

3. If you answered yes to this question for any of the items on your list, these are problems that you need to solve rather than pushing away. If you truly can take action, you will need to at least start in order to alleviate your emotional distress. The skill of pushing away is only effective if you can convince your mind that the problem is not solvable. So if it *can* be solved, don't push it away; start trying to solve it. For the items on your list that can't be solved immediately, you can use this skill.

4. For the problems remaining on your list that can't be solved now, close your eyes and try to picture in your mind an image that represents the problem. For example, this could be the image of a person you're having a difficulty with, or you could visualize the person's name or other words that represent the problem.

5. Next, visualize a box and see yourself putting your problem into the box. Put a lid on the box and tie the lid on with string. I tell people to go all out with this skill in order to convince their mind that the problem must be put away for the time being. So from here, picture yourself putting the box on a high shelf in a closet. Shut the closet door and imagine yourself putting a padlock on the door or even chaining it shut. Imagine whatever you need to in order to send the message to your brain that this problem is off-limits right now (Linehan 2003a).

The skill of pushing away, or any other skill you may use that actually has you trying to avoid thinking thoughts or feeling emotions, can be a helpful skill for some people. As mentioned earlier, though, sometimes trying to push the thoughts and emotions away just makes them come back harder. So this skill should be used sparingly, almost as a last resort. And of course, as with all of the distracting skills, you need to make sure you're only using it temporarily. Regular use of these skills turns into avoiding, which will ultimately make the situation worse.

DISTRACT YOURSELF WITH NEUTRAL THOUGHTS

Have you ever heard someone tell you to count to ten when you're angry? The idea behind this technique is that, by focusing on the numbers as you count, you're distracting yourself from the emotion. This usually helps to reduce the emotion's intensity. Distracting yourself with neutral thoughts uses this same idea. By focusing your attention on neutral thoughts that have nothing to do with your urge or the crisis at hand, you can decrease the intensity of your emotions and the urge connected to them. Neutral thoughts can be anything that won't trigger more emotions. Here are some examples:

- Counting

- Singing the alphabet song

- Singing the national anthem

- Saying the names of objects out loud as you look around the room

- Reciting poetry or saying nursery rhymes

- Praying

- Repeating a neutral mantra to yourself (for example, "om")

TAKE A BREAK

Often, taking a break when emotions are high can help you to get through the crisis situation without making it worse (Linehan 1993b). Taking a break may involve attempting some of the mindfulness exercises in chapter 2, which may help you to relax (for example, progressive muscle relaxation). Some people find that they are able to engage in imagery techniques that help them to relax, such as imagining themselves in a safe place (for example, in a room in their mind where they may feel safe) or picturing themselves in a favorite place (for example, at a favorite vacation spot). This kind of visualization can induce relaxation, can help to calm you, and can help you to not make the situation worse.

There are many other ways you can take a break from your problems. For instance, you can take a day off work, or take an extended lunch hour. Get someone to babysit your children for a couple of hours while you go get a manicure. Order takeout instead of cooking dinner. Have a massage or take a hot bath. Don't vacuum the house, even if you had planned to do it today. Taking a break can really help, but make sure you don't break too often or for too long. Consider whether your breaks are interfering with your important responsibilities and causing you more harm than good (Linehan 1993b). The occasional break can be very beneficial to help alleviate stress, but only when used sparingly and appropriately. Otherwise, they too turn into avoidance and can make the situation worse. Can you think of some small ways that you could take a break the next time things get difficult?

_____   _____

_____   _____

_____   _____

Reexamining Your Urge

So, those are the DBT distress tolerance skills that help you to get through a crisis situation without making the situation worse. Once you have used these skills to help you not act on your urge, you'll want to rerate your urge to see if it has come down in intensity. If it has stayed the same or become stronger, do your best to set your timer for another fifteen minutes, again promising yourself not to act on the urge for that period, and go back to practicing the skills in this chapter. If your urge has decreased to a tolerable amount, give yourself a pat on the back and go about your day.

WRAPPING UP

Having bipolar disorder means that you have more painful emotions to deal with than most people. When you engage in self-destructive behaviors to help mitigate those feelings, you tend to get caught in a vicious cycle. You behave in ways to help you feel better, but those behaviors usually generate more pain, either because you judge yourself for acting on the urges or because you destroy relationships when you do these things. Using healthier coping skills will help you to act in more effective ways, which means less for you to judge yourself about and more health in your relationships.

Over the next few days, think about these distress tolerance skills and use the exercises you've completed throughout this chapter to make your own list of skills that sound viable for you. This list should be as long as you can possibly make it so that you have lots of options when you're in a crisis. Remember, you probably use some of these skills already. So start by writing these down and then brainstorm other variations that seem helpful. Keep this list with you, or keep it in a place where you can easily access it. When you're in a crisis and emotion mind takes over, it can be very difficult to remember the kinds of things that might distract or soothe you. Having a list handy with concrete suggestions you can use in a crisis can give you a plan to follow when your emotions are high and your thinking may be clouded. So write your skills down, and when in crisis, pull out your list and start at the top. If you find that the first skill on your list isn't distracting your thoughts from the crisis, move on to the next until you feel the crisis has passed.

Following is a summary of the framework you can use to put your new skill set into action. Use this summary in conjunction with your personal skills list to help you get through the crisis without making it worse.

SUMMARY OF URGE MANAGEMENT

1. When you first notice an urge, set a timer for fifteen minutes and make a commitment to yourself to not act on the urge for that period of time.

2. Pull out your cost-benefit analysis exercise for the urge you're experiencing, and remind yourself of the reasons you don't want to act on the urge.

3. RESISTT acting on the urge: reframe, mindfully engage in activities, do something for someone else, generate intense sensations, shut out the situation, think neutral thoughts, and take a break. Use your personal skill list to help you remember which skills work best for you.

4.   Re-examine your urge after fifteen minutes. If it remains intense, try to set the timer for another fifteen minutes and continue using skills to resist acting on the urge. If it has disappeared or at least come down to a tolerable level, get on with your day.

Remember that the idea behind these skills is only to get you through the crisis *without making it worse*. They will not necessarily make your problems go away or make you feel better (Linehan 1993b). It's helpful to practice these skills when you're not in a crisis so that they come more easily when you're in trouble. The more comfortable you are with them in noncrisis situations, the more easily you can access them in times of distress.

As I mentioned earlier, if you're distracting from your thoughts and emotions regularly, you are no longer distracting—you're avoiding. Likewise, if you're distracting yourself from problems that can be solved, this is avoidance. Avoiding things inevitably does more harm than good.

Finally, while there are times when you need to take care of yourself by distracting so that you don't do something to make the situation worse, it's also important to have some awareness of what your distressing thoughts are about. Are they continuously about the same things? Do you see patterns or themes in the thoughts that get you into crisis? Identifying your triggers is just as important as being able to deal with crisis situations. Knowing what triggers you can help you identify when you may be heading for a crisis, allowing you to use the distress tolerance skills in this chapter to prevent yourself from getting to that point.

In the next chapter, we will begin looking at emotions themselves, and you will learn about ways to decrease and even change emotions, which will further help you to improve the quality of your life.

CHAPTER 6

Why We Need Emotions

Emotions can be incredibly uncomfortable, and often we just want to get rid of them. Trying to get rid of emotions, however, usually doesn't work and is generally not in your best interests. What will be helpful, though, is to have a bit more control over them. In this chapter, we'll look at how emotions are generated in people with bipolar disorder and the things that you might be doing to maintain those emotions. Next, I'll teach you some things you need to know about emotions—what emotions are, how to identify them, the connection between our emotions, thoughts, and behaviors, the different types of emotions, and why we need them. This is the groundwork you'll need to know in order for you to understand and be able to practice the skills I'll teach you in chapter 7, which will help you to control your emotions.

THEORIES OF EMOTIONS IN BIPOLAR DISORDER

When I first introduce the topic of emotions to clients and suggest that there are skills that you can use to help you control your emotions more effectively, I often get this response: "I've been told that bipolar disorder is a biological illness and that chemicals in my brain are involved. So how can I control my emotions if it's chemicals that are creating them?" This is an excellent question, and one that is not easily answered. If you recall from chapter 1, it's still unknown what the exact causes of mood disorders are or the role that the brain plays in them.

One theory that has been suggested is the kindling theory (Frank and Thase 1999). This theory holds that, while the first episodes of bipolar disorder are generally brought on by stressful events, as the illness progresses it takes less and less stress to trigger new episodes. If this is the case, over time it may be very difficult to determine what the triggering event was, which may create the illusion that mood episodes come out of the blue or are triggered by something happening in your brain.

Michelle, for example, a forty-nine-year-old woman recently diagnosed with bipolar disorder, had been quite severely depressed for some time. Her psychiatrist had just started her on a medication to help stabilize her mood, and Michelle immediately felt her depression lift. A week after this improvement, however, Michelle's mood suddenly crashed again. Upon exploring this dramatic mood shift, we were able to identify that a memory had triggered some anxiety for Michelle, and this emotion had led to some self-judgments: "Oh great, I thought I was over this. What's wrong with me?" This lowered Michelle's mood, which she coped with by spending her weekend in bed. This coping strategy led to even more self-judgments ("There's another weekend I've wasted"), as well as having the effect of increasing her emotion mind behavior (as discussed in chapter 4). You can see here that there was a trigger for Michelle's mood—a memory—and then her negative thoughts about the memory, the emotions, and herself sent her mood spiraling down into a depression.

Problems with regulating emotions, or *emotion dysregulation,* seems to be an additional contributing factor to the emotional problems experienced by people with bipolar disorder (Green, Cahill, and Malhi 2007). People who experience emotion dysregulation are more sensitive to things (in other words, they will react to things emotionally that other people would not); their emotional reactions tend to be more intense than those of someone without these problems; and it takes them longer to return to their baseline, or usual mood state (Linehan 1993a).

Research on why people are susceptible to depression relapse supports both of these theories, focusing on habitual patterns of negative thinking that people fall into. These thinking patterns trigger depressed mood, which may seem to come out of nowhere if you're not aware of your thoughts. The low mood leads to more negative thinking, which further depresses your mood, leading to yet another vicious cycle (Segal, Williams, and Teasdale 2002). While this research focused on unipolar depression, it's safe to say that these same patterns can be seen in many people experiencing bipolar depression. The good news is that this means there's something you can do to prevent and shorten these episodes. You are not a helpless hostage to the chemistry of your brain!

But before we get to the skills that will help you learn to deal with your emotions, there are some things you first need to learn about emotions.

EMOTIONS: THE BASICS

The first thing I need to clarify here is that mania and hypomania are not emotions but *states.* They consist of emotions but are also much more than that. So while the majority of the information that I will teach in this section doesn't specifically relate to these states, I will point out when skills can be helpful in reducing the emotions you experience while manic or hypomanic. This in turn may have the result of reducing the intensity of the state. Now let's take a look at what an emotion is.

What Is an Emotion?

We often use the words "emotion" and "feeling" interchangeably. This is inaccurate, because it implies that an emotion only consists of how we feel. Emotions are quite a lot more than that and have been referred to as "full-system responses" (Linehan 1993a). In other words, they include bodily reactions (changes in both body chemistry and body language) and thoughts (including images, memories, and action urges), as well as the way we feel. In addition to experiencing the feeling of anger, for example, we also experience bodily reactions such as an increase in our heart rate and tension in our muscles. Our thoughts generally become angry and often judgmental about the situation, and these thoughts are often accompanied by an urge (for example, to attack verbally or physically). So emotions are not as straightforward as just feeling something but include many other responses as well.

The experience of an emotion varies from person to person, although some responses are universal, such as crying when you're sad or smiling when you're happy. You may find that you have different experiences of the same emotion in different situations. Regardless, it's important to be aware of how you typically experience emotions, since it is well-known that people who are able to identify their emotions are better able to manage them. If you can't name what you're feeling, it's very difficult to figure out what to do about it. Consider your own experience of emotions: Do you have a hard time identifying any? Do you sometimes know you're feeling upset or bad, but you can't pinpoint the exact emotion you're feeling or where it came from?

To help you learn to identify your emotions, I've provided a worksheet to help you assess how you experience six basic emotions. If you don't know how you experience a specific emotion, you may need to wait until you experience that emotion before you can complete the chart. When you find yourself having that emotion, really pay attention to as much detail as you can and write it down. The first column lists six different emotions that you'll explore. For each, in the second column describe situations or events that trigger that emotion in you. In the third column, describe physical sensations, body language, and facial expressions that you typically experience in association with that emotion. In the fourth column, record the types of thoughts you generally experience along with this emotion, including memories, images, and judgments. Next, in the fifth column, record the urges you experience with that emotion. What do you feel like doing when you experience that emotion? In the sixth column, record your behaviors: what you actually do when you feel that emotion. And finally, in the right-hand column, record the consequences of that emotion; for example, you may judge yourself for having the emotion. Also record any consequences of the behavior you engage in as a result of that emotion. I've included an example for anger in the first row.

If you don't know how one or more of these emotions feels, read the list of feeling words provided after the chart, and see if this helps you identify what emotion you are experiencing. In the lists of emotion words, you'll see that I've included shame and guilt under the same heading, as the experience of these emotions is usually the same. The difference is that we feel shame when we think other people are judging us for what we've done, and we feel guilt when we're judging ourselves for what we've done. As a result, we often feel these emotions together.

GETTING TO KNOW YOUR EMOTIONS

Emotion	Your Triggers	Bodily Reactions	Thoughts	Urges	Behaviors	Consequences
Example: Anger	When someone criticizes me	My jaw clenches, my heart beats quickly, and I become flushed.	I become very judgmental and sometimes imagine myself becoming violent.	I want to yell and scream and physically act out in other ways, like throwing something.	I usually yell at the person criticizing me.	I often feel stupid and embarrassed later for the way I behaved. I think I judge myself for feeling angry and get angry at myself for feeling that way.
Anger						
Happiness						

Emotion	Your Triggers	Bodily Reactions	Thoughts	Urges	Behaviors	Consequences
Sadness						
Anxiety						
Love						
Shame and Guilt						

Anger Words

Annoyed
Frustrated
Bitter
Aggressive
Betrayed
Hurt
Combative
Deceived
Disapproving
Enraged
Furious
Hateful
Ignored
Infuriated
Jealous
Outraged
Obstinate
Rejected
Mad
Irate
Aggravated.
Indignant
Hostile
Vicious
Offended
Cross
Agitated
Disgusted
Resentful
Incensed
Exasperated
Displeased
Impatient
Bothered
Dissatisfied
Disturbed
Fuming
Livid

Happiness Words

Joyful
Ecstatic
Excited
Euphoric
Amused
Blissful
Calm
Cheerful
Content
Confident
Delighted
Eager
Relaxed
Glad
Honored
Hopeful
Pleased
Pleasant
Proud
Satisfied
Triumphant
Relieved
Exuberant
Jubilant
Jovial
Comfortable
Fulfilled
Overjoyed
Elated
Exhilarated
Thrilled
Charmed
Tranquil
Serene
Thankful
Inspired
Grateful

Sadness Words

Sad
Grieving
Abandoned
Defeated
Depressed
Hopeless
Worthless
Despairing
Inadequate
Lonely
Melancholy
Miserable
Negative
Powerless
Helpless
Gloomy
Cheerless
Heartbroken
Distressed
Unhappy
Glum
Dejected
Low
Disheartened
Despondent
Forlorn
Sorrowful
Dull
Dreary
Somber
Anguished
Hurt
Woeful
Pessimistic
Mournful
Regretful
Troubled
Disturbed
Remorseful

Anxiety Words

Afraid
Anxious
Stressed
Worried
Nervous
Fearful
Concerned
Disturbed
Frightened
Troubled
Overwhelmed
Panicked
Petrified
Terrified
Threatened
Unsettled
Frantic
Tense
Fretful
Apprehensive
Restless
Edgy
Jumpy
Uneasy
Perturbed
Uncomfortable
Bothered
Distressed
Alarmed
Distraught
Scared
Startled
Uncertain
Unsure
Frazzled
Jittery
Uptight
Overwrought
Disconcerted

Love Words

Affectionate
Lovestruck
Infatuated
Smitten
Adoring
Worshipful
Devoted
Caring
Yearning
Fond
Fancy
Tender
Passionate
Ardent
Amorous
Loving
Romantic
Besotted
Aroused
Desirable
Kind
Attracted
Lustful
Longing
Alive
Accepted
Appreciative
Beautiful
Complete
Committed
Lovable
Connected
Sensual
Attractive
Intimate
Cherishing
Magical

Shame and Guilt Words

Ashamed
Remorseful
Forlorn
Embarrassed
Regretful
Foolish
Dishonored
Sorry
Disgusted with self
Humiliated
Penitent
Dirty
Mortified
Repentant
Inferior
Uncomfortable
Contrite
Rejected
Disgraced
Apologetic
Incompetent
Degraded
Rueful
Awkward
Guilty
Wretched
Vulnerable
Blamed
Pitiful
Self-conscious

After engaging in this exercise, if you're still unsure about what emotion you're experiencing, feel free to ask people you trust how they experience these emotions and see if this helps you to figure out your own emotional responses. Finally, if you're still unsure, you can keep reading and come back to the chart later, when you have more of an understanding of emotions. Now let's look at the connection between our emotions, our thoughts, and our behaviors.

The Emotion-Thought-Behavior Connection

One difficulty that people often encounter when they begin to examine their emotions is determining the difference between an emotion and a thought. For example, when I ask a person how she felt in a situation, she may respond by saying, "I felt that I was being criticized" or "I felt that he should have understood how I was feeling." If you look closely, you'll see that she didn't actually describe an emotion, but instead stated what she was thinking about the situation. One reason for this confusion is that your thoughts and feelings are so interconnected that it can be difficult to distinguish between the two. Have a look at the following diagram, which is the typical way the connection between emotions, thoughts, and behaviors is described in cognitive behavioral therapy (CBT):

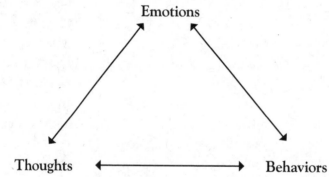

Looking at this diagram, you can see that your emotions trigger thoughts and behaviors, your thoughts trigger emotions and behaviors, and your behaviors trigger emotions and thoughts. So you can see why it's so easy to get the three of them confused. Let's look at an example: Patricia had a disagreement with her supervisor at work, and this led to the *emotions* of hurt, anger, and disappointment. These emotions led to more *thoughts* about the situation. She began considering looking for a new job and started thinking about other times her supervisor hadn't treated her very well. These thoughts led to more *emotions*. Her anger increased as she thought about the unfairness of the situation and as she recalled those other times she had been treated disrespectfully. All of these emotions and thoughts led to Patricia deciding to leave work early (*behavior*), saying she wasn't feeling well. Because so many emotions, thoughts, and even behaviors can be going on at the same time, it can be easy to mix them up. For example, in talking about her experience, Patricia may state that she *feels* like she has to get a new job, when this is actually a thought.

It is extremely important when you're working with your emotions to learn to differentiate between emotions, thoughts, and behaviors, and to remind yourself that these are just experiences or sensations, that they are not facts. If Patricia had taken the time to sort these things out, she may have been able to use skills to act in a more effective way. She could have recognized that just because she thought she was being disrespected did not actually mean her supervisor disrespected her, and then she could have determined that just because she had the thought that she should leave didn't mean that she must follow through and leave work early.

The following is an exercise to help you learn to differentiate between emotions, thoughts, and behaviors. Look at each statement, and in the space provided, write down if the statement is indicating an emotion, a thought, or a behavior. The answers are provided on the next page.

Thoughts, Behaviors, and Emotions

1. I'm an idiot!

    _____

2. I'm worried about my job security.

    _____

3. I'm angry at my sister for not inviting me to dinner.

    _____

4. I threw the TV remote across the room.

    _____

5. I'm disgusted with myself for having to be hospitalized again.

    _____

6. I really want to use drugs right now.

    _____

7. I'm starting a new treatment group and am anxious about meeting new people.

    _____

8. I cancelled the night out with my friends that I'd planned.

    _____

9. I really wish I didn't have bipolar disorder.

    _____

10. I stopped taking my medication.

    _____

(Answers: 1. thought 2. emotion 3. emotion 4. behavior 5. emotion 6. thought 7. emotion 8. behavior 9. thought 10. behavior.)

Being able to tell the difference between emotions, thoughts, and behaviors will help you to control your emotions. You'll come to see that just because you have a thought or an emotion doesn't mean that this is a fact. For example, the thought "I'm stupid" is just a thought, not a fact. Likewise, just because you *feel* helpless doesn't mean that you *are* helpless. Just because you feel worthless or unlovable doesn't mean these things are true. Emotions and thoughts are not facts; they are simply your experience of a situation. Once you can recognize this, you'll also come to see that just because you have an emotion or thought, you don't necessarily have to act on it. This awareness gives you more control over yourself, which in turn means that you'll be able to act in more effective ways that won't fuel your emotions.

Another concept that can help you to gain this control is what CBT theorist Aaron Beck called *automatic thoughts,* in which we are constantly talking to ourselves in our minds about what we are experiencing. We talk to ourselves about how we feel physically and emotionally, what our senses are telling us, what our perceptions or beliefs are about a situation, and so on. According to Beck, these automatic thoughts shape how we feel about a situation, which in turn impacts how we behave. The tricky part about automatic thoughts is that we rarely pay them any conscious attention. We're often not fully aware that they are occurring because they happen very quickly, almost like a reflex, and yet they seem realistic and believable (Beck 1976). The result is that we often act as though these thoughts are facts. Let's look at an example.

■ Shirley's Story

Shirley had left her friend Buddy several telephone messages and still hadn't heard back from him after a few days. Her automatic thought was that their friendship obviously didn't mean as much to Buddy as it did to her, which triggered feelings of hurt and anger. You can see here how Shirley had an automatic thought about the situation: "Our friendship isn't important to Buddy," which she took as a fact. Believing that this thought was true is what triggered the painful emotions for her. If Shirley had been aware that this was an automatic thought, she would have had the opportunity to evaluate it and choose for herself what to think about the situation. For example, she may have observed the thought "Our friendship isn't important to Buddy" and then refuted that statement by saying something to herself such as "That's not necessarily true. I don't know yet why he hasn't returned my calls. He may be away, or something may be wrong so that he hasn't had the opportunity to return my calls."

You can see from this example that the way we think about or interpret situations is often what triggers an emotion about the situation. Because automatic thoughts are so habitual, you may not be able to control them. However, you do have control over how you respond to these thoughts, and so you *can* change the way you feel.

Mindfulness of Internal Experience

To assist you in becoming more aware of your automatic thoughts and differentiating between thoughts and feelings, take a few minutes now to practice a mindfulness exercise. You'll want to keep these exercises short when you're beginning, as they can be very difficult to do. But feel free to increase the amount of time as you become more comfortable with them.

Set a timer for five minutes. Sitting quietly, just begin to notice your internal experience. Mentally note whatever comes into your awareness. Label whatever you notice as thoughts, emotions, or physical sensations. If you have the thought "This is really hard," label it as a thought. If you notice you're feeling bored, label this as an emotion. Just describe to yourself whatever you experience. You will become much more aware of the internal dialogue that goes on in your head and how automatically this occurs as you do these kinds of exercises.

Until you are able to separate thoughts from feelings, it will be helpful for you to practice the above mindfulness exercise at least once a day for a few minutes. Writing down the thoughts and emotions you observe can also aid you in learning to tell the difference between the two. For this purpose, I've provided the following Observing Thoughts Diary for you to use when you notice strong emotions. Completing this kind of diary or log can help you to identify what automatic thoughts may have triggered your emotions.

Begin by writing down as much detail as you can about the situation, sticking to facts only. Be specific, describing what happened, where you were, and who you were with. As well as you're able, leave your interpretation and judgments out and state only what really happened. Sometimes you may find that you don't know what triggered an emotion, and this is fine. When this happens, it's likely that an internal experience of some sort occurred (such as a thought, a physical sensation, or another emotion), and this is what triggered your current emotion. If you can't identify what the prompting situation was for your emotion, fill out the other columns in the chart. This might help you to identify the prompting event.

Next, write down any emotions you're feeling. You may only have one, or you may notice several. Do your best to identify all of them. In the third column, write down as much as you can about the automatic thoughts you are experiencing. Keep in mind that these might not present as just thoughts but could also be images or memories. Finally, use arrows to indicate any connection you can see between the specific thoughts you're having and the emotions that are being triggered for you, as demonstrated in the example provided.

Observing-Thoughts Diary: Example

Situation	Emotions you are experiencing	Thoughts you were having just before you started to feel these emotions
• I was sitting at my desk, alone in my office, and received an e-mail from my supervisor reprimanding me for something I had done that I thought would be helpful.	• Hurt • Anger • Disappointment • Anxiety	• What a mean thing for her to say. I was only trying to be helpful. • She doesn't like me. She wishes I'd just quit. • She's self-centered. • I'm going to have to find a new job.

Observing-Thoughts Diary

Situation	Emotions you are experiencing	Thoughts you were having just before you started to feel these emotions

Now that you are developing more awareness of your automatic thoughts, are more able to differentiate between your thoughts and feelings, and are learning to see that thoughts and feelings are not facts, the next thing you need to learn about is the different types of emotions.

PRIMARY AND SECONDARY EMOTIONS

There are two different kinds of emotions: primary and secondary. Primary emotions are those that you experience in response to an event. For example, you feel grief when someone dies or you feel happy when you go out with a group of friends and enjoy yourself. Often you'll experience primary emotions in response to your interpretation of an event. For example, you feel anxious because you have to do a presentation in front of a group of people and your interpretation is that they will be judging you.

On the other hand, secondary emotions are the emotions you experience in response to other emotions—how you feel about the way you feel. For example, you may not like to feel angry, and so you have a secondary emotion about anger. You may feel angry at yourself for feeling angry or you may feel guilt, anxiety, or sadness for feeling angry, depending on your automatic thoughts about the emotion.

Quite often, how we feel about our feelings stems from messages we got about these emotions as we grew up or even as we developed relationships with significant people in our adult lives. Some people grew up in homes where they weren't allowed to express anger, for example, and so as adults they may not like anger, or they may even fear it. In talking about how feelings were expressed in Cameron's childhood, for example, he came to realize that the anxiety his father demonstrated whenever Cameron expressed anger caused him to begin stuffing his anger instead of expressing it assertively. Cameron was able to see that, as an adult, he tends to express his anger in passive-aggressive ways that aren't helpful for him. He also realized that this behavior stems from the discomfort he feels with the emotion.

Think about the following questions to help you identify the automatic thoughts you have about emotions, which cause you to feel a certain way about your feelings.

AUTOMATIC THOUGHTS AND SECONDARY EMOTIONS

Anger

1. Are you "allowed" to be angry? (In other words, do you acknowledge your right as a human being to have this emotion, or is it one you "shouldn't" have?)

_____

_____

_____

2. What were the messages you received about anger as a child?

_____

_____

_____

3. Has there been anyone else in your life who shaped the way you feel about anger?

_____

_____

_____

4. What automatic thoughts (including images and memories) do you have about this emotion?

_____

_____

_____

5. How do you typically feel about yourself when you get angry? (Remember to think about how you feel about the emotion itself, not any behaviors you may engage in when you're feeling it.)

_____

_____

_____

Happiness

1. Are you "allowed" to be happy? (In other words, do you acknowledge your right as a human being to have this emotion, or is it one you "shouldn't" have?)

_____

_____

_____

2. What were the messages you received about happiness as a child?

_____

_____

_____

3. Has there been anyone else in your life who shaped the way you feel about happiness?

_____

_____

_____

4. What automatic thoughts (including images and memories) do you have about this emotion?

_____

_____

_____

5. How do you typically feel about yourself when you feel happy? (Remember to think about how you feel about the emotion itself, not any behaviors you may engage in when you're feeling it.)

_____

_____

_____

Sadness

1. Are you "allowed" to be sad? (In other words, do you acknowledge your right as a human being to have this emotion, or is it one you "shouldn't" have?)

_____

_____

_____

2. What were the messages you received about sadness as a child?

_____

_____

_____

3. Has there been anyone else in your life who shaped the way you feel about sadness?

_____

_____

4. What automatic thoughts (including images and memories) do you have about this emotion?

_____

_____

5. How do you typically feel about yourself when you feel sad? (Remember to think about how you feel about the emotion itself, not any behaviors you may engage in when you're feeling it.)

_____

_____

_____

Anxiety and Fear

1. Are you "allowed" to be anxious or afraid? (In other words, do you acknowledge your right as a human being to have this emotion, or is it one you "shouldn't" have?)

_____

_____

_____

2. What were the messages you received about anxiety or fear as a child?

_____

_____

_____

3. Has there been anyone else in your life who shaped the way you feel about anxiety and fear?

_____

_____

_____

4. What automatic thoughts (including images and memories) do you have about this emotion?

_____

_____

5. How do you typically feel about yourself when you become anxious or afraid? (Remember to think about how you feel about the emotion itself, not any behaviors you may engage in when you're feeling it.)

_____

_____

_____

Love

1. Are you "allowed" to feel love? (In other words, do you acknowledge your right as a human being to have this emotion, or is it one you "shouldn't" have?)

_____

_____

2. What were the messages you received about love as a child?

_____

_____

3. Has there been anyone else in your life who shaped the way you feel about love?

_____

_____

4. What automatic thoughts (including images and memories) do you have about this emotion?

_____

_____

5. How do you typically feel about yourself when you feel love? (Remember to think about how you feel about the emotion itself, not any behaviors you may engage in when you're feeling it.)

_____

_____

_____

Are there other emotions you need to consider these questions for? Think about these questions for any other emotions that might be troublesome for you. You can photocopy them, or just answer them on a separate sheet of paper.

After completing this exercise, you're probably beginning to develop some awareness of how you feel about your feelings and why you feel this way. Keep in mind that this exercise is not meant to lay blame at anyone's feet for your difficulties with emotions. But sometimes understanding where your beliefs and attitudes come from can help you to let go of those same beliefs and attitudes, especially if they're actually doing you more harm than good. For example, now that Cameron can see that his dislike of anger stemmed from his father's discomfort with it, he can learn to be more comfortable with it and can begin to express his anger in more healthy, assertive ways.

Sometimes people have a hard time figuring out what they're feeling because they've pushed their emotions away for so long. In addition, you may be confused about your feelings because you're experiencing both primary and secondary emotions at once. When you have a bunch of emotions going on at once, it can get pretty overwhelming and you can have a hard time figuring out what you're feeling and why. One thing that can be helpful is to remind yourself that the emotions are there for a reason.

WHY WE NEED EMOTIONS

As unpleasant and uncomfortable as they can be at times, emotions play a very important role in our lives. We talked a little bit about this when we looked at emotion mind, but it's important to remember that the goal of DBT is not to get rid of emotions. Emotions are neither good nor bad; they are simply there to perform a function. Let's take a look at some of the purposes emotions serve.

Emotions motivate you because some of them are signals for you to do something. Anger, for example, is a sign that there is something occurring that you don't like and may need to change. It motivates you to do something about the situation. Fear also motivates you by preparing you to flee, fight, freeze, or faint in order to survive when you're being threatened (Beck, Emery, and Greenberg 1985).

In these situations, you're motivated not only by the thoughts you have about your emotions but also by the biological changes that take place in your body. For example, anger increases your blood pressure and causes your muscles to tense up, readying you for action. Fear also does this, priming you to flee the situation or to stay and fight. While there are times when these emotions may seem inconvenient, remember that these responses have helped us to survive as a species.

Emotions inform you about social events or conditions, usually things that you want to change in some way (Campos et al. 1989). In other words, an emotion gives you information about what's happening in a situation so that you can change it to suit your own needs. For example, anger alerts you that there is something you deem to be unfair about a situation. Shame may be there to inform you that you've done something that doesn't align with your morals and values, which may impact your social standing in some way.

In addition, your emotions may act as a communication to yourself, signaling "the occurrence of events relevant to important goals" (Oatley and Jenkins 1992, 59). For example, when someone shouts, "Fire!" fear kicks in and gets you moving before your brain has time to even think about how to respond.

Emotions also help you communicate with others more effectively, in part because the emotions other people experience help you to interact with them on a social level (Ekman and Davidson 1993). In other words, by recognizing how someone feels, you can empathize with him or her and act in a way appropriate to his or her emotion.

Your own emotion can motivate you to speak (as mentioned earlier in the example of anger, which motivates you to try to change something in your environment) and can also evoke "complementary and reciprocal emotions in others" (Keltner and Haidt 1999, 511) allowing other people to understand and empathize with your emotions. Because of the facial expressions and body language associated with emotions, you often don't have to tell someone what you're feeling. If you're crying, most people will know that you're sad. If you're frowning and your hands are clenched into fists, people will conclude that you're angry. As humans, we instinctively recognize these emotions in others.

These are just some of the functions of emotions that have been identified by researchers. What all of these things boil down to is that we need our emotions and they all serve a purpose. For people with difficulties regulating their emotions, however, they can at times seem unbearable. So we'll be looking at things you can do to help yourself tolerate emotions more effectively in the next chapter.

WRAPPING UP

In this chapter, you've learned a lot about emotions in a general sense: that emotions are more than just feelings; how to identify emotions; the difference and connection between emotions, thoughts, and behaviors; the different types of emotions (primary and secondary); and that emotions are a necessary human experience and always serve a function. You've also been learning about your own emotions, including automatic thoughts that lead to attitudes you have about certain emotions and how you tend to experience these emotions.

So now you might be thinking, "Okay, I have all of this information, but what do I *do* about my emotions?" In the next chapter we'll look at some skills that will help you gain more control over your emotions. A reminder, though, to take your time working through this book. The information in the next chapter won't be as helpful if you don't practice getting to know your own emotions, so make sure you're continuing to use the skills you've learned so far. These include practicing mindfulness to help you get to know yourself and your emotions better.

CHAPTER 7

What to Do About Your Emotions

In chapter 6, I gave you a lot of information about emotions. That was background information you'll need to help you put into practice the skills you'll learn in this chapter. In this chapter, I'll teach you some skills that will help you tolerate your emotional experiences and reduce the intensity of your emotions so that they become more bearable. If you've worked your way through the exercises in the last chapter, you have more of an awareness of how you experience emotions. So now that you're becoming more familiar with what you're feeling, let's start to look at what you can do about it.

VALIDATION

Generally, if you're experiencing an uncomfortable emotion, you don't want it to stick around. That's because it's uncomfortable, of course. Ironically, this desire to get rid of unpleasant emotions can cause you to behave in ways that cause the emotion to stick around or even become more intense. Invalidating yourself is one way you might do this.

What this means is that you either judge the emotion or judge yourself for having it—and this results in more emotions. Remember learning about secondary emotions, how you feel about your feelings? When you invalidate yourself for having primary emotions, you generate secondary ones. Let's look at an example. Lamont ran into Marcus, a friend he hadn't seen in a very long time. While they were catching up, Marcus told Lamont that he had recently gotten married, and he and his wife were now expecting their first child. Lamont caught himself feeling envious of his friend and quickly told himself not to be ridiculous and that he should be happy for Marcus. Then he felt guilty and angry with himself for feeling envious.

As you're reading this, you may be thinking, "Well, he's right. He shouldn't be jealous of his friend." And while you might agree that you often experience emotions you don't want to have, like Lamont, if you invalidate them—judge them or judge yourself for having them—the only thing that happens is that you end up feeling more pain. Have you ever tried to just stop feeling something? It's quite a lot like telling yourself to stop thinking something. Not only does the feeling not go away, it often gets stronger. Let's look at Lamont's situation to see why.

Envy (primary emotion) + Invalidation =

Envy (primary emotion) + Anger and Guilt (secondary emotions)

As you can see from this equation, when you invalidate your emotion (for example, when Lamont tells himself he shouldn't feel envious), you not only have the original emotion to deal with, but all sorts of other, secondary emotions get triggered as well.

You might be wondering why we do this to ourselves if it just causes more pain. I think this kind of invalidating response to uncomfortable emotions is often a reflex for us. If something causes pain, we have automatic thoughts judging the experience as bad, and we try to get rid of it. But for many people, this is also a habit that stems from being in an invalidating environment for a length of time at some point in your life, most often in childhood. Again, this is not to lay blame at the feet of your parents or anyone else in your life. Invalidation can occur in a family even when no one is the "bad guy," but rather because there are difficult-to-resolve issues. For example, perhaps yours was a family where emotional temperaments were very different. Maybe you grew up with parents and siblings who were easygoing and not as highly emotional as you may have been due to your bipolar disorder. Because of your difficulties regulating your emotions, your "easygoing" family may have become frustrated with you and could have started to ignore your behavior. They probably didn't realize this was painful for you, but they didn't know how else to manage the situation. However, their tactic resulted in your feelings being invalidated, which may have had the effect of increasing your emotional outbursts in order to get your needs taken seriously (McMain, Korman and Dimeff 2001).

Invalidation can also occur because people are unaware of the consequences their words can have. In addition, parents tend to raise their children in relation to the way they were raised, and patterns of behavior can go on for generations before someone realizes that maybe it's not very healthy. We hear parents invalidating children all the time:

- "Don't be silly. There's nothing to be afraid of."

- "Stop crying or I'll give you something to cry about!"

- "You're not hurt—you're fine."

- "It's not nice to be angry."

From these examples, you can see that quite often the parent isn't intentionally being hurtful. The invalidating statement may be coming from a lack of understanding of the child's emotional response, from their own emotions (such as frustration or anger), from a desire to comfort the child, and so on. But invalidation can also happen without words, perhaps as a result of a parent's attitude. For example, some parents allow or disallow the expression of certain emotions. Recall the example of Cameron, whose father unintentionally invalidated his anger by becoming anxious about it, sending Cameron the message that it's not okay to be angry.

Here's another example: Khalid described his mother as domineering and explained that he grew up just knowing that he was not to disagree with her or express negative emotions. Quite often, the way parents interact with each other is enough to teach their children their expectations, without the parents having to vocalize these messages. In this example, every time Khalid's father became angry, his mother would cry and tell him how hurtful he was to her. This taught Khalid that to be angry was mean. As an adult, Khalid fears anger and avoids it.

Some people have experienced sexual or physical abuse, which are severe forms of invalidation. One result of this sort of abuse is that the child learns to trust someone else rather than his own internal experience, or he learns to keep his emotions to himself to avoid painful consequences.

For other people, adult relationships can lead to self-invalidation. For example, Barbara's first husband was verbally abusive and controlling. Over time, Barbara began invalidating herself and became dependent on her partner to tell her what she should be thinking and feeling.

These are just a few examples of how a person can be invalidated. Regardless of how it happened, if you self-invalidate, at some point you learned that your own internal experience is something that you are unable to trust. Once you learned to distrust your own experience, you likely started to look to others in situations to see what they felt in an effort to determine if your emotions were right or wrong. As with Marcus's experience with envy, you learned to pass judgment on your emotions and try to get rid of them if you believed they were wrong.

For those with bipolar disorder, the situation may be even more complex. People with this illness have learned over time that they actually *can't* always trust their emotions, and this means they can have an especially difficult time validating themselves. Not only do you have to deal with severe mood swings that often seem to come without warning, but you may often hear invalidating messages from well-meaning loved ones. They may think they're helping when they say things like "Calm down; you're becoming manic" when you are simply excited about a new opportunity, or "You need your meds adjusted; you're getting depressed" when you're simply sad over the end of a relationship.

So yes, again, because of your bipolar disorder, you face an additional challenge of learning to distinguish "normal" emotions and reactions from those that are symptoms of your illness. First and foremost, however, remember that you must validate whatever emotion is present before looking for answers or trying to change the emotion.

How to Validate

So how do you validate? Validating your emotions basically just means giving yourself permission to have them. It doesn't mean you like to feel that way or that you don't want the feeling to change. It simply means acknowledging the presence of the emotion and allowing yourself to have it. It is being nonjudgmental with your emotions.

In the example with Lamont, if he could say to himself, "I feel envious of my friend," and leave it at that instead of adding judgments, the equation would change:

Envy (primary emotion) + Validation = Envy (no secondary emotions)

In this instance, Lamont would still feel envy, but he would have no reason to feel anger or any other painful secondary emotions. So you can see that when you validate your emotions, you don't trigger painful secondary emotions. Yes, the original emotion remains, as illustrated above. But when you have just one emotion, it's much easier to get to wise mind and figure out what you can do to change it than when you're stuck in emotion mind, dealing with multiple emotions. Remember this order, though: *validate first, then problem solve.*

How are you at validating your emotions? Take a few moments to review the exercise Getting to Know Your Emotions, in chapter 6. This will help you see if there are patterns in the way you deal with emotions and will help you determine where these patterns may have come from. As I mentioned earlier, when you know how a behavior or attitude started for you and you can see that it's no longer helpful, it's usually easier to change. And remember that all emotions serve a purpose and are there to help us, so validate them.

Now take some time to complete the following exercise to help you with validating your emotions.

LEARNING TO VALIDATE

1. Thinking about your emotions in general, write down some of the messages you currently say to yourself that are invalidating. These are usually automatic thoughts and can be difficult to catch, so have patience with yourself and start to pay close attention to your thoughts when you're experiencing emotions. I've started you off with some examples:

   - *I shouldn't be feeling sad. What's wrong with me?*

   - *This is stupid! Why do I feel so angry?*

   - *I'm feeling excited. I must be getting manic.*

   - _____

   - _____

   - _____

2. Next, look at the ways you invalidate yourself. Can you come up with some statements that counter your invalidating messages?

   - *Sadness is a natural human emotion. There's nothing wrong with me for feeling sad.*

   - *The anger is here for a reason, and I have every right to feel it.*

   - *There are going to be times when I feel excited about things. Is the excitement I'm feeling now a typical emotion, or could it be the start of a manic episode?*

   - _____

   - _____

   - _____

3. Can you think of any other statements you can say to yourself that would be validating of your emotions?

- *I give myself permission to feel this way.*

- *I deserve to feel happiness.*

- _____

- _____

- _____

It can be very helpful if you carry this list of validating statements with you so that you can read it to yourself when you're feeling a strong emotion that you have trouble validating. Remember, when you aren't validating your emotion, you end up triggering more emotions for yourself, which makes it really hard to access wise mind.

How to Stop Avoiding Emotions: WATCH Them

Some people take self-invalidation one step further and actually avoid certain (or all) emotions. Is this you? Think about it carefully. Do you tend to "stuff" specific emotions? Do you try to pretend the emotions aren't there or consistently distract yourself (in healthy or unhealthy ways) when you begin to notice them? Or maybe you're even to the point where you automatically shut off from these emotions without even meaning to. If you notice yourself shutting down because of an emotion, try using the following acronym to help you experience it instead of avoiding it. Remember that avoiding actually just makes the feeling more intense and often makes it stick around longer. The following acronym, based on the DBT emotion regulation skills (Linehan 1993a), will help you to stop avoiding your emotions.

<u>W</u>atch: Watch your emotions. Mentally note your experience of each emotion, how it feels physically, thoughts that accompany it, and so on.

<u>A</u>void acting: Avoid acting immediately. Remember, it's just an emotion, it's not a fact. It doesn't require you to necessarily do anything about it.

<u>T</u>hink: Think of your emotion as a wave. Remember that it will go away on its own as long as you don't try to push it away.

<u>C</u>hoose: Choose to let yourself experience the emotion. Remind yourself that it's in your best interests and will help you work toward your long-term goals to not avoid the emotion.

<u>H</u>elpers: Remember that emotions are helpers. They all serve a purpose and are here to tell you something important.

By using this acronym to help you stop avoiding your emotions, you'll not only get to know the emotions better, but you'll be able to manage them more effectively. Remember, it's hard to figure out what to do about the emotion if you're unsure about what you're feeling.

INCREASING POSITIVE EMOTIONS

Another skill that's very helpful in regulating your emotions is the DBT skill of increasing positive emotions (Linehan 1993b). For the majority of people with bipolar disorder, major depression and breakthrough symptoms of depressed mood are the most problematic part of the illness (Thase 2005). In this section, we'll look at ways of improving your mood or, at the very least, making the depression a little bit more tolerable.

Pleasurable Activities

Trying to increase pleasurable experiences (preferably doing at least one of these things each day) when your mood is depressed can be very effective in alleviating the sadness, but it can also be extremely difficult to do this. Quite often, people say they don't feel like it, they don't have the energy, or they aren't motivated. And, absolutely—when you're depressed, these things are true. The problem is that it's very unlikely your mood is going to improve until you start to do some of these enjoyable activities. So now you're stuck in a vicious cycle.

Motivation often doesn't come until you start the activity you're trying to get motivated to do. You may not feel like doing the dishes, but once you get started it's not so bad. You may not feel like going out for a walk, but once you get outside you may end up going further than you intended.

The same principles apply to doing pleasurable activities. Once you start doing the activity, you might actually enjoy yourself, and this will help to improve your mood overall. So now the question becomes what can you do that will be enjoyable? This question can be especially difficult to answer when you're feeling depressed and nothing seems like it will bring you pleasure or change the way you feel. If getting out and kicking up your heels feels like too big a task, try to think of things that may help calm or soothe you or activities that might bring you some peace or contentment.

If there are things you've tried in the past that have improved your mood, trying those is a good place to start. It can also be helpful for you to review the lists of distracting and distress tolerance skills in chapter 5. Some of those things may be enjoyable for you. Make sure you choose things that you can do immediately, in the short term. The idea here is not that these activities are going to make your depression disappear. I'm asking you to think smaller. Think about it as a possible way of making you feel even just a little bit better for a time. Take a moment and make a list of things you used to enjoy doing, and things that you might possibly like to do now. I've started you off with some examples:

- *Having coffee with a friend*

- *Sitting outside in the sunshine*

- *Playing with your pet*

- *Sitting in a park, watching children play*

- *Watching a funny movie*

- *Spending more time with people you care about*

- _____

- _____

- _____

- _____

Ideally, you'll be trying to do at least one activity every day that brings a little bit of pleasure, contentment, or satisfaction to your life. If doing this feels too difficult, remind yourself that this is something that will help you feel better in the long run. Only you can take steps to change your mood.

Setting Goals

While doing pleasant activities in the present is very important, it's equally important to make changes in your lifestyle so that pleasurable things are occurring on a regular basis. One way of doing this is by looking at your long-term goals (Linehan 1993b). Think about changes you might like to make in your life. There might be some fairly big changes you'd like to strive for, like getting a job, going back to school, or moving. But keep in mind that smaller goals can be just as effective and rewarding—the main thing is that you have goals.

If you haven't considered this before, you may have no idea what your goals are. Don't judge yourself for this; just think about it very carefully. I often get people to start by thinking about this question: If you could do absolutely anything you wanted, what would it be? Then work your way to realism from there. Sydney, for example, said that if she could do anything she wanted, she would go to Tibet to study mindfulness with monks. Going to Tibet wasn't realistic for her, but she did look into mindfulness groups in her area and found one to join.

SETTING GOALS

The following worksheet can help you to narrow down your long-term goals.

1. List any interests you have ever had, even if you never acted on them. This is brainstorming, so write down anything that comes to mind. I've started you off with some examples:

    - *Learning a new language*

    - *Taking up a sport*

    - *Exercising*

- *Reading*

- *Photography*

- *Learning to dance*

- *Collecting something*

- *Developing new friendships*

- _____

- _____

- _____

- _____

- _____

2. If you were able to come up with more than one idea, is there a specific one that you would like to start with?

_____

3. After you've chosen one, do some research to find out what's realistic for you. For example, money often prevents us from pursuing these kinds of things. So if you can't take a Spanish class, can you afford to buy a book to teach yourself? Can you find sites on the Internet that you can learn from? Likewise, let's say you'd like to learn yoga. If it's not feasible for you to go to classes, maybe you can buy a videotape or DVD, or borrow one from the library, and learn to do it at home on your own. Jot down some ideas here.

_____

_____

_____

4. What would be some first steps you may need to take toward accomplishing your goal? (For instance, see if the library lends yoga videos, make a phone call to inquire about how to find out how many credits you need to complete your high school diploma, and so on.)

_____

_____

_____

_____

5.   What is the first step you're going to take to work toward your goal?

_____

_____

After you've taken that first step, you'll know more about what you need to do to progress closer to your goal. Remember to take it step-by-step and set small goals so that they will be achievable; you don't want to set yourself up for failure. (For example, if you haven't worked for three years, deciding to get a full-time job is likely not realistic, and you may not succeed.)

Just like incorporating pleasant activities into your life can seem like a chore when you're feeling depressed, looking at goals may seem pointless and too taxing. Remember that making these kinds of changes in your life will help to improve your mood in the long run. So take it slow if you need to; just make sure you do it!

INCREASING AWARENESS OF EMOTIONS THROUGH MINDFULNESS

You may have noticed that when you're feeling depressed or anxious or are experiencing other painful emotions, you have no trouble focusing on that experience. You can get very caught up in that emotion, and you probably also find that the emotion brings you into the past, triggering memories of previous times you've felt like this, which fuels the emotion and keeps it going. For example, Michael woke up on a February morning and noticed that he wasn't feeling himself. His mood was low, he didn't want to get out of bed to go to work, and he wasn't looking forward to the dinner he had scheduled with his family that night. As he lay in bed thinking about these things and how low he was feeling, Michael's mind took him back to the last time he had suffered a major depressive episode, about the same time last year. He started dwelling on these memories: how awful he had felt, how much weight he had gained from staying at home so much and turning to food to comfort himself, and how the weight gain had made him feel even worse about himself.

Without realizing it, Michael had gotten himself stuck in a line of thinking that only made him feel worse. It is likely that, had he been mindful of the current moment and the emotions he was feeling in the present, he may not have felt better, but he wouldn't have felt any worse. This is one example of increasing your awareness of your emotions through being mindful (Linehan 1993b).

How to Do It

I like to think of emotions as tornadoes. Like a tornado, when our emotions become intense they feel like a force of nature that can be very difficult to contend with and that can cause a lot of destruction in our lives. Increasing awareness of your emotion helps you to not get caught up in the whirlwind of your emotions. Your goal is to watch the tornado as it happens, from a distance. This does not mean disconnecting from your feelings or avoiding or blocking them. If you were stand-ing at a distance watching a tornado, you would still feel the wind and the rain. The difference is that instead of being caught up in that tornado and being spun out of control, you could watch the tornado from the ground, where you're relatively safe. Mentally noting your emotions is one way to get this distance and prevent yourself from getting caught up in the tornado.

Mentally Noting Your Emotions

You may want to set a timer for five minutes or so, as being mindful of your emotions can be dif-ficult and you may have the urge to quit after just a few moments. Sitting quietly, begin noting to yourself whatever emotions arise within you and describing the impact each is having on you. Notice and label any physical sensations that come up, and note any thoughts that come into your aware-ness about the emotion. If you notice you're becoming anxious as you sit, just describe to yourself how it feels to be anxious. If you notice pain anywhere in your body, simply describe it to yourself. Remember that these are all just a part of your experience, and nothing you notice requires action. You can simply note these things and see what happens next.

As you continue to practice these kinds of exercises, you'll find that you can actually put enough distance between you and the emotion that you don't get sucked up into its vortex. Mentally noting the emotion means that you aren't judging it, and you aren't attaching specific meaning to it. Quite often, when we can simply acknowledge the presence of an emotion, it will actually dis-sipate on its own.

Another analogy you can use here is the image of waves (Linehan 1993b). Imagine your emo-tions are waves lapping at the shore. Try to picture them in your mind as they build, peak, and then recede again; they don't stay around forever. Like waves and tornadoes, you can't push emotions away, so don't try to avoid them. At the same time, don't try to cling to them or try to keep them around. Increasing your awareness of your emotions simply means that you are acknowledging their presence as they come and go. Practicing validation and acceptance of your emotions will also help you to not get caught up in them.

Increasing awareness of your emotions is also an important skill to practice with positive emo-tions. People tend to be quite good at throwing themselves into feeling painful emotions but often have difficulties doing the same with positive ones. Especially when you're feeling down, you may find that you're so focused on how bad you feel that you miss any good feelings that might come your way. Does this sound familiar?

■ Demetri's Story

Demetri swore that he hadn't had a moment's respite from his depression since it began two weeks ago. When we reviewed activities he had done in the last twenty-four hours, however, he realized that there had been small moments that he had enjoyed: watching his dogs run in the park, watching his eight-month-old daughter sleep, seeing a comic on television who made him chuckle. No, those moments didn't bring him out of his depression, and yes, they tended to be brief. But Demetri realized that he had forgotten those periods of peace or calm because he had been so focused on the negative feelings. Once he discovered this, Demetri was able to pay more attention to those positive moments, which he said made the depression just a little bit more tolerable.

Write down some positive experiences you've had over the last twenty-four hours. Remember, we're not necessarily looking for things that made you happy. But can you think of times when you felt at least somewhat content, satisfied, or at peace?

■ _____

■ _____

■ _____

How did you do? If you weren't able to identify any positive experiences, you can be pretty certain that this is a skill you need to concentrate on and practice. Chances are, there were moments over the last twenty-four hours that helped you feel these positive emotions, but you simply didn't notice them because you weren't paying attention.

Sometimes what makes it difficult to be mindful of positive emotions are worry thoughts—worry about when the positive event will end, worry about how you might feel when it's over, worry about whether or not you deserve this happy moment, worry about when you'll become depressed or manic again. The list goes on and on (Linehan 1993b). In fact, I don't think I've worked with one person with bipolar disorder who hasn't had worries about when the next episode will happen. Now, I'm not saying, "Don't worry, be happy." Bipolar disorder can be a debilitating illness that can have extreme negative consequences, whether due to the emotions themselves or because of impaired judgment and damaging behaviors that occur as a result.

What you need to remember, however, is that every moment you spend worrying about when your next episode will occur and what will happen is a moment in which you've missed out on your current emotion. On average, people with bipolar disorder spend almost one-third of their adult lives with symptoms of depression (Thase 2005). Do you really want to miss out on the peaceful moments when they *are* there?

Increasing awareness of your emotions through mindfulness is also going to help you learn to differentiate between emotions that are "normal" and those that are related to your bipolar disorder. As I've mentioned before, you're going to experience emotions such as excitement outside of mania or hypomania, and you're going to be sad from time to time outside of depressive episodes. You need to be asking yourself the question "What is the difference between feeling sad and feeling depressed?" Or "What differentiates normal excitement from the excitement I feel when becoming hypomanic or manic?" You may be able to recognize, for example, that when you're feeling sad, you are able to connect the emotion to a specific situation, whereas when you become depressed, you may not be able to identify a specific trigger for this mood. Or you may find that whatever emotion you are experiencing is less intense when it's not connected to your bipolar disorder, or that it lasts longer when it is connected to the illness. For some people, the key to differentiating between emotions in this way is the physical experience of them. These are just some examples of what you may notice, but you'll have to do your own investigating since emotions are different for everyone.

Using the same emotions we looked at in chapter 6, I've provided a chart for you to help with this self-assessment. Again, you may need to experience each of these emotions before you complete the chart, so that you can practice being mindful of them and get as much information about them as possible. But try to complete the chart now, using memories of the emotions if necessary. Then you can return to this exercise and try it again when you've been able to be more mindful of the emotions listed.

Be as thorough as you can. It doesn't matter how long it takes you to complete the chart; what matters is that it's accurate and provides you with additional insight into how your emotions feel, both when you're experiencing an affective episode and when you're simply experiencing an emotion.

SYMPTOMS OF EMOTIONS WORKSHEET

Emotion	How I typically experience this emotion	How I experience this emotion when in a bipolar episode
Anger		
Happiness		
Sadness		
Anxiety and Fear		
Love		
Shame and Guilt		

So far in this chapter, you've learned some skills to help you improve your awareness of your emotions. You've also learned about the importance of validating and accepting your emotions and how this can help to decrease their intensity, and you've started to learn to differentiate between emotions that are being caused by your illness and those that are simply normal emotions. This next skill will also help you decrease or even change your emotion in certain situations. It's called acting opposite to your urge (Linehan 1993b).

RESISTING URGES THAT FUEL EMOTIONS

As I mentioned earlier in this chapter, emotions usually have urges attached to them. For example, if you feel angry, the urge is to attack (verbally or physically); if you are depressed, the urge is to withdraw or isolate; when you feel anxious, you usually want to avoid whatever is causing the anxiety. Quite often, you go along with this urge because it feels like the right thing to do. If you were to stop and look at this from wise mind, however, you would realize that acting on these urges is often not in your best interests and can serve to intensify the emotion you were trying to get rid of. If you verbally attack the person you're angry with, for example, you're actually fueling your anger and likely not acting in a way that's consistent with your morals and values, which can trigger negative feelings toward yourself later on. Isolating yourself when you're depressed causes you to feel more alone and hopeless, intensifying your sadness. And avoiding situations that cause you anxiety only increases your anxiety in the long run.

Acting Opposite to Your Urge

The skill of acting opposite to your urge has you do exactly what it sounds like: identify the urge attached to your emotion and then do the opposite. Once an emotion has served its purpose (for example, has alerted you to something that needs to be changed), it often gets in the way of you being able to act effectively. Let's take the example of you being harshly criticized by your boss, which triggers anger. The anger has served its function of alerting you that you don't want to be treated in this way, but it can get in the way of you being able to effectively communicate that message to your boss. If you can act opposite to your urge to decrease your anger, it will help you to be more effective. Here, you see that you aren't stuffing your emotion, but rather doing something to help you express it. If your opposite action is to avoid (such as with anger), it's important to remember that you will likely have to go back to address the problem. If the problem doesn't get resolved, your emotions about the situation won't get resolved either and may continue to build. The result of this is that at some point you will either explode with the emotion (for example, by yelling at the person), or you'll end up doing something else that won't be helpful for you (like ending the relationship when this isn't really what you want). In the example above, you would choose to avoid your boss until your anger decreases, but later you have to go speak to him to let him know that you don't like the way he spoke to you. Otherwise, you may end up exploding at your boss, quitting your job, or doing something else that you'll later regret.

So using this skill has you doing the opposite of what your urge is, which can sometimes reduce the intensity of your emotion. Instead of verbally attacking when you're angry, acting opposite to that urge may have you "gently avoiding" that person instead (Linehan 1993b, 161). Or if this is someone you can't avoid—such as your boss—acting opposite may mean that you're simply civil to the person. Engaging in either of these behaviors may have the effect of actually reducing your anger. At the very least, it won't add fuel to the fire.

Something else you need to know about acting opposite to your urge with anger is that usually the urge you experience with this emotion isn't just a behavioral one. When you're angry, chances are you're judging the person or situation in some way. What this means is that you have to do the opposite action both in your behavior and your thoughts (Linehan 2000). In other words, if you're practicing acting opposite to your urge by being civil to your boss while you're angry with him, your anger isn't going to decrease if you continue to think, "You jerk, you don't deserve for me to be civil to you," or something along those lines. Thoughts like these are still adding fuel to the fire. So if you're going to use this skill, you have to commit to doing it and practice it on every level. While you're being civil, you also need to think nonjudgmental thoughts. This will bring your anger down.

Now let's look at the example of depression. If your urge when depressed is to withdraw and isolate yourself, what would acting opposite be? It would probably be reaching out in some way, either making an effort to be around others or calling someone on the telephone.

When feeling anxious, most people tend to avoid whatever is causing the anxiety. I'm going to talk a lot more about anxiety in chapter 8, but for now just remember that acting opposite with anxiety would mean that you have to approach whatever is triggering the anxiety for you. In other words, if you're fearful of going into social situations, using this skill would mean that you purposely put yourself into a social situation. As with anger, however, you can approach a situation physically but still avoid it mentally. You have to make sure you practice the skill completely (Linehan 2000). If you go to a social situation but you avoid interacting with anyone while you're there, this is still avoidance. Approaching would mean that you not only have to go to the event, but then you have to interact with people while you're there (Linehan 1993b).

Acting opposite to your urge when you feel shame and guilt can also be extremely useful. The function of these emotions is to alert you to times when you aren't acting in accordance with your morals and values. If shame or guilt come up at other times, you need to act opposite to the urge. Remember in chapter 5, when we looked at activities that help you feel calm and soothed? I mentioned that many people experience guilt when they take care of themselves in this way. The urge that often accompanies shame or guilt is to stop doing the behavior triggering the emotion. In this case, that would mean discontinuing the soothing behavior. But these kinds of self-care skills don't go against your principles, so your guilt over them is misplaced and unhelpful. So when you're feeling guilt or shame when you're not doing anything to warrant these emotions, you need to continue to engage in the behaviors, and over time the shame and guilt will dissipate.

Acting opposite to how you would normally act when experiencing emotions you know to be related to hypomania can help you to come out of that state instead of escalating to mania or crashing into depression. When you're becoming hypomanic or manic, you probably have the urge to seek out stimulating activities. This will only feed into the mania, so acting opposite would be avoiding stimulation and doing activities that are relaxing, calming, and soothing instead.

Sometimes people confuse this skill with stuffing their emotions or pretending they're not experiencing them. I want to emphasize that this is not the purpose of this skill. Acting opposite to your urge is only used when it's not effective for you to continue to feel an emotion—in other words, you've experienced the emotion and you know why it's there, but now it's getting in the way of you reaching a goal and acting from wise mind.

It can be helpful to write down events after they've occurred to help you analyze how you used a skill or how you might use it in the future. For this purpose, I've provided the following worksheet. As usual, make sure you provide as much detail as you can to help you analyze how skillfully you acted in this situation. You may find you were quite effective, or you may discover that there were negative consequences that might have been avoided if you hadn't acted on your urge.

OPPOSITE-TO-EMOTION ACTION WORKSHEET: EXAMPLE

Situation (What was the event that prompted the emotion?)	Emotion (What emotions did you experience?)	Action Urge (What was the urge attached to the emotion you experienced?)	Action Taken (What was the actual action you took?)	Aftereffects (What were the consequences of the behavior? For example, did emotion mind go up or down? Did you get your needs met? Did you have regrets?)
I decided to practice self-soothing by taking a hot bath.	Guilt	Get out of the bath and do something productive	Made myself stay in the bath for the full 20 minutes I had given myself.	My guilt gradually decreased. I met my goal of soothing myself, which I know is in my best interest in the long run. I have no regrets.

OPPOSITE-TO-EMOTION ACTION WORKSHEET

Situation	Emotion	Action Urge	Action Taken	Aftereffects
(What was the event that prompted the emotion?)	(What emotions did you experience?)	(What was the urge attached to the emotion you experienced?)	(What was the actual action you took?)	(What were the consequences of the behavior? For example, did emotion mind go up or down? Did you get your needs met? Did you have regrets?)

WRAPPING UP

In this chapter you've learned some skills you can practice to help you tolerate your emotions, as well as skills to reduce the intensity of your emotions to make them more bearable. As with all of the other skills you've learned so far, mindfulness is a very big component of making these skills work, since you can't change something until you know it's there. Hopefully you're starting to develop some awareness regarding your attitudes toward your emotions and how you currently try to cope with them in ways that might not be so effective.

Make sure you're working on increasing your awareness of your emotions so that you can learn to identify them more accurately and then validate them. As best you can, increase the amount of pleasurable activities you engage in, identify goals for yourself, and be mindful of whatever emotions you experience. Finally, start thinking about ways you could be practicing acting opposite to your urges so that you can decrease the painful emotions you're experiencing. Remember that you will get the most out of this book by working your way through it slowly, practicing the skills taught in each chapter, and completing the exercises and worksheets I've provided for you.

In the next chapter, we're going to look at one specific emotion, anxiety, which is often a problem for people with bipolar disorder and which can severely impact your ability to function in life.

CHAPTER 8

The Additional Challenge of Anxiety Disorders

It is very common for people with bipolar disorder to also experience anxiety. In fact, one study reported that at some point in their lives, 51.2 percent of people with bipolar disorder will also experience some type of anxiety disorder (Simon et al. 2004). These authors also reported on the implications of having an anxiety disorder co-occurring with bipolar disorder, which included a shorter period of time with stable mood, higher rates of suicide attempts, higher rates of drug and alcohol problems, and poorer quality of life and ability to function in life roles such as working and parenting.

So you can see that having an anxiety disorder as well as bipolar disorder can greatly impair your ability to work toward a higher quality of life. It can be very difficult to differentiate between anxiety that's part of your bipolar disorder and anxiety that's a separate disorder. If you experience anxiety and haven't spoken with your doctor about these symptoms, it's very important that you do so, since having a separate anxiety disorder may affect the medications your doctor prescribes and the type of psychotherapy you need.

In this chapter, you'll learn some information that will help you to understand your anxiety better. Whether you have an anxiety disorder or anxiety is simply a part of your bipolar disorder, there are things you can do to help you cope with the anxiety and possibly even reduce it. First, let's look at how we distinguish between "normal" or functional anxiety and dysfunctional anxiety.

FUNCTIONAL VS. DYSFUNCTIONAL ANXIETY

Anxiety is a normal human emotion, and we all have times when we feel anxious. Anxiety may kick in when we have to give a presentation at work or in school, when we're talking to someone we're attracted to, or when we learn to drive a car. There are many times when it is perfectly natural that we feel anxious, fearful, or nervous. So a very basic question we need to start with is what is functional anxiety and when does anxiety become a disorder?

In general, *functional anxiety* is connected to a specific situation. For example, you may feel anxious about giving a presentation, but once it's over, the anxiety dissipates. With *dysfunctional anxiety*, you may not be able to identify what triggered the anxiety, and the emotion may not be time limited. In other words, you may have a general sense of anxiety that doesn't seem to be connected to a specific situation, or the anxiety doesn't go away even when the situation has come to an end.

A second indicator of dysfunctional anxiety is that it may be much more intense than a typical anxiety response. Functional anxiety is uncomfortable. For example, when you're thinking about giving a presentation, you may experience a racing heart, shakiness, and even nausea. However, dysfunctional anxiety can become so intense that you have a panic attack, which I'll describe shortly. Finally, you can tell that anxiety is dysfunctional if it is interfering with your life in some way; for example, with your ability to perform at work or school or to engage in social activities or relationships.

Can you think of examples of situations in which you have experienced functional anxiety?

_____

_____

_____

What about situations in which you've had anxiety that you'd consider to be dysfunctional?

_____

_____

_____

The Function of Anxiety

As you learned in the last chapter, all of our emotions serve a purpose. Anxiety comes to tell you that there is something dangerous in your environment that may be a threat to you, and the emotion mobilizes you either to stay and fight or to run for your life. When your brain senses danger, your sympathetic nervous system gets triggered. This is the system in the body that is responsible for your fear response and is essentially the way your body prepares to defend itself.

The activation of this system leads to the production of adrenaline, which causes an increase in your heart rate and the strength of your heartbeat. This speeds up the rate at which blood flows and directs the blood to places it is needed the most in order to help you flee or fight (for example, to the large muscles in your legs and arms so you can move more quickly).

However, if you have experienced these symptoms, you know that they are uncomfortable and can be quite scary, and looking at your thoughts about these sensations, you may find that you catastrophize about them. *Catastrophizing* or having *catastrophic thoughts* about your anxiety sensations means that your thinking immediately jumps to the most awful thing that these physical sensations of anxiety could be indicating. In other words, you have anxiety thoughts about the sensations you experience, which in turn makes you feel more anxious. For example, when your heart starts to race, you may think, "Oh my God, I'm going to have a heart attack." In the following chart, take a look at some of the sensations that accompany anxiety, then write down any catastrophic thoughts you can identify when you experience them.

Matching Sensations to Thoughts

Anxiety Sensation	Catastrophic Thoughts
Rapid heartbeat, heart palpitations	
Shortness of breath, tightness or heaviness in the chest	
Dizziness, light-headedness	
Nausea, diarrhea	

Now that you've been able to identify if you have any catastrophic thoughts about anxiety sensations, it's important to help you understand these sensations a little bit better so you can work on decreasing your anxiety. As we discussed earlier, the sensations that accompany anxiety are there for a reason—to do certain things in our body when our brain thinks we are in danger. So now, let's take a look at some of the ways in which this process affects us.

PHYSIOLOGICAL EXPLANATIONS FOR ANXIETY SENSATIONS

Anxiety Sensation	Physiological Explanation
Rapid heartbeat, heart palpitations	Increased adrenaline due to the fight-or-flight response—your body preparing to either fight or flee the situation.
Shortness of breath, tightness or heaviness in the chest	Contraction of muscles surrounding the chest cavity due to increased sympathetic nervous system activity.
Dizziness, light-headedness	Constriction in the arteries in the brain due to redirection of blood flow to larger muscle groups.
Nausea, diarrhea	Digestion processes stop due to redirection of blood flow to major muscle groups.

(Bourne 2000)

Looking at these explanations, you probably have a better understanding of how this emotion—and the sensations that accompany it—is really quite helpful. The sensations that are triggering more anxiety and catastrophic thinking in you are the same sensations that save our lives in dangerous situations. It's just that these sensations occur whether or not there is something actually threatening to you in the environment. In other words, whether you're anxious about doing a presentation, about going to a social event, or because someone has just shouted "Fire!" and your life may be at risk, these same sensations will occur. Think of anxiety as acting the same way a light switch does: it's either off or on; there's no in-between (Denisoff 2007).

Anxiety operates in this way for obvious reasons. There are times when you don't want to have to think about a situation before you react in order to protect yourself. When you hear an alarmed voice shouting, "Fire!" you don't need to stop and think about the message the person is trying to convey and how you should interpret it. Rather, your fear response automatically kicks in and your body quickly reacts, turning in the other direction and fleeing without you having to consider what you should do in the situation.

Here's another example: You're walking down the street alone, and as you pass an alleyway someone jumps out, points a gun at you, and demands your money. Do you need to stop and think about this? Probably not. Your fear response kicks in, and your body automatically hands over your money. When you consider anxiety from this perspective, you can probably see that it is an incredibly useful emotion meant to help us survive. Sometimes, however, people begin to experience anxiety outside of situations that are actually threatening to their safety in some way. This is when anxiety becomes dysfunctional or turns into a disorder, and you need to do something about it.

TYPES OF ANXIETY DISORDERS

There are many different anxiety disorders outlined in the *Diagnostic and Statistical Manual of Mental Disorders* (APA 2000). Here we'll look at three of the anxiety disorders that more commonly co-occur with bipolar disorder: generalized anxiety disorder, social anxiety, and panic disorder. Next, we'll look at how the skills you've already learned can help you cope with anxiety sensations. Finally, I'll teach you some specific techniques to help you cope with the anxiety that may be preventing you from living your life to the fullest.

Generalized Anxiety Disorder

Generalized anxiety disorder (GAD) is a chronic, persistent state of worry about specific stressful life circumstances, such as finances, relationships, health, family members, or work or school performance. If you have GAD, you spend a lot of your time worrying about these things, and you experience a lack of control over your worrying. In other words, you can't stop yourself from getting caught up in these thoughts.

To be diagnosed with GAD, the anxiety must have been ongoing for at least six months, and you must experience a minimum of three of the following symptoms: restlessness, problems with sleep, being easily fatigued, muscle tension, irritability, and problems with concentration. Many people can fit into this category at times, so it's important to remember what distinguishes functional from dysfunctional anxiety: if you have GAD, the anxiety triggered by your worries is more intense than is warranted by the situation, it may interfere with your ability to function, and the anxiety doesn't dissipate when the stressful situation is over.

■ Kevin's Story

Kevin was thirty-seven years old and had been living with bipolar disorder and GAD for most of his life. His bipolar was currently under control and his mood was stable, but his anxiety was so high that he was unable to work and was on a disability pension. Kevin described a general, constant sense of foreboding or worry. He said he was never able to pinpoint one specific thing that caused this feeling of dread, but he admitted to constant worry about many things. Some of Kevin's worries included ending up back in the hospital because of his bipolar symptoms, or doing things like gambling or using drugs, as he had in the past, which would make his life even more difficult. Kevin was also able to identify worrying that he wouldn't be able to stretch his pension to last the whole month, that his car would break down and he'd lose what little bit of freedom he had left, and that his parents, who had been a great source of emotional and financial support to him, would die.

The result of these constant worries was that Kevin was unable to sleep at night without the aid of a sleeping pill. He had a hard time concentrating and remembering things, he was often irritable, and he found it very difficult to enjoy anything he did because he was so caught up in his worries about the future.

It is estimated that 18.4 percent of people with bipolar disorder will experience GAD at some point in their life, as opposed to a rate of just 5.1 percent of people in the general population (Simon et al. 2004).

Take a moment and consider whether any of these symptoms of GAD feel familiar to you. Below, write down any thoughts that come up or any GAD symptoms that you experience:

_____

_____

_____

Social Anxiety

Social anxiety, also known as *social phobia*, involves an intense fear of being in social situations or in other situations where there is a possibility of being judged by others. This could include situations such as going to a dance or a get-together at a friend's house, attending a treatment group for bipolar disorder, or being at the mall. Social anxiety also occurs as a fear of doing things such as speaking, writing, or eating food in public, using public bathrooms, and a general fear of crowds. The primary fear with social anxiety is that you will somehow embarrass yourself in front of others—for example, by saying or doing something that will cause others to think that you're crazy, stupid, or weird.

You may be thinking that many people have some of these fears. Many of us are concerned about what others think of us, and many of us are afraid of public speaking, so what makes this an anxiety disorder? Again, it goes to the intensity of the emotion, its connection to a specific event or situation, and the extent to which it limits you. You may worry somewhat about what others think of you, but when this worry causes you to avoid social situations, triggers panic attacks, or compromises your ability to function in other ways, it is dysfunctional anxiety. Or you may have a fear of speaking in public, but if this is dysfunctional anxiety, you'll recognize that the fear is more intense than the situation warrants, the anxiety may not dissipate when the situation is over, or it may interfere with your ability to fully function in your life.

In addition, people with social anxiety often experience what is called *anticipatory anxiety*, which means that they spend a lot of time having anxious thoughts about the event before it happens or catastrophizing about it. Once in the anxiety-provoking situation, the socially anxious person tends to focus on the things that worry her the most. For example, if she starts to blush or sweat, this becomes the focus of her attention, and dwelling on this sensation causes the anxiety to increase.

The other thing socially anxious people tend to focus on is trying to detect signs of negative judgment from others. In other words, they monitor the people around them, waiting for a sign that they've said or done something to make them look foolish. This constant monitoring of the environment takes a lot of energy and also increases anxiety.

■ Roop's Story

Roop was thirty-four years old, had been living with bipolar disorder most of his life, and successfully sold real estate for a living. A few months before, Roop's wife had told him she wanted to separate, and she had taken their three-year-old son with her. As a result, Roop wasn't seeing his son very often, and this was causing him a lot of pain. He hadn't been sleeping well as a result of the stress in his life.

One evening he was taking a couple to see a house, and he began to feel anxious about the showing. He began to worry that the couple he was meeting would notice that he was having a hard time concentrating or would see the shadows under his eyes from lack of sleep. Then Roop began to experience more intense fear that if they noticed these things, the couple might think he was crazy or weird and would decide not to buy a house from him.

Although that evening went quite smoothly, these became regular worries for Roop. Every time he was showing a house, he began to worry that people would somehow see he was having difficulties in his personal life and would judge him for this in some way. He further worried that this would cause people to decide not to use him as an agent, and this would greatly impact his livelihood. Roop's anxiety got so intense that he began to consider going into another line of work.

Here you can see that Roop's fears, although connected to stressful situations that were actually occurring in his life, were far out of proportion to reality. The fact that he was considering quitting his job when nothing catastrophic had actually happened, as well as the fact that the anxiety wasn't limited to a specific situation, were indicators that this was dysfunctional anxiety. When Roop's anxiety started causing him to avoid social events as well, he realized that the anxiety was getting out of control and consulted his doctor, who diagnosed him with social anxiety.

Social anxiety is one of the more common anxiety disorders, occurring in approximately 13.3 percent of the general population, but in 22 percent of people with bipolar disorder (Simon et al. 2004).

Does Roop's experience sound familiar to you? Do you see some of his symptoms in yourself? Below, jot down any thoughts about your symptoms and whether they may indicate social anxiety:

_____

_____

_____

Panic Disorder

A *panic attack* is an intense episode of anxiety during which you experience multiple physical sensations such as rapid heartbeat, dizziness, nausea, trembling, sweating, shortness of breath, tingling in your hands and feet, and visual disturbance. In addition to these physical sensations, you may experience fears of going crazy, dying, or losing control, or thoughts of needing to escape the situation. At least four of these symptoms are present in a full-blown panic attack (APA 2004).

Many people have panic attacks and don't actually have panic disorder. Put simply, *panic disorder* is actually a fear of the panic attacks themselves. Have you ever noticed that paying attention to a sensation makes it seem much more bothersome? For example, when you're driving and your foot starts to itch, you can't scratch it, and as you keep driving it seems to get worse because it's all you can think about. The same happens with anxiety sensations. The more you focus on them, the more intense they become, and this often leads to an increase in your anxiety because the sensations seem more intense. For example, if you have a moment of dizziness that you negatively interpret as a symptom of a panic attack, this can trigger anxiety in you and actually start the panic attack. In this way, anxiety is often a self-fulfilling prophecy.

In panic disorder the attacks are triggered by a fear of the sensations themselves, so it often seems to people that their panic attacks come out of the blue, since the attacks aren't related to any specific situation. What's actually happening is the person is experiencing some kind of physical sensation. Her brain (now highly sensitized to these kinds of sensations because of previous panic attacks) interprets this sensation as a symptom of a panic attack, and this is what actually triggers the attack. The attacks seem to come from nowhere because the person is often not aware that she just experienced a physical sensation that her brain interpreted as dangerous.

To be diagnosed with panic disorder, you must have had at least two panic attacks, one of which was followed by a minimum of one month of persistent concern about having another panic attack (APA 2004).

■ Makenna's Story

Makenna was twenty-three years old when she had her first panic attack. She had been working very hard on a presentation for a psychology class, and so she'd been staying up late at night and taking caffeine pills to give her the extra boost she needed to keep going. When the time came for her to present, she got up in front of the class and her heart began to race so quickly and beat so hard that she thought it was going to pop right out of her chest. When this thought occurred to her, she became frightened, and this quickly escalated into a full-blown panic attack. She began shaking and sweating, it became difficult to breathe, and she was convinced she was going to die. She was taken to the hospital and was told that her symptoms had been a stress reaction.

Knowing that she would still have to present to the class, Makenna became anxious that she was going to have a panic attack again. Her brain became much more sensitive to her body sensations, so that whenever something happened that it identified as out of the ordinary (for example, if her heart sped up) Makenna's brain would automatically interpret this as dangerous, resulting in the triggering of a panic attack.

The lifetime rate of panic disorder in people with bipolar disorder is 17.3 percent, while people without bipolar experience panic disorder at a rate of only 3.5 percent (Simon et al. 2004).

Do you think you may be experiencing panic disorder? Note any possible symptoms below:

_____

_____

_____

UNDERSTANDING YOUR ANXIETY

Now you have a better understanding of these three types of anxiety disorders, and you may be able to identify that you have some symptoms of one or more of these disorders. Keep in mind that not only do anxiety disorders frequently co-occur with bipolar disorder, but you can also have symptoms of a variety of anxiety disorders as well. For example, many people with GAD or social anxiety also have panic attacks, people with panic disorder can have symptoms of social anxiety and GAD, and so on. So don't worry too much about which category you fall into. Just be aware of what symptoms you're experiencing, since these are the targets of treatment.

Panic attacks are quite common and can be experienced even by people without an anxiety disorder. Because misinformation can make dealing with anxiety very difficult, in the next section we're going to look at some myths about panic attacks. I will provide you with some facts to clear up any misunderstandings you may have, which will help you to cope more effectively with your anxiety.

Addressing Faulty Beliefs About Anxiety

There are a lot of myths that people come to believe about anxiety—and specifically about panic attacks—that can make reducing anxiety much more difficult. I'm going to list a few of these faulty beliefs here, and I want you to think about each one and answer the questions below the myth to get you considering how realistic it is. Then I'm going to provide some facts to help dispel each of the myths. Keep in mind that the degree to which you believe each of these will probably vary depending on whether you're in emotion mind or wise mind. If you want, you can answer each question from the perspective of both thinking styles.

Myth 1: If I have a panic attack, I could have a heart attack and die.

■ On a scale from 0 to 10, how much do you believe this to be true? (0 = not at all, 10 = completely believe it) _____

■ Do you know anyone who has ever died from a panic attack? Have you yourself ever suffered a heart attack because of the panic?

_____

_____

■ Can you think of a time, outside of having a panic attack, when your heart was racing but it didn't scare you? Think of being on a roller coaster or being very excited about some good news you received. If you play sports in which you exert yourself, you probably experience a fast heartbeat regularly. Or you may recall a time when you were extremely frightened and this caused your heart to speed up, but you were so focused on the frightening experience that you didn't pay much attention to your internal experience.

_____

_____

_____

Fact: A healthy heart can beat two hundred beats per minute for days without being damaged in any way (Bourne 2000). Having said that, I strongly recommend that you see your doctor for a full physical examination if you haven't done so, and if you experience panic attacks. Although a panic attack won't cause a heart attack, it's important that you make sure your symptoms can be attributed to panic attacks and are not indicative of some kind of physical problem.

Myth 2: I could faint during a panic attack.

- On a scale from 0 to 10, how much do you believe this to be true? (0 = not at all, 10 = completely believe it) _____

- Do you know anyone who has ever fainted because of a panic attack? Have you yourself ever passed out because of the panic?

_____

_____

Fact: Fainting is caused when the blood rushes from your head. During a panic attack, the fact that your heart is pumping harder, increasing your circulation, means that it is very unlikely that you're going to faint (although it's not impossible). If you haven't fainted during a panic attack before, chances are it won't happen. The dizziness and light-headedness you may experience is likely due to constriction in the arteries in your brain, so your brain isn't getting as much blood as it's used to.

These sensations can also be caused by hyperventilating, which you can stop by covering your nose and mouth with your hands (or with a paper bag if you prefer, although this isn't necessary). Although when you're hyperventilating it feels like you can't breathe, the real problem is that by overbreathing (breathing quickly and shallowly), you have decreased the levels of carbon dioxide in your body. So covering your nose and mouth allows you to rebreathe the air you've just exhaled, restoring the carbon dioxide levels in your system to normal and stopping the hyperventilating.

Myth 3: I'll lose control if I have a panic attack.

- On a scale from 0 to 10, how much do you believe this to be true? (0 = not at all, 10 = completely believe it) _____

- Do you know anyone who has ever lost control because they had a panic attack? Have you yourself ever lost control because of the panic?

_____

_____

- What exactly is your fear here? What does losing control mean to you? Some people fear they'll lost their balance and fall over. Others fear they'll go crazy. Still others are concerned they might lose control of bodily functions and, for example, vomit in public. Can you identify what your specific fear is?

  _____

  _____

- Now ask yourself if the panic attacks you've experienced have ever resulted in your feared outcome. _____

Fact: Since anxiety is such an uncomfortable emotion, people tend to catastrophize about what anxiety can lead to. Sometimes panic can make you dizzy and can cause your limbs to tremble and feel weak. In general though, these sensations aren't so severe that you would fall over, and they don't usually come on so quickly that you would be unable to do something to prevent this from happening, such as quickly sitting down (even if you have to sit on the floor). The same applies to feeling nauseated. Just because you feel nauseated due to the anxiety, that doesn't mean you'll actually vomit in public. If these things have happened to you in the past, you can try to plan for them in the future. For example, if you're feeling nauseated, it may be a good idea to know where the nearest washroom is. As with fainting, it's good to remember that if it hasn't happened to you in the past, chances are slim that it will happen in the future.

If you have the fear that you're going to go crazy, please know that it is unfounded. Even though this is a common fear during panic attacks, possibly due to the feelings of unreality and disorientation that can occur due to the reduced blood flow to your brain, no one has ever gone crazy because of a panic attack (Bourne 2000).

Some people also worry about how they look to others during a panic attack. Typically, however, your perception of how you look in these situations is quite out of proportion with reality. Just because you feel really awful doesn't mean that it's apparent to others. Something that can help you to get some perspective on this is to have a friend or family member videotape you when you're having a panic attack so that you can see what you actually look like. You might be surprised. I've had clients sitting in my office tell me they were having a panic attack in that present moment, and they barely looked anxious. Remember that your perceptions don't always match reality.

Myth 4: I'll stop breathing and suffocate.

- On a scale from 0 to 10, how much do you believe this to be true? (0 = not at all, 10 = completely believe it) _____

- Do you know anyone who has ever stopped breathing because of a panic attack? Have you yourself ever stopped breathing during a panic attack?

  _____

  _____

Fact: Even though sometimes during a panic attack you might feel like you're having a hard time breathing, this is often due to hyperventilating, which was mentioned in myth 2. The tightness in your chest that makes it feel hard to breathe can also be caused by tightening of your chest and neck muscles due to your anxiety. These uncomfortable sensations will pass. It can also be helpful for you to know that your brain has a built-in reflex that will force you to breathe if your body isn't getting enough oxygen (Bourne 2000). The fact is, you will not stop breathing because of a panic attack.

How Your Thinking May Be Contributing to Your Anxiety

Now that we've cleared up some of these myths about anxiety and you have a better understanding of the sensations that accompany it, let's turn to a discussion of the way your thinking contributes to the emotion.

In the stories you read earlier in this chapter of peoples' experiences with anxiety, you can see that each person's anxiety was out of proportion to the situation he or she was facing. Sometimes the brain becomes more sensitive to stimuli in the environment, and it starts sending messages to the sympathetic nervous system when it doesn't really need to. You've probably heard about those lights that turn off and on when you clap your hands. Picture this: You install these lights, thinking how convenient they'll be. You clap once, the lights come on; you clap twice, they turn off. But what if, after you've installed them, you drop something on the floor and the lights come on? Or let's say you've come home after a harrowing trip to the grocery store, and when you drop your grocery bags on the counter top, the lights go off? The system is too sensitive and is being triggered accidentally, when you don't want it to be. The same thing can happen with anxiety. Your brain can become overly sensitive to what it perceives in the environment, and it alerts your fear response when it doesn't need to. So how do you get it to stop? First, look at the following flowchart (Denisoff 2007), which shows you how you got stuck in this cycle to begin with.

This flowchart starts with a situation. Remember from chapter 6 that there is always a trigger for our emotions. The situation itself is usually not what leads to the emotion, although this is sometimes the case. For example, the death of a loved one automatically brings on feelings of grief. There is no interpreting or thinking that takes place in this instance—you go straight to emotion. Most often, however, this is not the case.

Instead, emotions are usually triggered by your interpretation of or automatic thoughts about a situation. For example, someone you love dies, and after a while, when you can think straight again, you begin thinking about how young she was (interpretation), and that it's not fair that she died (interpretation), which leads to the emotion of anger. Here's another example: You're at a party, and you find yourself sitting on a couch alone. You may start to interpret this in a negative way: no one there likes you; they find you boring; they don't want to talk to you. These automatic thoughts are going to lead to negative emotions such as sadness, hurt, or perhaps anger. So remember, it's usually your *interpretation* of a situation that leads to an emotion.

To continue with the flowchart, interpretations can be positive or neutral. (For example, if I'm going to a party, I might think it's going to be fun and that it will be nice to have a night out.) When this is the case, as the chart shows, there is no anxiety and therefore no further steps to be taken. When interpretations are negative, though, they usually lead to painful emotions such as anxiety.

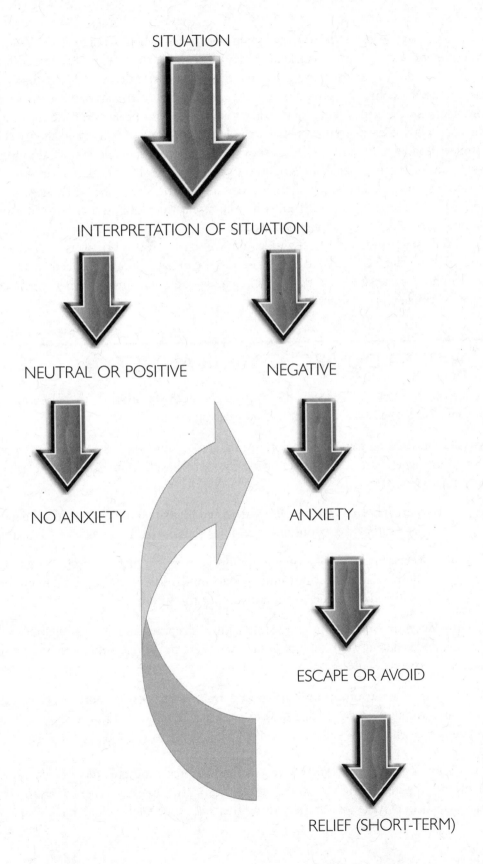

SITUATION

INTERPRETATION OF SITUATION

NEUTRAL OR POSITIVE   NEGATIVE

NO ANXIETY   ANXIETY

ESCAPE OR AVOID

RELIEF (SHORT-TERM)

The next level of the flowchart illustrates that when anxiety is triggered by your negative interpretation, your instinct is usually to try to decrease the anxiety because it's uncomfortable. You may try to do this by escaping the situation you're currently in and avoiding similar situations in the future. Escaping the situation certainly does decrease the anxiety in the short term because it provides relief. The problem is you've just taught your brain that you can't tolerate the situation, and this actually increases your anxiety in the long run, making it more likely you'll continue to avoid similar situations in the future. In other words, you've just made your brain more sensitive to that situation, so the next time the situation occurs, your brain will alert your fear response and you'll become anxious. Likewise, avoiding anxiety-provoking situations will relieve anxiety in the short term, but in the long run this results in your world shrinking as you have to avoid more and more situations in order to avoid feeling anxious.

You may be starting to get an idea now of what you need to do to decrease your dysfunctional anxiety or to turn down your level of sensitivity. That's right: you need to *stop avoiding* and start approaching those situations that you find yourself anxious in—in other words, act opposite to the urge accompanying your anxiety.

WHAT TO DO ABOUT YOUR ANXIETY

A lot of the work you've been doing throughout this workbook to help with your symptoms of bipolar disorder will also be helpful in decreasing your anxiety.

Mindfulness. Being mindful is helpful in reducing anxiety in all sorts of ways and can be effective in treating general anxiety disorder and panic disorder. Here are some examples of how mindfulness can impact anxiety:

- Mental noting of anxiety sensations can help you to accept and validate these sensations rather than continuing to fight them, which causes more anxiety.

- Regular practice of formal mindfulness exercises such as those presented in chapter 2 can have the effect of calming your mind and decreasing the amount of time you're feeling anxious due to thinking about the future.

Caring for your body. Improving your eating, sleeping, and exercise habits, avoiding drugs and alcohol, and reducing your caffeine intake will help to decrease the activity of your emotion mind, including anxiety.

Awareness of your emotional state and behaviors. Being aware of when you are in emotion mind and avoiding situations due to your anxiety will allow you to use skills such as acting opposite to your urge, which will help to decrease your anxiety in the long run.

A lot of the information you've read in the preceding chapters on emotions is also going to go a long way in helping you to reduce your anxiety. Take a moment now to consider how you're currently dealing with your anxiety using the skills you've learned so far.

DBT SKILLS AND ANXIETY

Since you started working through this workbook, have you noticed any kind of change in your anxiety level? _____

How often are you practicing mindfulness? _____

If you are practicing mindfulness regularly (a minimum of once each day for at least five minutes), what are you noticing? For example, is it helping you to feel calmer or more relaxed? Have you noticed an improvement in your concentration? Is it helping you to fall asleep at night? Is it helping you to become more aware of your anxiety sensations?

_____

_____

Have you cut down on your caffeine intake? _____

How else are you working on reducing the amount of time you spend in emotion mind? For instance, are you exercising, cutting down on drugs or alcohol, or working on improving your eating habits?

_____

_____

Are you practicing acting opposite to your urge to help you cut down on the extent to which you are avoiding things?

_____

Are you validating your emotions to prevent secondary emotions such as anxiety from arising?

_____

List any other skills you are using that have decreased your anxiety:

_____

_____

Take a moment to congratulate yourself on the work you've done thus far on these powerful skills. However, even if you're practicing all of these skills regularly, you may find they just aren't enough and your life is still being impacted by your anxiety. If this is the case, use the space below to list some ways your life would be different without anxiety. For example, Makenna from our previous example set a goal for herself to finish her college degree, which meant that she would have to look at setting smaller goals, including getting over her anxiety about doing presentations.

Keep in mind that you may not find your anxiety is limiting you, either because you've already been using skills to help you stop avoiding, or because you simply never started avoiding to begin with. Regardless, make sure you take some time to carefully evaluate the impact of anxiety on your life.

Below, list the ways your life would be different if you didn't suffer from anxiety. I've provided some examples to get you started.

- *I could go shopping at the mall.*

- *I could drive on the highway.*

- *I could take public transit.*

- *I would have more friends because I would go out more often.*

- _____

- _____

- _____

The items we're going to focus on here are things that you're avoiding because of anxiety. If you aren't currently avoiding anything, I would encourage you to read over the rest of this chapter anyway, so that you understand more about why you want to continue not avoiding.

Exposure Therapy

If you are currently avoiding certain situations in your life, the rest of this chapter is for you. This is where a specific cognitive behavioral therapy technique called exposure therapy comes in. *Exposure therapy* is exactly what it sounds like: you stop avoiding the situations that trigger your anxiety and actually expose yourself to them in order to teach your brain that there is nothing in the situation that is actually threatening. The result is that your anxiety will decrease as your brain gradually accepts the stimuli as nonthreatening and it stops alerting your fear response.

Some people do exposure therapy with a professional, which works well in many cases. However, I'd like you to establish a goal to learn how to do it on your own. In this way, you can become your own therapist, approaching situations that trigger anxiety regularly without needing professional support. This will give you more flexibility in the work and will help to increase your confidence around anxiety issues.

Before you panic at the thought of doing this kind of work, let me assure you that, while it is uncomfortable work to engage in, we're not going to just jump right in. I'll be teaching you some things that will make it a little bit easier on you. Also remember that, while the discomfort will only last a little while, the benefits you'll see will be long-term. Reminding yourself of this notion—short-term pain for long-term gain—can make the process more bearable. Exposure therapy isn't for everyone, though, so first you need to assess whether or not this is something you are ready and willing to do.

IS EXPOSURE THERAPY RIGHT FOR YOU?

Although exposure therapy is extremely effective in treating anxiety, it may not be your treatment of choice right now. What's great about exposure is that it will increase your self-confidence and feelings of mastery and will improve your quality of life by reducing your fear of sensations and situations that are currently causing anxiety. It will allow you to get back to work or school and any other activities you've avoided because of the anxiety.

On the other hand, exposure therapy is uncomfortable. You will likely experience some symptoms such as fatigue, tension, irritability, and difficulties sleeping after doing an exposure session (Denisoff 2007). Remember, this is short-term pain for long-term gain. However, there is one aspect of exposure that can be a deal breaker: exposure therapy requires a lot of time and commitment on your part. You will need to set aside approximately ninety minutes a day, five out of seven days, for each situation you're addressing (although you don't have to do situations consecutively—you can take time off in between). You need to make sure this is something you can commit to and that it won't interfere with responsibilities such as work or child care. If you can't commit to this right now, you'll need to come back to it later. It's okay to acknowledge that you feel unable to make this commitment now. But do remember that the longer you wait, the more your world will tend to shrink as your brain becomes more sensitive and you have to avoid more and more situations in order to not become anxious.

Last but not least, it's important for you to be sure that you are medically fit to do exposure therapy. It's never safe to assume that the sensations you experience are caused by anxiety. So make sure before engaging in this kind of treatment that you have seen a doctor and have been given a clean bill of health.

If you've decided to give it a try, keep reading. If it's not going to work for you right now, come back to it when it's more realistic. Now let me tell you some of the things we know about anxiety that will help you in doing exposure therapy.

THINGS TO KNOW ABOUT ANXIETY AND EXPOSURE

You've already learned that anxiety is a normal human emotion that prepares us for immediate action in dangerous situations or situations that the brain perceives as dangerous. Reminding yourself of this can help you stop fighting the sensations and can reduce your fear of them.

Another helpful thing for you to know is that anxiety is self-limiting. As soon as your brain triggers your sympathetic nervous system because it has perceived a threat in the environment, the sympathetic nervous system sends a message to another system in your body called the parasympathetic nervous system, which is the system that turns the anxiety off (Denisoff 2007). So remind yourself as soon as you start to feel the anxiety that your body is already working to shut it down—it just takes some time to do this.

The final thing you need to know about how your body responds to anxiety is something called *habituation*. When you repeatedly expose yourself to something that causes fear, your anxiety decreases over time. Think of it as your body getting bored because it's being exposed to the same thing for a long period of time. You've probably had a similar experience with physical sensations. For instance, you may have taken baths that started out so hot that you thought you'd burn yourself. But after a few moments the heat of the water was not only tolerable, it felt nice. Or what about jumping into a cold lake or pool and experiencing the shock of the cold, but after a few minutes, your body has grown accustomed to the physical sensations and it feels good (or at least tolerable). Just as your body gets bored with these physical sensations and stops sending you messages about them, it also gets used to the feeling of anxiety. In other words, when you expose yourself to and remain in anxiety-producing situations, the anxiety will decrease on its own.

Keeping these facts in mind, I'm now going to teach you how to do exposure therapy to help you reduce your anxiety. In this section, I'm first going to teach you some basic elements of exposure therapy. Next, I'll describe how to do exposure therapy for panic disorder, known as *interoceptive exposure*. This helps you get used to the physical sensations associated with anxiety so that your brain stops reacting to these sensations by triggering panic attacks. I'll then teach you how to do exposure therapy for external situations you're avoiding due to anxiety.

HOW TO DO EXPOSURE THERAPY

The first thing you need to know is how to rate your anxiety. We use a scale called the *subjective units of distress scale*, or SUDS. This basically means that you rate your level of anxiety on a scale from 0 to 100. Following is a chart that gives you an idea of what different ratings on the SUDS might mean.

SUDS Level	Description of Anxiety
0	Fast asleep; no anxiety present
15	No anxiety; feeling relaxed
25	Some stress due to normal life stressors; not uncomfortable
35	Increasing anxiety; some discomfort
45	Increasing sensations of anxiety causing more discomfort (for instance, heart rate increasing, difficulties keeping thoughts off the anxiety-provoking situation)
55	Anxiety somewhat interferes with functioning (for example, difficulty in concentrating, sweating, worry thoughts)
65	Anxiety continuing to increase, becoming more uncomfortable and distracting
75	Anxiety making it difficult to function (for instance, stammering, concentration becoming very difficult, heart racing, limbs trembling)
85	Increasingly uncomfortable, difficulty thinking straight because of anxiety, sweating, blushing, and so on
100	Full-blown panic attack (for example, visual disturbance; feeling faint, weak, and nauseous; difficulties breathing; tightness in chest).

If you have panic disorder, meaning you're fearful of the panic attacks themselves, you *must* treat this first with interoceptive exposure. (If you don't have panic disorder, you can skip this part and move on to the next section, which instructs you on creating a hierarchy. If you're not sure, try the exercises below and see how much anxiety they provoke.)

TREATING PANIC DISORDER WITH INTEROCEPTIVE EXPOSURE

You'll remember that panic disorder is a fear of the fear itself. It's not a situation triggering your anxiety but the physical sensations of anxiety that cause the fear. *Interoceptive exposure* is a technique that has you purposely generate the sensations you're afraid of in order to expose yourself to them and let your brain habituate to them. Make sure before you try any of these exercises that you have medical clearance from your doctor.

Interoceptive Exposure Techniques

Here is a list of ways to generate anxiety sensations. Many of these exercises generate more than one sensation. Try all of these exercises to see which ones most accurately stimulate the sensations you are fearful of. In the blank with the heading "Anxiety" beside each exercise, rate your anxiety level from 0 to 10, where 0 is no anxiety, and 10 is intense anxiety. Under "Similarity," rate how similar the sensation is to when you experience the sensation during a panic attack.

	Anxiety	Similarity
Dizziness, light-headedness, altered vision		
Shake your head from side to side	_____	_____
Put your head between your knees, then sit up suddenly	_____	_____
Hold your breath for thirty seconds	_____	_____
Hyperventilate (breath rapidly and deeply) or breath through a straw	_____	_____
Shortness of breath, rapid heartbeat, sweating, flushing		
Run on the spot, do jumping jacks, skip rope, or climb stairs	_____	_____
Sweating, difficulties breathing		
Sit in a hot, stuffy room	_____	_____
Wear too many layers of clothing	_____	_____
Stand in the bathroom with the shower running as hot as possible	_____	_____
Trembling, shaking		
Tense your whole body for one minute	_____	_____
Spotty vision		
Stare at a light until your vision alters	_____	_____

Feelings of unreality

Stare at yourself in the mirror   _____   _____

Stare at your hand   _____   _____

Once you've gone through each of these exercises and rated the level of anxiety and similarity of the symptom generated by each one, you can create a hierarchy of symptoms to be induced based on how much anxiety they triggered for you and how similar the experience was to when you have the sensation during a panic attack. If you had sensations that didn't trigger anxiety or weren't at all similar to those you experience during a panic attack, cross them off the list. Your hierarchy should start with the least anxiety provoking and end with the activity that triggered the most anxiety. Next, starting with the least anxiety-provoking sensation, follow the exposure therapy instructions in the "Graphing Your SUDS" section, later in this chapter.

You need to be aware that this work will be tiring, and you will likely feel similar to the way you feel after you've had a panic attack. So try to ensure you're doing the work on days that you don't have other major obligations or commitments. Thinking of these consequences, people often want to avoid doing this kind of work, which is understandable. Remember, though, that until you have treated your panic disorder effectively, you won't be able to do exposure therapy with other situations. This is because every time you approach a situation, you'll experience anxiety due to your fear of the sensations, not due to anxiety about the situation itself.

CREATING HIERARCHIES FOR ANXIETY-PROVOKING SITUATIONS

If you don't have panic disorder, or if you've already treated it using the above interoceptive exposure techniques, you'll need to make a hierarchy of the external situations that trigger anxiety for you. Go back and review the goals you wrote down a few pages ago and choose one. These are things you'd like to do if anxiety weren't a factor. Next, use the blank hierarchy provided to fill in situations that would trigger SUDS ratings at each level, from lowest to highest. For example, if your goal is to stop avoiding social situations, think about different situations that trigger anxiety for you and write them in the hierarchy according to what you expect each SUDS level to be. You can look at the two sample hierarchies I've provided to help you construct your own.

While making this list, remember that a degree of anxiety is quite natural with many things—having to do presentations or take exams, for example. So try to think of those situations that you avoid altogether, that trigger more intense anxiety, or in which the anxiety seems to be higher than what is warranted in the situation. You'll notice that the hierarchies below start at a SUDS of 35, since this is the level at which the anxiety starts to become more uncomfortable.

Sample Hierarchy: Social Phobia

SUDS	Description of Situation
35	Going to a gathering with my partner, at a friend's house, with people I know
45	Going to a gathering without my partner, at a friend's house, with people I know
45	Going to a small social event with my partner and best friend, where I don't know anyone else, and not talking to people I don't know
55	Going to a small social event, sitting with my partner and best friend and a couple of people I don't know, and not initiating conversation with strangers
60	Going to the same social event as in 55, but by myself, and not talking with anyone
65	At the same social event as in 55, starting a conversation with someone I don't know
75	Hosting a get-together at my house, with my partner, for two or three friends
85	Hosting a get-together at my house, by myself, for two or three friends
100	Being the center of attention (by telling a story or giving a speech)

Sample Hierarchy: Going to the Grocery Store

SUDS	Description of Situation
35	Heading to the grocery store alone and driving by the store
40	Parking in the parking lot with my friend
45	Parking in the parking lot of the grocery store by myself
50	Walking into the store with my friend
55	Walking into the grocery store alone
65	Being in the store with groceries in the cart, which makes it more difficult to leave the store if I have to
75	Standing in line to pay, with my friend
85	Standing in line alone, with no one behind me
90	Standing at the checkout, initiating conversation with the cashier
100	Standing in line alone, with people in front of and behind me, which makes it difficult to leave the store in a hurry if I need to

Take your time completing your own hierarchy, making it as accurate as you can. You may have more than one situation for each level on the SUDS, which is fine. You'll want to aim for a total of ten to fifteen situations for each hierarchy.

Keep in mind that exposure therapy isn't possible with all situations. For example, it won't be possible to get on an airplane frequently in order to desensitize yourself. And you don't want to put yourself in dangerous situations, like walking in the dark by yourself. So make sure you're being safe and realistic with your hierarchy. Because the anxiety can get in the way of logical thinking, if you aren't sure about your hierarchy ask someone you trust for help. If you do have intense fears of things that you can't do real-life exposure with, there are other options such as exposure to photographs or videotapes, role-playing situations, and imaginal exposure. While a detailed discussion of these techniques would go beyond the scope of this book, you can check out Edmund Bourne's book *The Anxiety and Phobia Workbook* (2000) for more details on these helpful tools.

My Hierarchy

SUDS	Description of Situation
35	
40	
45	
50	
55	
60	
65	
70	
75	
80	
85	
90	
95	
100	

Now you have your list or lists of anxiety-provoking situations that you will be practicing exposure therapy with. Your next step is to choose which situation to start with. As a general rule, you'll want to start off with a situation that you've ranked at about 40 on the SUDS (Denisoff 2007). This is a low enough level of anxiety to ensure success, and at the same time it's high enough to provoke the required anxiety response and give you a sense of accomplishment for tackling the situation. If you start off with a lower SUDS, it's not going to be challenging enough; if you start off any higher, it may feel too difficult.

So what if you don't have a situation ranked at 40? Take the next highest one (perhaps, as in the above example, you have "Walking into the grocery store alone" ranked at 55). Next, think about something you could incorporate into that situation that might make it more tolerable. For example, "Walking into the grocery store alone" might become a 50 if you have a friend with you, and it may become a 40 if you go in the midmorning, when there tend to be fewer people shopping. Get creative!

Once you've got your starting situation, you need to make plans to go into that situation. Make sure you choose a time when you won't be rushed. The most important thing to remember about exposure therapy is that once you get into the situation, you *can't leave* until your anxiety comes down. If you leave the situation while the anxiety is still high, you continue to reinforce the message to your brain that you can't tolerate the anxiety and that the anxiety won't decrease unless you escape the situation.

GRAPHING YOUR SUDS

I've provided an exposure therapy graph that you can photocopy and use to keep track of your sessions. Don't be surprised if, when you first enter the situation or induce a sensation, your anxiety spikes to a level higher than you predicted. This isn't unusual, and the anxiety often drops to a more tolerable (although still uncomfortable) level relatively quickly. Put a dot on the graph where your anxiety starts, and add a new one approximately every five minutes (one to two minutes for interoceptive exposure or for situations that you might not be in for a prolonged period, like standing in line) at whatever your SUDS level is. The general guideline to keep in mind is that you need to remain in the situation or continue inducing the sensations until your SUDS rating comes down by half or to 30, whichever is higher. For example, if your SUDS starts at 55, you can stop the exposure when your SUDS reaches 30, even though it's not quite half. This is because to get below 30 may be quite difficult, given the anxiety of being in the stressful situation and all of the other stressors we experience in our everyday lives. Make sure you use a separate graph for each exposure session so that you're not comparing yourself to the last session, which can influence your perceived level of anxiety.

Exposure Therapy SUDS Graph: Example

Date: _September 24, 2008_   **Session #** _Two_

Exposure Therapy Situation: _Going to a gathering at a friend's house with my partner_

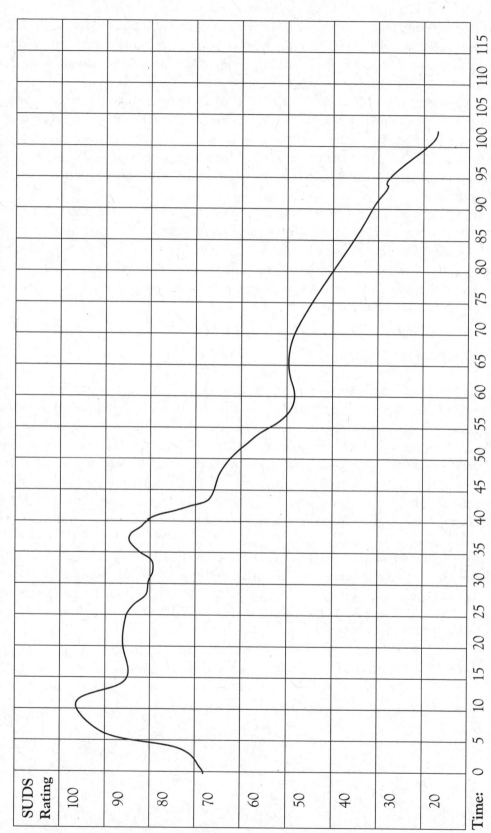

Exposure Therapy SUDS Graph

Date: _____

Exposure Therapy Situation: _____ Session # _____

SUDS Rating																								
100																								
90																								
80																								
70																								
60																								
50																								
40																								
30																								
20																								
Time:	0	5	10	15	20	25	30	35	40	45	50	55	60	65	70	75	80	85	90	95	100	105	110	115

MORE TIPS FOR EXPOSURE THERAPY

While you're doing exposure therapy, you want to try to remain in the present moment as much as possible. Don't distract yourself so that you're not experiencing the anxiety, as this defeats the purpose of the exercise. Remember, you're trying to retrain your brain that there is nothing in this situation that is a threat to your safety. If you're continuously distracting from the situation or your anxiety sensations, your brain won't learn that it's safe. It learns instead that you need to distract yourself in order to cope. As soon as you stop distracting, your anxiety is going to escalate again. So, you need to be mindful to your experience of anxiety in the situation, and you need to remain in the situation (or, with interoceptive exposure, continue inducing the sensations) until your anxiety decreases.

This also means that you can't take medication that you may normally take to quickly decrease your anxiety. This refers only to medication such as lorazepam (Ativan), clonazepam (Klonopin), diazepam (Valium), or other medication that you only take when you need it. It does not include antidepressants that you may take on a daily basis to help with your overall level of anxiety.

Take a moment to consider ways in which you would normally distract yourself when you're feeling anxious. The more aware you are of how you avoid feeling your anxiety, the more able you will be to not engage in those behaviors:

- *Take medication*

- *Avoid looking at people (or the thing causing anxiety)*

- _____

- _____

- _____

The last ingredient in helping your brain become bored with this experience is repeating the process approximately five out of seven days. Doing it consecutively is best, but not always possible. Make sure you graph each exposure therapy session, and by the fifth exposure, your anxiety will likely have come down substantially; you will have habituated. When this happens, you can move on to the next item on your hierarchy. If this happens sooner than the fifth session, it's best to complete all five anyway to ensure you are completely habituated.

If you find that after the fifth session you're still experiencing high levels of anxiety, you will need to evaluate more closely whether or not you are remaining present and mindful during the exposure or if you are distracting yourself from the experience in some way. If you believe you are being mindful and the anxiety is still not decreasing, you may want to go back and start with a different situation or seek help from a professional.

WHAT YOUR SUPPORT PEOPLE NEED TO KNOW

It can be extremely helpful to have a support person who will help you when you're first starting out with your exposure therapy sessions. The goal, though, is to get to the point where you can enter the situation on your own. If you have someone who is available to do this, there are a couple of things she will need to know.

Most importantly, she must not distract you from your experience of anxiety. Even if you seem very uncomfortable, talking to you to distract you is counterproductive and will hinder your ability to cope with the anxiety. This same idea applies to reassurance. When you're anxious, you may notice that you seek reassurance from others. This reassurance can sometimes help to decrease your anxiety, but again, if your support person is providing you with this reassurance, you're still sending your brain the message that you can't cope with the anxiety yourself—that you need reassurance from others to do so.

Instead, it will be most effective for you if your support person is able to remind you to be mindful of the anxiety and whatever sensations you're experiencing. For the most part, she should be relatively silent. But when she notices a change in you that might indicate a decrease in your anxiety (in your facial expression or body language, for example), she can ask questions like "Are you still being mindful of the anxiety?" or "Are you still focusing on being in this situation?"

If upon entering the situation your anxiety is much higher than you expected, your support person can help you to think of things you can temporarily incorporate into the experience to have your anxiety come down a little and make it easier for you to stay in the situation. For example, I did an exposure therapy session with a client named Anita, who had social anxiety. It was our first of the five sessions, and we were entering a cafeteria later in the morning, when we thought there would be fewer people there. Anita had estimated her SUDS would be about a 40, but when we got into the situation she rated her anxiety at about an 85, and she quickly became tearful. To try to lower her anxiety level, I suggested we sit in a booth that was located at the side of the cafeteria so we would be less visible to others. Anita was able to identify that sitting facing the doorway would lower her anxiety further. Finally, she avoided looking at the other people in the cafeteria until her anxiety became more tolerable, at which point she was able to start looking around the room and absorbing herself in the experience.

Your support person can also be your timekeeper, prompting you to put a dot on your graph at the appropriate time (or doing the graphing for you) by asking you what your SUDS level is. These kinds of questions will help you to stay focused on the experience, which is exactly what you need to do in order to desensitize yourself. Your support person can also remind you to practice saying your coping statements to yourself, which we'll discuss next.

COPING WITH THE ANXIETY

You can use coping statements about what you're experiencing to help you get through the exposure therapy experience, and this is often a good idea. Remember that it's your interpretation of events that's increasing your anxiety, so coping statements can actually help you change your automatic thoughts about the anxiety-provoking situation. Here are some examples of statements you can say to yourself to help you cope with anxiety. Have a look at them and then, considering your own personal experience of anxiety, write some of your own:

- *This feeling is uncomfortable, but I can cope with it.*

- *I can handle these sensations.*

- *I can get through this.*

- *I accept that this is anxiety, it's normal, and it's already shutting itself down.*

- _____

- _____

- _____

- _____

Notice that none of the sample coping statements has you avoiding your feelings. You're saying things to yourself about what you're experiencing, not distracting yourself from those things.

Mental noting can also be very useful to help you cope. Remember that this skill can help you to put some distance between yourself and the emotions, to help you reach wise mind rather than getting caught up in the emotions. Here's an example of mental noting while doing exposure therapy: "I'm entering the grocery store. My heart is racing, and I'm feeling anxious. My stomach is tight and my hands are sweaty." Talking to yourself about your anxiety in this way helps you to remain focused on the anxiety experience, and at the same time helps you to accept whatever sensations you're experiencing in the moment. We're going to look at this idea of acceptance further in the next chapter.

WRAPPING UP

You've learned a lot about anxiety in this chapter—what it does, why we need it, and how to reduce anxiety that's impacting your ability to function in life. If you need to do some exposure therapy to help you stop avoiding situations, I suggest that you continue working your way through the remaining skills in this workbook and work on the exposure therapy afterward, since some of the skills to come will also help you with your anxiety. Whatever order you decide on, remember to take your time.

In the next chapter, we'll take a more in-depth look at a skill called radical acceptance, which will further help you tolerate your emotions and can also reduce the number of unnecessary painful emotions you experience.

CHAPTER 9

Radical Acceptance

Have you ever noticed that there are things in your past that keep coming back to trigger painful emotions in you? Or do you sometimes dwell on situations that are occurring in the present that you have no control over, and that this also increases the amount of negative emotions you're experiencing? What about fighting emotions you might have? Do you still catch yourself invalidating some emotions, telling yourself you shouldn't feel that way, and trying to push the feelings away?

Whether you have bipolar disorder or not, sometimes there are things in life that are difficult to accept and that regularly create more emotional distress for you. When you have bipolar disorder, do you really need *more* emotional distress? In the last few chapters, we've been looking at emotions, how to tolerate them, and how you can sometimes change them. In this chapter I'll teach you a skill called radical acceptance, which will help you continue along this same path of reducing painful emotions when you can, and when this isn't possible, help you learn to tolerate them.

FIGHTING REALITY

Quite often we experience situations in our lives that are painful and sometimes even traumatic. As humans, our natural instinct is to avoid physical and emotional pain, to try to make it go away, or to fight it. So it's quite understandable that when something painful is happening in life, our automatic response is to fight it. It's almost as if we believe that if we deny it long enough, the pain will disappear. Take a moment to think of some situations you may have in your life presently or things that have happened in the past that you're fighting. Write them in the space provided. I've started you off with some examples:

- *I have bipolar disorder.*

- *I have to take medications on a daily basis.*

- *I was abused as a child.*

- *I can't work right now because of the frequency of my bipolar episodes.*

- *I'm an alcoholic.*

- *My relationship with my partner is over.*

- *I had an affair.*

- _____

- _____

- _____

- _____

- _____

- _____

Most of us can think of at least one situation in our lives that we fight. Next, in the space provided, write down some of the things you say to yourself when you're fighting the reality (Linehan 1993b) of the situation. Again, I've started you off with some examples:

- *It's not fair that this happened to me.*

- *Why me?*

- *I shouldn't have to go through this.*

- _____

- _____

- _____

- _____

- _____

- _____

Now I want you to choose one of the situations you listed above, and I want you to think very carefully about the emotions that arise within you when you fight the reality of that situation. Read the fighting-reality statements you've also written above, and really think about how unfair the situation is. Tell yourself that it shouldn't be happening, that it's not right, and so on. Then, in the blanks below, write down any emotions that come up as you do this. Rate each emotion from 0 to 100, where 0 means no emotion, and 100 means the emotion is incredibly intense:

Emotion	Rating	Emotion	Rating
_____	_____	_____	_____

You've probably written down some negative emotions such as anger, frustration, bitterness, resentment, or pain. These are typically the emotions that come up in us when we fight reality. Fighting reality creates suffering. This isn't to say that you shouldn't have emotions about difficult situations; remember, the goal of DBT is not to get rid of emotions or to help you learn how not to have them. But when you fight reality, you increase the amount of unnecessary painful emotions that get triggered, which creates suffering. Accepting pain actually helps to decrease the amount of suffering in your life (Hayes 2005). Pain is a necessity in life; suffering isn't!

What Is Suffering?

Pain is a natural part of being human; you can't escape it. There are always going to be situations that arise in your life that cause pain. For example, the death of someone you love will cause the emotional pain of grief. Being diagnosed with bipolar disorder may cause pain for various reasons: perhaps you're grieving the person you were or could have been, or maybe you've lost someone or something because of the illness. There are an infinite number of situations that will cause anxiety, sadness, regret, disappointment, and every other difficult emotion you can think of. This is what we call pain.

Suffering comes when you can't accept the pain in your life, so you focus on trying to deny the reality that's causing the pain. Essentially, suffering is pain amplified because of your inability to accept the pain. So when someone you love dies, for example, your pain turns to suffering if you refuse to accept it. You no longer just feel grief; you also feel anger, sadness, despair, and perhaps many other emotions.

The good news in all of this is that there are yet more painful emotions you can reduce by practicing skills and especially by using the skill of radical acceptance.

WHAT IS RADICAL ACCEPTANCE?

Radical acceptance is about accepting something with your body, mind, and soul—accepting it completely rather than halfheartedly. Accepting it with all of yourself, rather than just with your mind. This is why it's radical—because you're doing it with your entire being (Linehan 1993b).

Now before we go any further, I want to clarify exactly what acceptance means. A lot of people have a hard time with this skill simply because of the language. There is often a misconception that acceptance is the same thing as approval—that if you accept something, it means you want it to be that way. Actually, acceptance is nonjudgmental. If you accept something, it doesn't mean that you're saying it's good or bad. Acceptance means that you're simply acknowledging reality as it is. *Radical acceptance* is "the willingness to experience ourselves and our life as it is" (Brach 2003, 4). Let's look at an example.

■ Andrew's Story

At age twenty-one, Andrew had recently been diagnosed with bipolar disorder. In our first session, he talked a lot about how unfair it was that this had happened to him. He constantly asked, "Why me?" and insisted that it wasn't right, that he was just starting his life and that this was going to interfere with his ability to reach goals he had set for himself. When I introduced the idea of accepting his diagnosis and the fact that bipolar disorder was a part of his life, Andrew argued that if he accepted that he had bipolar disorder, it would mean that he was okay with it. Andrew had the idea, like many people, that acceptance meant approval.

What acceptance really means is that you are acknowledging reality. So in Andrew's example, saying he accepts that he has bipolar disorder doesn't mean that he likes it, that he doesn't want it to be any different, or that he's okay with it. It simply means that he acknowledges that this is reality. You can dislike something and still accept it. In fact, radical acceptance of our experience is the shift that must take place in order to open the way to genuine and permanent change (Brach 2003). In other words, you can't change something *until* you have come to accept it. Think about it: If you're continuously fighting the reality of a situation (like having bipolar disorder), you're not going to be doing things to help minimize the impact of the disorder, such as regulating your sleep habits or taking medication daily. Instead, you'll be fighting the reality and essentially pretending it doesn't exist (which, by the way, also takes a lot of energy). Once you come to accept the situation, you can do something to change it, like educating yourself about the illness so you understand what it will mean for you, taking your medications, and starting to take better care of yourself so that you can continue to live a high-quality life.

So if you find that you shy away from this skill because of the language, change it. If you can't get past that word "acceptance," think of it as "acknowledging reality" instead. One client I worked with just used the phrase "It is what it is" to help her accept.

Now that you have a better sense of what it means to accept, think of the same situation you were thinking of for the preceding exercise, when you were fighting reality. With that situation in mind, write some accepting statements about that situation below. I've provided some examples to start you off:

■ *It is what it is.*

■ *I don't like that this happened, but it did.*

■ *This is the way my life is now.*

■ *I acknowledge that this is the reality of my life.*

■ _____

■ _____

■ _____

■ _____

Now I want you to try another experiment. I want you to continue to think about the same situation as in the last exercise, and as you do so, read the list of accepting statements to yourself. Read them slowly and carefully, thinking about each of them and applying them to the situation you've been fighting. Then I want you to write in the following spaces any emotions that come up for you as you do this, and again rate each emotion from 0 to 100, where 0 means no emotion, and 100 means the emotion is incredibly intense:

Emotion	Rating	Emotion	Rating
_____	_____	_____	_____
_____	_____	_____	_____
_____	_____	_____	_____

You probably still had some negative emotions to put in these blanks. Remember, the pain is natural and won't simply go away when you're dealing with a difficult situation. But I'm guessing that the intensity of the painful emotions might have been lower this time. Go back and compare these emotions and their intensity to the list you created earlier in this chapter. Do you notice anything? Is there a difference in the emotions you listed? Did you perhaps have fewer negative emotions in the second exercise or notice that the intensity of your emotions was lower? Again, the emotions are still going to be there—they don't magically disappear. But generally speaking, when you can get to acceptance with a situation, the emotions will be more tolerable. If you noticed the emotions increased or stayed the same in the second exercise, you might want to try it again. Pay attention to whether or not you're *really* working on radically accepting or if you're holding back and still fighting.

You've probably had situations in your life that were really difficult and that you may have fought at first, but that you gradually came to accept. These might be things like the death of a loved one, the end of a relationship, or the loss of a job. Take a moment and write down some of the situations that you have already accepted in your life:

- _____
- _____
- _____

Thinking back on these situations, can you recall the difference between how you felt when the situation had just happened and you hadn't yet accepted it, compared to how you felt once you had come to accept that situation? You'll likely remember that the pain didn't just miraculously stop, but that it became a little bit more tolerable. You may recall, for example, that you began thinking about the situation less frequently, that you felt depressed or sad about it less often, that you were able to stop using substances to cope with those emotions, that you self-harmed less often, that your anger decreased, and so on. In the space below, make some notes below about the effects that accepting had on your life:

- _____
- _____
- _____

Hopefully by now you're at least considering the possibility that radical acceptance might just make a difference in your life. So now let's look at how you would actually practice this skill.

HOW TO PRACTICE RADICAL ACCEPTANCE

Radical acceptance is a difficult skill to practice, and there are a few things you need to know before you start working on it. The first thing you need to understand is that the more painful a situation is, the more difficult it will be for you to accept (Linehan 2003d). Let's say, for example, you have to move. Your spouse recently took a new job in a different part of the country, and you are relocating. Let's also say that you really like where you live right now. Imagine you're living in your dream house, and you have a lot of friends in your current neighborhood. You get together with them regularly for social activities, and your kids play with their kids. Perhaps you're also working at a job or doing volunteer work you really enjoy. Do you think it will be easy to accept that you're leaving all of these things behind? Even though you may know it's a positive change—your partner has been promoted, which means more income and status within the company—it will be hard for you to accept that you must leave because there will be pain involved.

Now let's imagine the opposite is true: You're moving from your current neighborhood, which you dislike immensely because there is gang activity nearby, there has recently been a string of break-ins in the neighborhood, and you've just never felt safe there. You never really got to know any of your neighbors very well, and you didn't take the time to get involved in the community. How difficult do you think it would be to accept this situation? Probably not so difficult, since there's very little pain involved. This is exactly how radical acceptance works. The more painful the situation you're trying to accept, the more difficult it will be and the longer it will take.

This brings us to the second thing you need to know about radical acceptance: This is not a skill that you can accomplish overnight. Some situations are going to take you a very long time to accept, while others will take a short period of time, depending on how painful they are. In addition, you may find that you get to the point of acceptance with a situation, and then something happens to get you fighting reality again. For example, you may have come to accept that you have bipolar disorder. But then you have another depressive or manic episode and need to be hospitalized, and you find yourself fighting it once again. This is natural.

It may get frustrating, though, so I encourage you to try to think of it in this way: When you're working on trying to accept a painful situation, you may find that you can only accept it for about thirty seconds each day. Even if this is the case, those are thirty seconds in the day that you are *not suffering*. Gradually, that time is going to increase to thirty minutes, to three hours, and so on, until you've fully accepted it. But regardless of how long it takes, if you're working on radical acceptance, you're decreasing your painful emotions and making life more tolerable for yourself.

Steps Toward Radical Acceptance

The following are the four steps you take to practice radical acceptance. First, you need to decide if this is a situation you want to accept. Sure, I've told you it's going to help, but that doesn't mean you have to practice this skill. You have to make that decision for yourself.

Once you've decided to radically accept something, the second step is to make a commitment to yourself to radically accept it. Essentially, this is you promising yourself that from this day forward, you're going to do your best to radically accept the situation. Before you know it, however, you're going to be fighting reality again. You'll probably find yourself thinking that it's not fair and wondering why the heck you should accept it when it so clearly shouldn't have happened in the first place.

The third step is noticing when you start fighting reality again.

The final step is turning your mind back to acceptance (Linehan 2003d).

I think of practicing this DBT skill as those internal arguments we often have with ourselves. Lots of people have these kinds of arguments around dieting, so let's look at that as an analogy. Step one is the decision. You decide you want to lose weight. In step two, you make the commitment to yourself that, starting right now, you're dieting. No more junk food. Shortly after making this commitment, however, your boss brings in a cake to celebrate the retirement of one of your coworkers, and the internal argument starts: "Okay, I'll just have one piece of cake, and *then* I'll start the diet." Step three is when you notice that you're fighting with yourself over your original commitment. And the final step is turning your mind back to the commitment: "No. I promised myself that I was going to stop eating junk food, and I'm committed to that. I'm not going to eat any cake."

This same process happens with radical acceptance. You make the decision to radically accept a situation, and then you make the commitment to yourself that, as of this moment, you're working on radically accepting it. A moment later, you're saying to yourself, "Why on earth should I accept it? It's not fair!" As soon as you notice that you've gone back to fighting reality, you need to turn your mind back to radical acceptance and remind yourself of your commitment. You may need to turn your mind back over and over again in the course of just a few minutes.

Let's look at a situation that would be much more difficult to accept than dieting. André had been physically abused by his father when he was growing up, and this was something that he constantly struggled with as an adult. André understood that accepting what had happened didn't mean it was okay or that he forgave his father. He could see that fighting reality was taking up a lot of his energy, and that this was regularly triggering a lot of anger and bitterness in him. So he made the commitment to himself that he was going to work on accepting the fact that he had been physically abused as a child.

Shortly after making this commitment, André heard his thoughts turning to the old pattern of fighting reality: "But he shouldn't have treated me that way, it's not fair. And it's not fair now that I have to do so much work to get over it when it shouldn't have happened in the first place." As soon as André heard those familiar thoughts running through his head, he was able to turn his mind back to acceptance by reminding himself of his commitment and why he wanted to do this: "I know it's going to be helpful for me in the long run if I can accept that this is what happened. I want to work on radically accepting this so I can decrease my painful emotions." A few moments later, André noticed himself fighting reality again, and he repeated the process of turning his mind.

Just like any of the other skills you've learned, you don't practice radical acceptance for someone else. It's not about forgiveness, for example; you're not radically accepting to put someone else's mind at ease. It's simply about whether or not you want to continue expending so much energy and having so many painful emotions about something that's out of your control. What happened in the past is out of your control. Sometimes situations in the present are out of your control (when they aren't out of your control, they're going to be much easier for you to accept). So continuing to fight reality just exhausts you. It doesn't actually accomplish anything productive.

Here are some examples of situations that you can begin to practice radical acceptance with. Remember that it's usually best to start by practicing with situations that aren't too painful. Starting this way will allow you to accumulate evidence that you can practice this skill and that it does reduce suffering. Providing this evidence to yourself can build up your level of confidence so that you can then begin to work your way up to the more painful situations in your life.

- The next time you find yourself stuck in traffic, practice radical acceptance: "It is what it is."

- When you go to fill up your vehicle with gasoline, rather than complaining to yourself about high gas prices, practice radical acceptance.

- When you have to stand in a long line, radically accept that you have to wait.

- When your plans have to change because of poor weather, radically accept this.

When you start thinking about practicing this skill, it can be helpful to make a hierarchy of situations you want to work on accepting. Below, list as many situations as you can think of that you are currently fighting—things that trigger painful emotions for you when you think of them (use an extra page if you run out of room):

- _____

- _____

- _____

- _____

- _____

Next, beside each situation you've listed, rate the intensity of the pain that comes up when you think about it. Use a scale from 1 to 10, where 1 is very little pain, and 10 is highly intense. Finally, identify the lowest-ranked situation and start trying to practice radical acceptance with it. Once you've made some progress with this first situation, you'll want to gradually work your way up to the more distressing situations. In this way, you come armed with the knowledge that you can practice radical acceptance, and you'll see from experience how it can be helpful. Give yourself time, and be patient with yourself. Remember that acceptance can take a long time to get to—but it's well worth the trip!

So, we've talked a lot about how radical acceptance of situations can be helpful. But there is another time you'll want to practice this skill: when you can't change your emotions and you have to tolerate them somehow.

RADICAL ACCEPTANCE OF YOUR EMOTIONS

Radical acceptance can be extremely helpful when you're experiencing painful emotions that you can't change. Accepting your emotions means feeling the pain without resisting it, without judging yourself for having the feeling, and without following the urge to act on the emotion (Brach 2003). Just like when you're fighting a situation, fighting emotions makes them even more painful. Let's look at anxiety as an example. Let's say you start experiencing sensations of anxiety; for example, your heart starts beating rapidly and your breathing becomes shallow. Out of habit, you start right in on fighting the feelings, thinking things like "No, I can't have a panic attack right now. I won't let it happen". However, you may have noticed that this struggle usually only makes the anxiety worse. Radically accepting the anxiety, on the other hand, makes it more tolerable. Yes, the anxiety is still there, but it doesn't get stronger when you accept it, like it does when you fight it and try to make it go away.

People often fight feelings of depression with thoughts like "I shouldn't feel this way," "This is stupid," or "Why can't I just get over this?" How do you think these kinds of thoughts end up making you feel? Probably, since you're judging your emotion, you're going to feel angry with yourself for the way you're feeling. Or perhaps you feel more anxious or even sadder. The point is, by fighting your emotions this way, you make them stronger. Remember when we talked about the importance of validating your emotions? Radical acceptance can help you do this. Stop fighting them and accept whatever emotions you're experiencing. They're neither good nor bad—they just are. Researchers demonstrated this point by providing just ten minutes of acceptance training to people with panic disorder. They found that these people were more able to face their anxiety than others who were taught to distract from and suppress their thoughts and emotions (Levitt et al. 2004).

Let's look at how radical acceptance might help with hypomania and possibly with manic episodes as well. As I noted earlier in this book, not everyone has awareness of when they are in a manic episode. If you do have such awareness, or if you notice you're hypomanic, you might fight this reality: "Oh no, this can't be happening again! It's not fair. I was doing so well." Again, these kinds of thoughts are going to trigger emotions such as anxiety, anger, and sadness, which can make the state you're in worse. Remember, when you're manic or hypomanic, you want to decrease stimulation, not add to it with agitating feelings like anxiety and anger. So you can simply acknowledge the reality of the affective state you are in, and then see if there's anything you can do to help yourself become less stimulated.

Stefan was someone who participated in one of my bipolar disorder groups, and after learning the skill of radical acceptance, he reported that he was actually able to use this skill very successfully when he was having a visual hallucination associated with mania. Instead of fighting it, Stefan was able to accept that this was his reality right now—that he was in the middle of a manic episode and was seeing something that wasn't actually there. In this way, he was able to remain calm and prevent other emotions, such as anxiety, from arising, which would have made the situation far more difficult for him to cope with.

Try writing down some accepting statements you can say to yourself when you're feeling an emotion you don't like, or a state, such as a manic, hypomanic, or mixed episode. If you have difficulties with this, you can refer back to the validating thoughts statements you came up with in chapter 7. I've also provided some examples to help:

■ *This is just anxiety. I can tolerate it.*

■ *I'm experiencing a hallucination right now. I've been through this before, and I can get through it now.*

■ *I'm feeling angry right now. It's uncomfortable, but it's here for a reason and I can deal with it.*

■ _____

■ _____

■ _____

■ _____

■ _____

In spite of how helpful this skill can be, it is often quite difficult for people to put into practice. To help with this, there's one more part to this skill that is important for you to know. That is the need to be open to the idea of accepting and willing to try it.

Willingness: Taking an Attitude of Openness

Sometimes people report that they understand how radical acceptance is going to help and why it would be effective for them to practice it, but they still can't make a commitment to work on it. This is often due to something known as *willfulness*, which is when we set ourselves apart from the fundamental essence of life, refusing to do what's effective and closing ourselves off from the possibilities (May 1987). It's when we throw up our hands and say, "I don't care anymore," "I give up," or "Whatever!" It's refusing to play the cards you've been dealt in the game of life or to do what you can with what you've been given. Sometimes, the tougher something is to do (like practicing radical acceptance or other skills), the more likely it is that we will be willful about it.

The opposite of willfulness is *willingness*, which refers to taking an attitude of openness toward life or agreeing to enter into life fully (May 1987). This is when you try your best to do what's most effective for yourself, try to solve a problem even when it seems unsolvable, or work on radically accepting something even when it's very painful. Willingness is trying to be more flexible (Hayes 2005) and opening yourself up to possibilities.

Think about things you do when you're feeling willful. For example, maybe you isolate yourself from other people or lash out at loved ones because your emotions are so intense. Or maybe you fall back into unhealthy coping skills, like using substances or self-harming. Think about how you close yourself off from possibilities, and write some of the willful behaviors you can identify in the space provided:

- _____
- _____
- _____

Now you'll be more able to recognize when willfulness arises within you. But how do you get to willingness when you're feeling willful? The first step is to simply notice that you're feeling willful. When willfulness does emerge, don't judge yourself for it. Instead, note it and radically accept that this is your current experience.

Next, think of willingness as opening yourself to the experience, to learning, to possibilities, to the universe. Expressing this attitude through your body can help you change willfulness to willingness. In other words, if you're trying to take an open attitude, show this with your body language. Take your unwilling posture and turn it into a willing one. Uncross your arms and unclench your fists. Instead, open your hands, holding your palms upward in an open posture. Smooth out the frown on your face, unclench your jaw, and try changing your expression to a half smile, with both corners of your mouth turning slightly up (Linehan 1993b). Research has shown that changing your facial expression actually sends signals to your brain about how you're feeling emotionally (Ekman and Davidson 1993). So if you can put a slight smile on your face, it can actually help you take a more open attitude.

Using willing language can also help you shed your willfulness. When you're feeling willful, remember, your attitude is one of nonacceptance, refusal, and denial: "No!" The opposite of this, telling yourself yes instead, can help you become more willing (Linehan 1993b). Try closing your eyes, taking some deep breaths, and using willing language—for example, "I can do this," "I'm all right," or "I'm going to try."

Remember that willfulness doesn't just occur with the skill of radical acceptance. It's useful to know about willfulness because it can come up frequently in life. The sooner you become aware that willfulness has arisen within you, the sooner you can work on changing this to willingness so that you can do what you need to in order to be effective.

DIFFICULTIES WITH RADICAL ACCEPTANCE

We've already looked at a couple of problems people run into with the skill of radical acceptance. These issues can become roadblocks to practicing the skill. Keeping in mind that this is a tough skill to master (or even to try), let's look at a few of the other misconceptions about radical acceptance that can sometimes get in the way of practice.

"If I Radically Accept, It Means I'm Giving Up"

Radically accepting something doesn't mean that you become passive about the situation you're trying to accept. This idea generally comes up with current situations, as people think that getting to the point of accepting the situation means they stop trying to do anything to change it. For example, I was working with Lisa, the mother of a twelve-year-old girl who had been having emotional problems for a few years. Lisa could see that she was spending a lot of time and energy simply wishing that her daughter didn't have to go through these difficulties and getting angry because she kept thinking how unfair it was that this had happened to her daughter. When I introduced the skill of radical acceptance to help reduce the painful emotions she was experiencing, Lisa expressed fear that this would mean she was giving up on her daughter. This is not at all the case! Radical acceptance means that you're giving up the negative emotions you're experiencing because you're no longer fighting the reality of the situation. It doesn't mean that you stop looking to solve the problem you're experiencing.

In another example, Tanya's brother was addicted to cocaine. She thought that radically accepting this would mean that she was giving up on her brother. Radical acceptance means that you stop fighting reality. This acceptance actually frees up the energy you've been using to fight the situation, so you end up with more energy at your disposal to try to solve the problem. For Tanya, this would mean saying to herself, "Okay, I acknowledge the reality that my brother is addicted to drugs. Now what can I do that will be most helpful for him?"

"How Can I Accept That I Will Have to Experience Depression for the Rest of My Life?"

Fah had been doing quite well for a number of months and admitted to me that he had actually been optimistic lately that maybe the depression wouldn't come back this time. So when his mood started to become low, he got very down on himself. I talked with Fah about radically accepting the fact that his mood was depressed, and he told me that he couldn't do it. He was afraid that he'd have to accept the fact that depression was going to continue to be part of his life, and that would just make him feel hopeless. I explained to Fah that you can't accept things that haven't happened yet. Radically accepting his depression meant only accepting that at the present time he was depressed. It had nothing to do with having depression in the future.

If you find yourself continuously going into the future and worrying about possible depression and other things, it's not radical acceptance you need to practice, but mindfulness—living in the present moment, not the future. The fact is, there are no guarantees of what will happen in the future. Bipolar disorder is such an unpredictable illness that you have no idea when or if the next episode will happen. Although there may be a strong likelihood of future episodes occurring, there are no guarantees, and there is no way of knowing if it will be in three weeks, three months, or three years.

If you're currently experiencing a depressive episode and find yourself fighting this reality, thinking something like, "Great. I thought this was over. It's not fair...," you only need to accept that, at the present time, you are experiencing depression. Trying to accept this will be difficult enough. Do you really want to add the pressure and pain of trying to accept that you're going to feel this bad for the rest of your life?

Another example occurred when Paul expressed difficulties radically accepting that his son may have bipolar disorder as well. He worried that he was to blame, knowing that bipolar is often in part an inherited illness, and he didn't want to see his son go through the same difficulties he had gone through in his life. I pointed out to Paul that, while he may have his suspicions, he didn't know for a fact that his son had bipolar disorder, so this wasn't something he could accept. However, he could work on radically accepting the behaviors he may have been seeing that he was interpreting as symptoms of bipolar disorder; for example, that his son was having troubles with mood swings, that he seemed to be angry a lot, and that he was withdrawing from friends and family. Those were the facts. If his son is diagnosed with bipolar at some point, then this too will be a fact that Paul will need to radically accept. But this was not the case at that time.

"How Can I Accept That I Am a Bad Person?"

Similarly, you can't accept judgments. Judgments are not facts. Julie brought this up in my bipolar group one day when we were discussing radical acceptance. She said she was having a hard time accepting something very painful. When I asked if she would share an example of what was giving her a hard time, she said she had been trying to accept that she was a bad person. Remember that another way of saying radical acceptance is "acknowledging reality." Judgments aren't reality— they are our perceptions of reality, but they aren't facts. So what I asked Julie to do was describe why she thought she was a bad person. She had a list of behaviors she had engaged in that in her mind were bad: she was addicted to drugs and alcohol; she lashed out at people who were trying to help her; and, in the past, she had had a problem with shoplifting. I explained to Julie that these were the facts that she needs to radically accept. Take the judgments out and work on accepting facts only.

"Some Things Are Just Too Awful to Accept"

Often people have difficulties with radical acceptance because the situation is just so painful, they don't want to accept it. If this is you, you need to ask yourself what's stopping you from trying to accept the situation. I often run into this with people who have experienced abuse in their lives, and they ask me how they can be expected to accept something so awful. First, you are not *expected* to practice anything. However, you might consider first that the way you've been dealing with things in your life until now hasn't been working for you, or you wouldn't have picked up this book. Second, remember that you practice radical acceptance for *yourself*. If you're working on this skill because you feel someone else expects you to, it's not going to work.

If you're trying to accept for yourself and you're still coming up against this reluctance, look a little closer at the thoughts you have about what it means to radically accept. Sometimes you'll discover that you're having difficulty with the language again; perhaps you're thinking of acceptance as meaning that you approve of the situation or that you forgive the person who hurt you.

Other times, however, it can seem to the person that the situation was just so painful they can't go there. Unfortunately, they're going there whether they want to or not. When you can't accept something, your mind has a painful tendency to bring you back to it over and over again. So, over time and with practice, radical acceptance can actually help you to think about a situation less. And even more important, when you're working on accepting your situation and your mind takes you back to it, there will be fewer emotions triggered and less intensity to those emotions.

If this is something you're struggling with, remember that the decision is ultimately yours. You can't practice radical acceptance unless you're doing it for yourself. If you're doing it because you're being told to, it simply won't work. Also, you have to have a degree of belief that this skill is going to help. Otherwise, you're just not going to want to put the effort into doing it.

■ Sebastian's Story

Sebastian was a client I worked with who had bipolar disorder and had been sexually abused as a child. The depressive episodes he experienced were usually quite severe and often resulted in him being hospitalized. He had been in the hospital for depression approximately six times by the time he was twenty-four and had made some serious suicide attempts. One of the things that Sebastian kept coming back to was the sexual abuse he had experienced and how unfair it was. Sebastian's mind often took him back to the horrible things that happened to him, and he would get caught up in fighting the reality of those experiences.

After a few months of working together, I could see that Sebastian was stuck. During every session he would go over and over how unfair it was that he'd had to go through those things and that no one had been there to help him. I pointed this out to Sebastian and he agreed that he just couldn't stop going back to those events; he said he felt like a broken record, repeating the same things over and over. So I taught him the skill of radical acceptance, and Sebastian agreed to try it. He struggled with this skill, and we went over many of the points I've written down here—that accepting what happened doesn't mean he forgives the person who abused him or that he approves of what happened or is okay with it. It also doesn't mean that all of his emotions about what happened are going to disappear, because this was a situation involving extraordinary pain for him.

Over time, as Sebastian kept working on this skill, he found that his mind took him back to those events less often. He also noticed that when his mind did go there, the emotions weren't as intense as they used to be when he was still stuck in the fighting-reality mode. Sebastian also reported that when his mind took him there, he was much more able to let the thoughts go and think about something else instead of continuing to dwell on the situation like he used to. Overall, he found that those past events had much less power over him than they used to, and he was thrilled.

Now, I want to emphasize that this took a long time for Sebastian to work on. Especially with such an emotionally loaded situation, radical acceptance can be extremely difficult and time-consuming. There are still times that Sebastian's mind turns back to those events and he falls back into the same thinking patterns. But those times are now outweighed by the times that he can turn his mind away from those thoughts and toward acceptance.

Sebastian reported that it was most helpful to pay attention to his behaviors. He realized that he had a tendency to engage in certain self-destructive behaviors when he was getting caught up in fighting acceptance. He would isolate himself and sometimes use drugs and alcohol to try to get rid of the painful emotions and thoughts. He would often turn to self-harming behaviors to try to distract himself from the emotional pain, and when these efforts failed, he would resort to suicide attempts.

At the beginning of this chapter, you identified some of the thoughts you have when you're fighting reality. Take a moment now to consider what kinds of behaviors you engage in when you are fighting reality:

_____

_____

_____

_____

_____

_____

When you notice yourself engaging in these behaviors, pull out your list of distress tolerance skills you made at the end of chapter 5 to help you get through the crisis. When there's a chance you could do something to make the situation worse, you want to distract yourself from those thoughts and just get yourself through it. Radical acceptance is a skill that is going to help you have fewer crisis situations, but it's unlikely to be really helpful as a short-term coping skill when you're right in the thick of it. When you've survived the crisis situation, go back to regularly practicing radical acceptance.

WRAPPING UP

In this chapter, you've learned about a DBT skill called radical acceptance. This is a skill that will help to reduce the number of painful emotions you have in general, and it can also help you to tolerate your emotions so that they won't overwhelm you and result in unhealthy or self-destructive behaviors. Radical acceptance is a very important skill, and it's also one of the more difficult skills to learn. So it's extremely important that you have patience with yourself. It will come—it just takes time.

One of the goals of this chapter was to help you understand how this skill will help reduce painful emotions, so I had you examine some things that may have happened in the past that you've already accepted. Remind yourself of these instances if you notice yourself becoming frustrated with your lack of progress with this skill. You have done it before, you can do it again, and you know from experience the difference this skill can make. So keep at it!

Also, don't forget about practicing radical acceptance with the bipolar states of depression, mania, hypomania, and mixed episodes. Accepting these things as they are occurring can reduce painful emotions that might lead to their escalation.

Finally, with radical acceptance, as well as with other skills, you learned about the importance of trying to adopt an attitude of openness. Being open to the possibility that skills might help you will reduce your level of resistance to practicing them. They do, after all, take a lot of energy and hard work. Recognizing when you're feeling willful and replacing this with willingness using some of the strategies mentioned earlier can make a big difference when you're trying to effectively use skills.

Mindfulness is an important part of practicing radical acceptance, since being in the present moment more often means you'll be more aware of your thoughts and notice more quickly when you're starting to fight reality again. To be even more effective with radical acceptance, you may want to go back to chapter 2 for a reminder of mindfulness exercises that involve observing your thoughts and practice them regularly.

In the next chapter, we're going to look at relationships in more depth, and you'll learn some new skills to help you be more effective in interpersonal situations.

CHAPTER 10

How to Be More Effective in Relationships

I've already mentioned that bipolar disorder can have serious consequences for relationships, and if you have bipolar disorder, you likely already know this all too well. When you're depressed and you isolate yourself, withdrawing from the people you care about, you damage relationships. When you're manic and you act in ways your loved ones don't approve of, like drinking, using drugs, or carelessly spending a lot of money, you damage relationships. Even outside of bipolar episodes, you can damage relationships—for example, getting caught up in emotion mind and lashing out at someone in anger.

But don't forget that your relationships can also have an effect on you. If you don't have enough relationships in your life, you may feel lonely, and this can lead to depression. If you have unhealthy relationships, this can also trigger painful emotions.

This chapter will teach you skills to help you change the way you interact with others in order to improve your relationships. While we're most concerned with the important relationships in your life, these are also skills that you can use on a daily basis to be more effective with people in general. First, let's take a look at the relationships you have in your life and the goals you might have in this area.

ASSESSING YOUR RELATIONSHIPS

Quite often people don't give a lot of thought to the relationships in their lives, which means that this is an area that may suffer. I've provided the following worksheet to help you assess the relationships in your life.

RELATIONSHIP ASSESSMENT

If you experience a crisis, do you have someone you can call for help? If so, who?

_____

Do you often find yourself in conflict with friends or family?

_____

Think about how often you go out with others to socialize (for example, going to the movies, out for dinner, dancing, or to a friend's house for a get-together). Are you satisfied, or do you feel that this is something you're missing out on and that you need to do more often?

_____

_____

Do you find it easy to apologize to someone when you know that you are in the wrong?

_____

_____

Are you able to ask people for help when you need it?

_____

Are you able to say no to others when they make requests of you that you don't want to comply with?

_____

Do you have any difficulties communicating with others (for example, expressing your opinions or feelings)?

_____

Do you have any unhealthy relationships you want to end but have been unable to?

_____

_____

Do you think your relationships are well-balanced, so that you and the other person are both giving and taking from one another?

_____

Consider the people in your life in each of the following categories, and write the names of the people with whom you currently have relationships. If you need more room, write on a separate sheet of paper.

Family

_____ _____ _____

_____ _____ _____

_____ _____ _____

Friends

_____ _____ _____

_____ _____ _____

_____ _____ _____

Mentors

_____ _____ _____

_____ _____ _____

_____ _____ _____

Professional Helpers

_____ _____ _____

_____ _____ _____

_____ _____ _____

Spiritual or Faith Community

_____ _____ _____

_____ _____ _____

_____ _____ _____

Now that you've thought about your relationships with these people, think about what goals you might have in terms of relationships. For example, are there some people you would like to improve your relationship with, and if so, in what way? Do you have enough close friends? Would you like to work on improving how you communicate with others? Take some time now to write down any goals or other thoughts that come to you:

_____

_____

_____

_____

As you work through this chapter, keep these goals in mind. You may develop new goals as you read the material. If so, be sure to write them down. And remember, everyone can benefit from improving their relationship skills.

THE IMPORTANCE OF RELATIONSHIPS

Have you ever lost a relationship—either because you ended it yourself or because the other person did—and then regretted that loss? Sometimes this is beyond our control. Romantic relationships, for example, can end because there's no chemistry or because the people in the relationship want different things. But quite often relationships end prematurely when they don't have to.

One reason for this is that many people take their relationships for granted and don't work to keep them healthy. Think of a relationship as being like a car. When you own a car, you take care of it to prevent it from breaking down. You get the oil changed, you have the tires rotated, and you have it tuned up now and then. If the car starts making a noise, you take it in and have it checked out. Relationships need to be treated in the same way; you have to put some effort into keeping them healthy or they break down.

Taking care of a relationship in this way means two things. First, as with your car, you do things that prevent problems from arising in the relationship. You call your friend regularly rather than waiting for her to call you all the time. You invite her to do things with you. This is maintenance. This is you preventing the relationship from breaking down.

The second way you keep the relationship healthy is by taking care of the squeaks as soon as you hear them. If your car starts making a loud noise every time you start it, you don't assume it will just go away or get better on its own. You get the problem taken care of as soon as possible so it doesn't get worse. In a relationship, as soon as you become aware of a problem, you need to address it. It won't get better on its own either. Rather, these kinds of problems tend to fester and build resentment if left alone too long.

Let's look at an example: Caleb and Chris had been close friends for a couple of years. Chris had recently met some new friends, and Caleb noticed he was hearing from Chris less and less. He started to realize that the only time he spoke with Chris was when he called him, and Caleb began to resent this because it felt like he was doing all the work in the relationship. This went on for a couple of months, and because Caleb didn't talk to Chris about his feelings, the problem went unresolved and his resentment continued to build. One day, Caleb decided he'd had enough and that he would no longer make the effort to stay in touch with Chris. A couple of months later, when he got a message from Chris, Caleb didn't return the call. If Caleb had addressed the problem when it arose, it's possible the two friends may have been able to save the relationship. However, these skills don't come with guarantees.

ENDING UNHEALTHY RELATIONSHIPS

Sometimes you'll come to see that people you've had relationships with are just not healthy people for you. For example, let's say that Caleb did speak to Chris about his feelings, but nothing changed in their relationship and Caleb continued to feel resentful. Or perhaps someone you are in a relationship with is aggressive or passive-aggressive (these communication styles will be discussed shortly) and regularly leaves you feeling like you've been bullied. Maybe you have a friend with an alcohol problem who insists on offering you drinks whenever you visit, even though she knows you're trying to stop drinking. Sometimes relationships become abusive and aren't healthy for you to remain in, even if you continue to love or care for the other person.

Over time, as you practice skills and build up your self-esteem, you may come to see that this person isn't ready or willing to change, and that you aren't willing to remain in the relationship as it is. When this happens, you will come to realize that you need to end the relationship. Although this can be very difficult, remember that not all relationships will survive, and you must do what is healthiest and most effective for yourself.

Now you may be wondering how you would talk to a friend about a situation that's making you uncomfortable, angry, or sad. Communicating about problems in relationships isn't easy, which is why we often avoid doing it. One thing that can contribute to making it so hard is that a lot of people think of addressing problems as a conflict or confrontation. When you identify a problem in your relationship, it's neither a conflict nor a confrontation—at this point, it's simply a problem. If you enter into a conversation thinking about it as a conflict, however, you might just turn it into one. There are ways of talking to people that make it more likely the discussion will remain just that—a discussion. But before I teach you these skills, it's important for you to become familiar with where you're at now in terms of your communication style.

COMMUNICATION STYLES

Let's take a look at how you tend to communicate. I'm going to describe the four typical communication styles, and I want you to consider which of these categories you fall into. You may find yourself relating to more than one category, depending on whether you're dealing with a personal or professional matter, who you're communicating with, and so on. This is fine. This evaluation isn't so much about labeling yourself as gaining awareness of your patterns.

Passive

People who communicate passively often don't communicate at all. If you're a passive person, you tend to stuff your emotions rather than expressing them. Perhaps you do this out of fear of hurting others or making them uncomfortable, or maybe it's because you don't believe your feelings or opinions matter as much as those of others, or both. Passive communicators usually have a fear of confrontation and believe that if they voice their own ideas or emotions, it will lead to conflict. If this is you, your goal is usually to not rock the boat, and so you sit back and say little. Being passive often results in allowing others to violate your rights, and it shows a lack of respect for your own needs. It communicates a message of inferiority. This style of communication may or may not negatively impact the other person in the relationship. For example, it may not bother the person, or the person may become uncomfortable with your lack of respect for yourself. Regardless of the impact on the other person, though, it will definitely have a negative impact on you over time. Usually passivity leads you to resent not having your needs met, and this will create difficulties.

Notes about how you may communicate in a passive way:

_____

_____

_____

Aggressive

Aggressive communication is about dominating and controlling others. It's about getting your own way, no matter the cost to others. If you are aggressive in your communication style, you're direct, but in a forceful, demanding, and possibly even brutal way. You tend to feel self-righteous, which fuels your aggression and leaves others feeling resentful, hurt, and often fearful of you. You might get your way, but if you do, it tends to be at the expense of others (and sometimes at your own expense, as you may experience feelings of regret, guilt, or shame for the way you behaved). An aggressive communicator doesn't care so much about how she goes about getting her needs met, even if she disrespects and violates the rights of others, as long as the result is in her favor. This communication style will have obvious negative impacts on your relationships, as others will often not tolerate being disrespected and mistreated for long.

Notes about how you may communicate in an aggressive way:

_____

_____

_____

Passive-Aggressive

Passive-aggressive communicators are people who don't directly express themselves. The passive-aggressive person shares the passive person's fear of confrontation but still makes attempts to get his needs met through indirect means. If this is you, your goal is to get your way, but you won't come right out and say it. Instead, you'll use techniques that more subtly express your emotions; for example, being sarcastic, giving people the silent treatment, slamming a door on your way out, telling someone you'll do something for them but then "forgetting" about it, and so on. You can see that in these ways, someone would certainly be getting a message across without actually having to say the words. If you behave passive-aggressively, you likely confuse others with your indirectness and lack of clarity as you say one thing but then send a contradicting message. Many of these techniques are thought of as manipulative, and they often have negative impacts on relationships.

Notes about how you may communicate in a passive-aggressive way:

_____

_____

_____

Assertive

Assertiveness is expressing your thoughts, feelings, and beliefs in a direct, honest, and appropriate way. It means that you demonstrate respect for yourself as well as the person you're communicating with, and you try to ensure that you're getting your own needs met while also trying to meet the needs of the other person as much as possible. If you're assertive, you effectively listen and negotiate so that others choose to cooperate willingly with you. After all, they feel that they, too, are getting something out of the interaction. When you communicate with others in this way, they will respect and value you because they feel respected and valued.

Assertive communication is the way we naturally express ourselves when we feel good about ourselves. When we have good self-esteem, we feel confident about ourselves, and we feel as though we have every right to express our opinions and feelings. This doesn't mean that if you have low self-esteem you can't practice this style of communication. In fact, if you can practice communicating assertively, it will actually improve how you feel about yourself. It will also improve your relationships and your interactions with others overall, which will also make you feel good about yourself.

Notes about how you may communicate in an assertive way:

_____

_____

_____

DIFFICULTIES WITH ASSERTIVENESS

So why do we often have problems asserting ourselves? Sometimes people feel that they don't have the right to assert themselves. This often happens when people have low self-esteem, and this, in turn, can be connected to having a mental health problem such as bipolar disorder. Think about this for a moment: Do you believe you have the right to speak up and state your opinion or to tell people how you feel? Or you may truly believe that you have a right to express these things, but you fear that your thoughts or emotions aren't valid. As we discussed in the section on emotions, this can especially be a problem in bipolar disorder, since your illness makes it difficult for you to trust your own experiences.

Another reason people have a hard time asserting themselves is that they often fear being disliked by or offending others. If you aren't used to communicating in this way (and sometimes, even if you are), it can certainly be uncomfortable. It's often much easier to keep it to yourself when someone says something hurtful to you. So you avoid the situation and pretend it didn't happen (passive); you verbally attack the person to protect yourself (aggressive); or you decide to stop talking to that person and give her the silent treatment (passive-aggressive).

These can all be solutions that are easier in the short term, but think about the long-term costs. Being passive leads to a buildup of resentment and a likely decrease in your self-esteem as you don't speak up about your feelings. Aggressive communication can lead to feelings of guilt and remorse afterward if you regret what you said. It can also lead to damaged relationships or the premature ending of relationships as other people get fed up with your disrespectful behavior. Behaving in a passive-aggressive way can lead to all of these outcomes.

Being assertive is often uncomfortable in the short term, especially until you become used to expressing yourself in this way. But in the long run, it leads to improved self-esteem as you feel good about yourself for respecting your own boundaries, as well as those of others.

HOW WE LEARN TO COMMUNICATE

Think back to chapter 6, in which we talked about emotions and the attitudes we develop about emotions based on past learning experiences. The same occurs with communication styles. We learn how to communicate by seeing others around us communicate. It can be very difficult for someone to be assertive if she has grown up thinking that she needs to communicate in a passive, aggressive, or passive-aggressive way in order to reach her goals. Let's look at an example.

■ William's Story

William idolized his father, who was a very important role model in William's life. William's father was an aggressive communicator, and so William learned that in order to be heard and respected by others like his father was, you had to be domineering and go after what you wanted. William thought he had to be aggressive about his needs and wants, regardless of the consequences to others. On the other hand, William had a younger brother, Nigel, who was quite fearful of their father's angry outbursts. Because of this, Nigel developed a passive communication style. He grew up fearful of his father's anger and learned that to avoid his father's anger he could simply stay quiet and not rock the boat. So although they grew up in the same environment, William and Nigel learned different communication styles based on their own unique personalities and temperaments.

Take a moment now to think about the communication styles you grew up with. Then answer the following questions.

FAMILY COMMUNICATION STYLES

Thinking about your immediate family members (or those people who were regularly in your household), can you identify if any were:

Passive _____

Aggressive _____

Passive-aggressive _____

Assertive _____

Did anyone in your family encourage you to not rock the boat (passive)?

_____

Did any family members regularly not express opinions or feelings about situations (passive)? Perhaps they usually said, "It doesn't matter to me" or "Whatever you guys want to do" when you were deciding where to go for dinner or what board game to play.

_____

Did any of your family members regularly have angry outbursts, when they may have called other people names or yelled at others (aggressive)?

_____

Did any family members seem like they always had to have their way or they would become angry and bully others into agreeing with them (aggressive)?

_____

Were there people close to you who would give you or others the silent treatment when they weren't happy about something (passive-aggressive)?

_____

Did you have family members who, instead of talking about their emotions, would slam doors or engage in other behaviors that told you, without words, that they weren't happy (passive-aggressive)?

_____

Did any family members talk to others about emotions—for example, telling others when they weren't happy with a behavior (assertive)?

_____

Were any of your family members able to express that they were angry without yelling, so that a discussion could happen and a resolution could be reached (assertive)?

_____

Hopefully you're starting to get a clearer picture of why you communicate the way you do. Remember that the reason for looking back into your history is not to find someone to blame for the problems you're experiencing, but simply to help you understand why you behave the way you do. You still need to take responsibility for making changes in your life. Figuring out where your patterns of communication came from can help you let go of them if they are unhealthy. Answer the following questions to help you identify what these current patterns are.

PEOPLE-SPECIFIC COMMUNICATION STYLES

Are there certain people in your life you tend to communicate with in these ways:

Passive _____

Aggressive _____

Passive-aggressive _____

Assertive _____

Do you notice that you have a tendency to assert yourself only in certain aspects of your life, such as personally, professionally, or on the telephone?

_____

_____

How do you see your communication style impacting your life in negative ways?

_____

_____

What are the positive impacts of the way you communicate?

_____

_____

Do people comment on how you communicate (for instance, make reference to how quiet you are, how aggressive or bullying you are, that they don't like the way you treat them, and so on)? If people haven't said anything about this spontaneously, you may want to check this out with some people you trust.

_____

_____

_____

By now you're probably developing a fairly accurate picture of how you communicate with others. Remember that we often use a variety of communication styles, depending on the situation and who we're communicating with. You may also be coming up with more relationship goals as you develop a more in-depth understanding of yourself and the way you communicate. It may be a good idea to go back to the beginning of the chapter and write down any additional goals that come to mind, thinking about these as we move on to the next section about when and how to be more assertive.

WHEN DO WE NEED TO ASSERT OURSELVES?

The quick answer to when you need to assert yourself is "Always!" Asserting yourself helps in relationships because it shows the other person that you have respect for him, as well as for yourself. It is a way for you to effectively maintain limits you set for yourself, as well as to negotiate conflicts without damaging relationships (McKay, Wood, and Brantley 2007). Communicating assertively also leads to improved self-esteem, as you learn to leave old, ineffective patterns of communication behind and begin to interact with others in a healthy way that will be more likely to meet your needs.

Apart from relationships, however, asserting yourself is simply a way of being more effective in the way you communicate, as you express yourself clearly and concisely. So whether you're interacting with a sales clerk at a store, your psychiatrist or therapist, your partner, a close friend, or a coworker, assertiveness will help you say what you want to say, be understood, and get what you want out of the interaction.

HOW TO COMMUNICATE ASSERTIVELY

By now you probably have a good understanding of why assertiveness can be helpful. Now you're probably asking the question "How do I do it?" Mathew McKay and his colleagues (2007) identified the following six interpersonal skills that will lead to more assertive behavior in relationships.

Knowing What You Want

First, you need to decide what your priority is in the situation you're in. Let's look at an example: Say you have a coworker who communicates in an aggressive way. After speaking with her, you often leave the interaction feeling as though you've allowed her to be disrespectful to you without saying enough to stick up for yourself. When interacting with that person, you need to decide which is most important: Do you have a goal you're trying to reach that she could help you with, or possibly prevent you from reaching? Do you want to improve the relationship you have with her? Do you want to feel good about how you handle yourself in the interaction, regardless of the other outcomes? Or do you want to be able to say no to a request she has made of you?

You'll find that sometimes more than one of these areas are priorities, and sometimes it's possible to achieve more than one of these at a time. At other times, though, you'll find that these priorities conflict, and you have to choose which is the most important. Whatever you decide on, it's very important that you be clear with yourself what your top priority is so that you can clearly communicate this to the other person. It's very difficult to get what you want if you're not sure what it is. Once you've decided on your priority, you'll be able to choose which skills will help you reach that goal.

Asking for What You Want in a Way That Doesn't Damage the Relationship

Following is what I think of as a recipe for assertive communication. If you follow it, as with any recipe, you aren't guaranteed of the outcome you're looking for. You can still make mistakes, even when you're following the recipe. The same happens with skills. Sometimes, even though you're doing what you're supposed to do, things can still get in the way of you having the outcome you were hoping for. When you follow a recipe, though, you have a better chance of the situation (or cookies) turning out the way you'd like than if you play it by ear. So here is the recipe for assertiveness:

1. **Nonjudgmentally describe the situation.** Once you've decided on your priority in the situation, you need to clearly describe the situation to the person, sticking to the facts. If you bring judgments into the conversation, the likelihood that you will meet any of your goals is going to decrease. For example, if your friend said something hurtful to you, you could describe the situation like this: "Earlier, when we were talking, you said you didn't like my sister." The description of the situation doesn't have to be lengthy; sometimes it may be one sentence long. The main thing is that you be clear and specific about what you're talking about. The other thing to keep in mind here is that, at this point, the problem you're discussing is neither a conflict nor a confrontation; it's simply a problem that needs solving.

2. **Describe what you think and feel about the situation.** Next, you need to tell the person what your opinion is on the matter and how you feel about it. To continue with our above example, your description of what you think and feel might go something like this: "I don't like the fact that you were critical of my family, and I'm feeling hurt."

3. **Assert yourself.** So far, you've nonjudgmentally described the situation and you've stated what you think and feel about the situation. The next thing you need to do is assert yourself by clearly asking for what you want; for example, "I would appreciate it if you wouldn't speak about my family that way in the future."

Let's look at an example: Ernie's supervisor at work is often quite critical of him, and Ernie usually leaves their interactions feeling as though he isn't speaking up for himself and doing what he needs to do to feel good about himself. His performance appraisal is coming up, and he's fairly certain, based on his past experience with his supervisor, that the appraisal won't reflect favorably on him. In this situation, Ernie has decided that his priority is to feel better about himself when the interaction is over.

When the day of his performance appraisal arrived, Ernie did some preparation to help him through the interaction. He knew it was coming, and he was fairly sure it would go like many of his previous interactions with his supervisor, leaving him feeling walked over and like he could have spoken up for himself more. So when Ernie's supervisor completed the appraisal and told Ernie how unhappy he was with his progress, Ernie was ready and responded assertively: "You've given me a poor rating on my performance appraisal (*nonjudgmentally describing the situation*). I don't believe that I deserve that rating, and it's frustrating to me that we don't seem to be on the same page with this (*expressing his opinions and emotions*). I'd like for us to get together to go over my job description and your expectations in various areas so that I can understand how to make the changes you're asking for (*asserting himself*)." At last, Ernie left an interaction with his supervisor feeling good about himself for the interaction and for having asserted himself.

Negotiating Conflicting Wants

An inherent part of being assertive is respect for the other person and a desire that everyone get something they want out of the situation, at least to some extent, whenever possible. So being willing to give something in order to get something can go a long way toward helping you reach your goals. Instead of focusing solely on your goals, change your focus to trying to reach a mutually agreeable solution where both of you are getting some needs met.

Getting Information

Knowing what other people want and understanding what they think and how they feel is also imperative in helping you to communicate assertively. When you're being assertive, you are just as concerned about the other person in the interaction as you are about yourself. So you need to know how she feels in order to treat her fairly and respectfully. Quite often we make assumptions about the other person, and these assumptions can damage the relationship and prevent us from being successful in our interaction. Rather than making assumptions about how the other person is feeling and what she's thinking, ask her about her wants, thoughts, and feelings so that you know you have accurate information that will help you proceed.

Saying No in a Way That Doesn't Damage the Relationship

Saying no can be difficult for people for a variety of reasons. Do you feel guilty if you say no? Do you feel like you should be complying with the person's request? In other words, do you judge yourself? Do you worry that the other person will be angry with you if you say no? Setting limits for yourself and sticking to them—even if it means saying no at times—means that you respect yourself. In addition, assertively saying no to the requests of others rather than giving in protects the relationship from resentment that would arise if you felt like you had to say yes when you really didn't want to.

Acting According to Your Values

Know what your values and morals are, and stick to them. When people ask you to do something that goes against your values, you aren't going to feel good about yourself if you agree to their request. Being truthful with yourself and the other person also falls under this category. Many of us, for example, have an urge to make up excuses when someone is asking us to do something we really don't want to do. It's perfectly okay to say no and to be honest about the reason, even if it's just because you don't want to. If you can be truthful and assertively tell the person you don't want to do what he's asking of you, your self-respect will increase.

ADDITIONAL SKILLS FOR ASSERTIVENESS

Depending on what your priority is in an interpersonal situation, you may have to use additional skills to be effective. Here are some further tips for assertiveness that will help you reach your goal without damaging your relationships. They will also help you to feel good about yourself after the interaction.

Mindfully listen to the other person. You'd be surprised at the difference mindfulness makes when you use it to listen to someone. Not only do you gain a much greater understanding of what he's trying to say, but quite often the other person notices that there's something different about how you're paying attention. He feels as though you're truly interested in what he's saying.

Use validation. Validating your own emotions and thoughts or beliefs about a situation, rather than judging them as wrong or criticizing yourself for them in other ways, will help to improve your self-esteem. But validation is also a great way to let the other person know that you're really trying to understand her perspective, you're listening to what she's saying, and you care. Remember that, just like when you're validating your emotions, validation doesn't mean that you approve of or agree with what's happening; it simply means that you acknowledge it or understand it. Here are some validating statements that can be helpful in interactions with others:

- I understand that you're angry (or other emotion).

- I realize that you believe...

- I get that you're feeling...

- I understand why you're feeling that way.

- I can see why you'd think that...

Validating is an especially helpful skill to use when someone is angry with you. It's very hard to stay angry with someone when they're telling you they understand why you're angry. This usually leads to a productive discussion of the problem, which can improve the relationship.

Think dialectically about the situation. The skill of thinking dialectically comes from DBT (Linehan 1993b) and refers to trying to see the bigger picture. In other words, you know your own viewpoint and why you think the way you do; thinking dialectically involves trying to see something from the other person's perspective.

You've probably heard the term "black-and-white thinking." Dialectical thinking is the opposite of this—it's trying to see the grays that fall in between black and white on the spectrum. It's trying to see the bigger picture. When you're thinking about something in this way, it helps to validate the other person because you have a better understanding of why they think or feel what they do. Thinking in this way can also help resolve power struggles, which will help you feel good about yourself after the interaction. This is because dialectical thinking helps you to consider that perhaps it's not that you're right and the other person is wrong, but you're both right and you're both wrong. Dialectical thinking helps you to get unstuck from that feeling of self-righteousness and see that there is no one truth (Linehan 1993b).

Adopt an attitude of openness. Being willing to engage in problem solving with the other person makes it easier for you to keep an open mind, to hear his perspective, and to work with him. It also helps the other person remain open, since he can see from your body language, your words, and your attitude when you're feeling willing. If you are willful in an interaction, this, too, comes across to the other person, and it's less likely to have a positive outcome. In addition, when you're taking an open attitude, it's easier for you to be lighthearted about the matter. If your goal is to improve the relationship, even if the problem is a serious one, you want to be gentle with the other person and try to make him feel comfortable—for example, by smiling at him or using humor. This is easier to do when you're adopting an attitude of openness.

Only apologize when you've done something you truly need to apologize for. Many of us have an inexplicable need to apologize for things we aren't responsible for, and this actually decreases your self-respect. It can also be a sign that you have low self-esteem to begin with. Think about it: if you're apologizing on a regular basis, you're regularly thinking and feeling like you've done something wrong. So try to limit your apologies to when they are truly warranted—for example, when you have done or said something to hurt someone.

Remember that in order to assert yourself you have to know what your goal is in a situation. You can't assertively say no to someone's request if you're not certain that you want to say no. Likewise, it's hard to know what to say to get your own need met if you're not clear on what your need is. In the next section, we're going to talk about something that often results in conflict: when things we want to do conflict with things that other people want us to do.

ENJOYABLE ACTIVITIES VS. RESPONSIBILITIES

Quite often, conflict arises with people around us because there is a disjunction between what we want to do and what other people want or expect us to do (Linehan 1993b). This has been referred to as the "I Want—They Want" ratio (McKay, Wood, and Brantley 2007). Here, I'll be using the term "enjoyable activities" to refer to things that are important to you because you enjoy doing them. They give you enjoyment or pleasure, and you do them just because you want to (the "I Want" part of the ratio). For example, for me, writing this book is an enjoyable activity. It's something that gives me pleasure, and I'm doing it because I want to, not because I have to. Other examples of enjoyable activities might be reading, going for a walk, watching a movie, or taking a yoga class.

On the other hand, I'll use the term "responsibilities" to describe the demands that are placed upon us by others—things that we must do and things that other people want us to do (the "They Want" part of the ratio). Examples of responsibilities might include paying your bills (you probably don't really want to, but others expect you to), mowing the lawn, cleaning the house, and going to work. So responsibilities are things you have to do. Sometimes there's an overlap; some things can be both an enjoyable activity as well as a responsibility. For example, attending Alcoholics Anonymous meetings can be an enjoyable activity because it's a social event, you have fun there, you know it's helpful for you, and you don't want to start drinking again. At the same time, it can be a responsibility. Your doctor may have told you that if you don't stop drinking, you'll develop cirrhosis of the liver; or your children may have told you that if you start drinking again, they won't have anything to do with you.

Going to work is another example of something that can be both an enjoyable activity and a responsibility. For most of us it's a responsibility because we have to work to pay our bills. But you may also really like your job and get a lot of satisfaction out of it, which could make going to work an enjoyable activity.

Take some time now to think about the things you do in life because you want to, and the things you do because you have to. Write them in the space provided. Be as thorough as you can, and use extra paper if you need more space.

Enjoyable Activities

_____   _____

_____   _____

_____   _____

_____   _____

_____   _____

_____   _____

_____   _____

_____   _____

_____   _____

_____   _____

Responsibilities

_____   _____
_____   _____
_____   _____
_____   _____
_____   _____
_____   _____
_____   _____
_____   _____
_____   _____

Your list should be fairly even. The number of enjoyable activities and responsibilities you have in your life would ideally be relatively balanced. If you have too many things you do in your life that are just for fun and not enough responsibilities, you won't have enough in your life to make you feel needed and to give you that sense of mastery we talked about in chapter 4. Too few responsibilities can result in low self-esteem and can be unhealthy, as you have too much free time on your hands to dwell on things and to engage in unhealthy behaviors.

On the other hand, if you have too many things in your life that you do because you must and not enough things you do because you want to, this can also lead to problems. Sometimes we spend so much time fulfilling obligations and responsibilities that we don't make the time to do things that are simply fun or enjoyable. This can result in high levels of stress, which can also result in unhealthy behaviors to cope with the stress, such as drug and alcohol abuse. So, as with all DBT skills, the trick here is to find a balance. This is where conflicts can arise and where the assertiveness skills you learned earlier can come in handy.

Quite often conflict occurs because you want to engage in an enjoyable activity for yourself, and others are placing demands on you (for example, you want to go swimming, and your partner wants you to help out with yard work). Or, when your priority of engaging in an enjoyable activity conflicts with someone else's enjoyable activity (for example, you want to go swimming, and your partner wants to play golf together), this can bring conflict into the equation. When this is the case, you need to decide what is most important to you in the situation. If you decide your enjoyable activity is more important, you then need to decide what your priority is in the interpersonal situation. That is, you need to decide what is most important to you in the interaction you'll have with the person who presents an objection to your desire or need. Is your objective in the interaction to reach your goal, saying no to the other person's request and engaging in your preferred activity? Is it to improve or keep the relationship at all costs? Or is it to feel good (or better) about yourself when the interaction is over? You then follow the recipe outlined earlier to help you communicate what you want in an assertive way.

When you're asking someone for something, it can be helpful to tell her what positive outcome may occur if she agrees to your request. In Ernie's case, he might point out to his supervisor the benefit of compromise. If they could reach a middle ground in terms of his performance and his supervisor's high expectations, Ernie might become more productive, since he would feel understood and valued. This would likely increase his morale at work.

You can see from this example that the positive outcome might not be something concrete—an increase in morale isn't really measurable. But on the other hand, it may be more concrete than it first appears. For example, if a mother tells her child that she will pay her for doing an extra chore, the money would be a positive outcome that's concrete and measurable. But quite often, positive outcomes will simply be how we feel about the other person as a result ("I would appreciate it"), or perhaps a positive impact on the relationship ("I think we'll fight less if I have more time to do some of the things I want to do").

In the same way, you can also point out negative consequences. Ernie could also mention to his supervisor that if they are unable to come to a compromise, he may have to look for work elsewhere (assuming Ernie is a good worker whom his employer wouldn't want to lose). Make sure these negative consequences don't turn into threats, though. In other words, the negative consequences must be things that are within your power and that you are willing to follow through on. And ideally, they would be things that will motivate someone to give you what you want.

Here's another example: Nancy wanted to increase the amount of time she was spending engaging in enjoyable activities. But in order to do so, she had to ask for help with some of her responsibilities. When she assertively asked her husband for help in this area, he didn't respond in the way she wished. So Nancy added the negative consequence that if he was unable to help her with some of her requests, one night each week he would have to fend for himself for dinner so that she would have more time to devote to her interests.

In general, though, if you can use a positive consequence rather than a negative one, people will tend to respond more openly to your request. You just have to try to find a positive outcome that they desire so that they'll be more motivated to do what you're asking.

Remember that one roadblock to effectively asserting yourself can be your lack of belief that you deserve to get your way. This can be especially true when it comes to enjoyable activities and responsibilities. Many people feel as if they don't really have the right to pursue enjoyable activities for themselves when there are responsibilities they also have to meet. Or you may fall into the habit of making sure everyone else gets to engage in activities that are enjoyable activities for them, even if it comes at your expense. Remember that all of us have the right and, in fact, the *need*, to do things for ourselves. If you're not tending to your need for enjoyment and nurturing, your resentment will build because others are getting their needs met at your expense, even if you're allowing this to happen. At some point, this will inevitably cause problems in the relationship. Doing things that are enjoyable for yourself is another way of taking care of yourself. So, your next task is to consider the following worksheet.

ENJOYABLE ACTIVITIES

Looking at your lists of enjoyable activities and responsibilities, do you need to increase one or the other to find more of a balance?

_____

If you answered yes to the above question, can you think of things that you could do in order to increase your enjoyable activities or responsibilities? Remember, increasing enjoyable activities might mean looking for a hobby or interest and asking others for help with your current responsibilities. Increasing your responsibilities might mean asking people if you can help out with their responsibilities.

_____

_____

What kinds of communication skills will you need to use to accomplish these goals?

_____

_____

When you know in advance that an interaction is going to occur in which you want or need to assert yourself, it can be very helpful to write yourself a script and practice what you'll say to the other person. This isn't about scripting the entire conversation, but rather helping you to get yourself used to the language you'll want to use to reach your goal. So take a moment to think about one of the interactions you'll be having in order to reach your goals. Then write out some thoughts about what you want to say to the person. I've provided an example to start you off.

Sample Situation

Your goal: *To tell my elderly parents that, rather than coming to visit them every day as I have been, I'm going to come over every other day instead.*

Person you will be interacting with: *My mother and father.*

Nonjudgmentally describe the situation: *For the last year or so I've been spending a lot of time with my parents, helping them out more as they've gotten older and can't do what they were once able to do.*

Express your opinions (and emotions, if appropriate): *I'm finding that spending so much time at my parents' house is taking me away from my responsibilities at my own home too much. This is causing me to feel stressed-out and irritable.*

Assert yourself by clearly asking for what you want or saying no to the other person's request: *I still really want to help my parents, but instead of coming over every single day, I will only be able to come over every other day, and sometimes less often, depending on my other responsibilities and how I'm feeling.*

Other skills to use or other things you'll want to say in this interaction: *I want to make it clear that I enjoy spending time with my parents and that I want to continue to do so. But I also need to clarify that I need to take care of myself and my relationship with my partner a bit more.*

Situation #1

Your goal: _____

Person you will be interacting with: _____

Nonjudgmentally describe the situation: _____

_____

Express your opinions (and emotions, if appropriate): _____

_____

_____

Assert yourself by clearly asking for what you want or saying no to the other person's request:

_____

_____

Other skills to use or other things you'll want to say in this interaction: _____

_____

_____

Situation #2

Your goal: _____

Person you will be interacting with: _____

Nonjudgmentally describe the situation: _____

_____

Express your opinions (and emotions, if appropriate): _____

_____

_____

Assert yourself by clearly asking for what you want or saying no to the other person's request:

_____

_____

Other skills to use or other things you'll want to say in this interaction: _____

_____

_____

Until you get comfortable with asserting yourself, you may want to write out these kinds of scripts in advance when you know these kinds of situations are going to happen. Practicing them—reading them over to yourself, role-playing with a support person, saying them out loud with different words—can also help you get used to being assertive.

Let me remind you that even when you are acting assertively, being nonjudgmental, clear, and specific, and being as skillful as you can possibly be, there's no guarantee that you're going to get your needs met. Sometimes, regardless of how effectively you act, people just don't want to do what you want them to, or they can refuse to take no for an answer. This can lead to conflict if you continue to assert yourself, and if someone is refusing to take no for an answer, you must continue to assert yourself. Having said that, however, being assertive makes it more likely that you'll get your needs met, and at the very least, you'll feel good about yourself for communicating in a way that's respectful to both yourself and the other person.

WRAPPING UP

Relationships are extremely important in our lives. We need people to support us and love us, and we need people to have fun with. When we don't have enough relationships in our lives, it can impact our mood and how we deal with crisis situations. In this chapter, I've aimed to help you assess the quality and quantity of relationships in your life and how effectively you interact in those relationships. You've learned some skills that will help you to be more assertive. Assertiveness will increase your effectiveness in interpersonal interactions while preventing damage to your relationships. At the same time, being assertive will help you feel good about yourself for acting skillfully.

You've also learned about the need to prioritize your goals in interpersonal situations and the need to balance things you do because you enjoy them with your responsibilities.

Many of the other skills you've learned in this workbook are also going to be helpful in your relationships. For example, being more aware of your emotions will help you to not lash out at others from emotion mind. Learning how to tolerate your emotions and how to cope with crisis situations in healthier ways will help those around you not burn out so they can be there to support you.

The next chapter is going to help your friends and family learn how they can improve their relationship with you. Keep reading, though, as you are still going to play a big role.

CHAPTER 11

Skills for Family Members of People with Bipolar Disorder

I frequently hear about the troubles families are having because of the illness their loved one is experiencing. Because of this and the turmoil I see families going through, largely because of bipolar disorder, I wanted to include a chapter in this book that will offer some guidance to families.

ENLISTING THE HELP OF FAMILY AND FRIENDS

I would suggest that you, the person with bipolar disorder, also read through this chapter, because you are the person who can best guide your loved ones in how they can support you. I've provided suggestions and guidelines here, but your family and friends need to hear from you how they can most effectively help. In fact, I think that your participation in this chapter is so vital that I want to start off by asking you to consider ways your family and friends can be most helpful to you; for example, by helping you monitor your symptoms of mania, by not constantly reminding you to take your medications, and so on. Then write these suggestions down in the space provided. Perhaps your family and friends are already doing things that you find supportive and helpful. Feel free to write these down as well, so that people will know what's effective and can continue to do it.

How My Loved Ones Can Support Me

- _____
- _____
- _____
- _____
- _____

- _____
- _____
- _____
- _____

Now that we know some of the things your family and friends can do to help you, I'm going to offer a few suggestions as well. If you were unable to think of ways others can better support you, keep reading and come back to fill in the blanks as you see things that you think would be helpful. At the end of this workbook, I'm also going to provide a list of resources, both for you and your family and friends, which will continue to help you learn to cope with bipolar disorder and other illnesses you might have.

While it will be helpful for you to keep reading, the rest of this chapter will be directed to your family and friends, and the term "loved one" will be used to refer to you, the person with bipolar disorder.

UNDERSTANDING BIPOLAR AND OTHER DISORDERS

Knowledge is power. The more you know about bipolar disorder—and any other mental health problems your loved one is experiencing—the better prepared you will be to help him. Bipolar disorder is such a complex illness that it's easy for the person with the diagnosis to feel alone and as though no one could possibly understand his experience. And while it's true that we can't possibly know what people with bipolar go through (unless we've had these experiences ourselves), we can educate ourselves so that we can better understand.

If you, the friend or family member of someone with bipolar disorder, haven't read through the rest of this workbook, you might want to do so. This will give you more of an understanding of the illness and the skills that your loved one is working on incorporating into his life in order to deal with his bipolar disorder. Actually, many of the skills presented in this book are valuable in helping anyone experience a higher quality of life, so you may want to practice the skills yourself—not only to show your support of your loved one and gain a better understanding of the work he's doing, but also to improve your own life.

Finally, having a greater understanding of any other illnesses your loved one might have is also extremely important. Unfortunately, bipolar disorder often doesn't happen by itself. It can co-occur with anxiety disorders, personality disorders, substance abuse problems, attention-deficit/hyperactivity disorder (ADHD), eating disorders, and many other illnesses. So educating yourself about any of these other problems your loved one may have is going to be important as well, especially because sometimes there are things that friends and family do that actually feed into the problems. For example, when someone has obsessive-compulsive disorder (OCD), he often engages in rituals or compulsive behaviors to try to decrease his anxiety. When you also engage in these behaviors at the request of your loved one, you are doing so in order to appease his anxiety, which means that you are feeding into the illness, or enabling him.

Enabling can also happen with other anxiety disorders. When your loved one is feeling anxious and regularly seeks reassurance from you, this reassurance reduces his anxiety. Or he may have trouble leaving the house by himself, so you make sure you're available to accompany him. Or your loved one may have social anxiety, so he avoids any kind of social situations where he doesn't know people and you won't go without him. Any of these scenarios (and more) prevents a person from learning that the anxiety goes away on its own. Instead, he comes to rely on your reassurance and other enabling behaviors to help him cope.

Another example is substance abuse problems. If your loved one has a drug or alcohol problem, you may find yourself covering up for him at work or school, for example, when he's too hungover or high to attend. Or you make excuses for him when he doesn't attend family functions or when his behavior gets out of control—the list goes on and on. The important thing to recognize in any of these kinds of situations is that when you enable someone in this way, you're doing him more harm than good. Trying to protect him in this way helps him continue to deny the existence of the problem rather than having to face it and work to make it better.

If your loved one has other disorders, you may want to consider attending some family therapy sessions or do more reading about those illnesses so that you can learn how to help your loved one most effectively.

EFFECTIVE COMMUNICATION IS KEY

Being able to communicate effectively with your loved one is of absolute importance in being able to support her. Assertive communication, which was examined in chapter 10, is most helpful, and I strongly suggest you read that chapter to help you with this. Even if you think you already communicate in an assertive way, remember that there is no such thing as being too effective in relationships—you can always improve how you interact with others. The following points are what I believe to be some of the most important things to remember in communicating with a loved one who has bipolar disorder.

Don't Invalidate Her Emotions

All too often, the tendency is to question the person's emotions, usually out of love and concern that she's going to experience another bipolar episode. Even though your heart is in the right place, being invalidated on a regular basis usually triggers anger in the person, which will only make the situation worse. In addition, being invalidated over time contributes to the person not trusting her own emotional experience, which can have devastating emotional effects. Even though she has bipolar disorder, she also experiences typical emotions.

One of the big tasks for a person with bipolar is to figure out which emotions are normal and which are due to bipolar disorder. This is something that will be very helpful for her to learn, and you can play a role in this. First of all, you can ask if you can help (and accept a no if that's what you get). And second, if she agrees to your help, you can ask questions about her emotions rather than making assumptions about them. Here are some examples of what not to say and some examples of what will be more helpful. I've left room at the end for you and your loved one to write your own examples. See if the two of you can identify ways in which you have invalidated her and how you can replace this with something more validating.

What *Not* to Say	What to Say
You need to calm down. You're going manic.	*I've noticed your speech is speeding up a little. Are you feeling okay?*
You look depressed. Have you taken your meds?	*You look a little sad right now. How do you feel?*
You're sleeping too much. You need to see your psychiatrist.	*You seem to be sleeping more. What do you think about that?*
You shouldn't be this angry. It must be your bipolar.	*Wow, you're really angry. What's going on?*
_____	_____
_____	_____
_____	_____

Asking questions in this way, rather than assuming from her behavior or words that you know how she's feeling, can serve two functions: it validates your loved one's experience while drawing her attention to something that she may not have been aware of, such as the fact that she is talking very rapidly. This provides her with an opportunity to assess her own experience, deciding if there is a problem or if this is just an emotion related to the current situation.

If your loved one is willing to accept your help, these kinds of questions can assist her in becoming more aware of her emotions, as well as of her body language, speech, and other behaviors that often express how a person is feeling. This increased awareness can help her get to know her emotions better—both regular emotions and those connected to bipolar disorder.

Be Nonjudgmental

Family and friends can become judgmental during a loved one's depressive episodes. You may not be able to understand how incredibly awful it feels to experience depression. I've heard clients describe depression as "the abyss" or the "black hole." When your loved one is stuck there, it's not going to be helpful for you to tell her what she *should* do to get out of it. She probably already knows what she could do to help herself; it's a matter of getting herself to do it. If you judge her because she hasn't showered in three days, this will only make her feel worse. Even if you don't say the judgments out loud to her, the judgmental thoughts often come out in a person's attitude, so try to take the judgments out all together.

Again, the most effective thing you can do is to ask how you can help. Express your concern; for example, "You've been really down for a few days, and you haven't been to work this week. Is there anything I can do that would help?" Aim at offering compassion and assistance without lecturing or blaming.

The same applies when your loved one is hypomanic or manic. Quite often her behavior can become disruptive or cause you to feel annoyed or irritated. If you criticize or blame your loved one, this can lead to a conflict, which could end in an escalation of the hypomania. Now, I'm not saying you need to just put up with any kind of behavior out of fear of making her worse. Obviously, if you need to leave the situation, leave. You do need to take care of yourself as well! Likewise, if your loved one is escalating to manic behavior and you fear for her (or someone else's) safety, you need to do what you have to in order to keep her safe, even if this means she's going to be angry with you for having her hospitalized.

We've talked about not judging when your loved one is experiencing mood problems, but what about outside of those times? Research has shown that regular negative communications, such as critical comments, lead to more severe symptoms for people with bipolar disorder (Altman et al. 2006). In other words, being critical and talking to your loved one in a judgmental way can actually have an impact on the severity of her symptoms of depression and, to a lesser degree, her symptoms of mania. It is not helpful! I strongly suggest that you read chapter 4, in which I talked at length about judgments and how to be nonjudgmental. I'll give you a few examples here of situations that might come up and how you can still express emotions and opinions about these things without judging or being critical of your loved one.

- I can see that you're very excited about the clothing you bought, but I'm feeling angry that you spent this much money, and I'm worried that you might be hypomanic right now.

- I think the decision you made was not in our best interests, and I'm disappointed you didn't consult me first, since this affects both of us.

- I'm concerned that you're spending so much time sleeping right now, and I'm frustrated that you're not helping out around the house while you're at home.

- I know that you're feeling depressed right now, but I'm feeling hurt that you won't talk to me about what's going on and that you don't want my help.

Hopefully you can see from these examples that not judging your loved one does *not* mean that you stop expressing your opinions and emotions about her behavior. Rather, it helps you to assertively communicate what you think and how you feel about a specific behavior the person engaged in. If she's agreeable, take a moment with your loved one to see if you can come up with some instances when you've been judgmental. Then think about how you could express the same information in a nonjudgmental way. Remember, when trying to be nonjudgmental you still want to express your opinions and emotions about the situation—without the judgmental language.

1. **Judgment:** _____

   Nonjudgmental statement: _____

   _____

2. Judgment: _____

   Nonjudgmental statement: _____

   _____

3. Judgment: _____

   Nonjudgmental statement: _____

   _____

4. Judgment: _____

   Nonjudgmental statement: _____

   _____

5. Judgment: _____

   Nonjudgmental statement: _____

   _____

Avoid Guilt-Trips

Sometimes, when nothing else seems to be working to get your point across or to get your need met, you may find yourself resorting to the guilt-trip. Simon's partner did this regularly, especially when Simon was going through depression. His partner, David, would try to get him out of the house to cheer him up, wanting to help Simon. In trying to do so, however, David would say things like "If you really loved me, you would come to the theater with me tonight." Although you can see that David's heart was in the right place and he really was trying to help Simon, this kind of guilt-trip always backfired. Simon may have ended up going out with David to appease him, but he also resented the guilt-trip and felt trapped into doing what David wanted him to. This took its toll on the relationship, as Simon's resentment built over time.

While guilt-trips may have the desired short-term effect (such as getting your loved one to do something you want her to), the long term effects are quite often negative, as your loved one will come to resent you for putting her in a position of feeling like she must comply with your request. Of course, you also have to keep in mind that this kind of communicating will often not even have a positive outcome in the short term. For example, rather than resulting in your loved one doing what you want, your guilt-trip could very possibly end in an argument and your loved one withdrawing from you even further.

So, communication is obviously very important, and you've read some tips here that will hopefully help you to improve your communication with your loved one who has bipolar. Take some time to have a conversation with your loved one about how the two of you communicate right now. In the space provided, see if you can collaboratively come up with a list of things that you tend to do well when you're communicating with one another, and then a list of things you think you need to work on. I've started you off with some examples.

Positive Things About the Way We Communicate

- *We don't yell at each other.*

- *We try to validate each other.*

- _____

- _____

- _____

- _____

- _____

- _____

Things That We Could Improve Upon in the Way We Communicate

- *More validation!*

- *Make fewer assumptions.*

- _____

- _____

- _____

- _____

- _____

- _____

RADICAL ACCEPTANCE

If you've read through this workbook, you already know all about the skill of radical acceptance from chapter 9. Sometimes it can be quite difficult to accept that this person you love has a mental illness. Parents might fight the reality that the future they wanted for their child is now less likely (for example, a university education and high-paying job). A spouse might fight the reality that the relationship he thought he was going to have with his partner has been replaced by something different. If the illness has just arisen, some people may fight the reality that the person they love has changed.

Sometimes people will fight the reality of the symptoms themselves—for example, denying that the person has a substance abuse problem or other addiction, trying to avoid seeing bizarre behavior when the person is becoming manic, and so on. There are many ways people can try to fight the reality of bipolar disorder, and however you do it, you spend a lot of energy and trigger many emotions for yourself.

Radical acceptance is not about liking the way things are, being passive, or giving up and not doing anything about trying to make the current situation better. In order to support your loved one, you must first accept that he has this illness. Only then, once you've acknowledged this reality, can you be open to learning about how you can make the best of your life with this person. How can you best support your spouse so that he doesn't end up back in the hospital? What can you do to make it more likely that your son might be able to one day graduate from college? How can you try to improve your life, and that of your loved one, if you continue to deny that there's a problem that needs to be considered? Let's look at an example.

■ Shannon's Story

Shannon was seventeen years old and had just started her last year of high school when she was diagnosed with bipolar disorder. She had not required hospitalization, but her mood was low enough at the beginning of the school year that she was having difficulty getting her work done on time. Shannon's parents took her to a psychiatrist, but when they were told the diagnosis, they fought it. They argued that there was no history in the family of mood disorders and that Shannon was likely just going through typical teenage problems. Shannon's grades suffered, she sometimes missed days of school at a time because of her depression and high levels of anxiety, and she didn't get the support she needed from her parents because they were too busy refusing to believe that their daughter could have a chronic mental health problem.

Now let's look at what could have been different. When Shannon was diagnosed with bipolar disorder in her last year of high school, her parents were devastated by the news. But what if they accepted the diagnosis and wanted to do whatever they could to help her? What if they accompanied Shannon to her school and spoke with her guidance counselor and teachers so that the staff was well-informed about Shannon's illness, how it might impact her, and what might be most helpful for her while she was at school? Due to this intervention, when her anxiety got really high at school, Shannon might have a place she could go to lower the stimulation level and help her calm down. Then she could eventually get back into class and not miss too much material. When her mood got so low that she was unable to go to school for a couple of days in a row, Shannon could speak with her teacher about handing in an assignment two days late. In short, by accepting Shannon's diagnosis rather than expending energy fighting it, Shannon's parents could help her deal with it, lowering the impact the illness had on her life.

Radical acceptance is not an easy skill to practice, and it takes time to get to the point of acceptance. But once you get there—even if it's only for short periods at a time—you will find that the painful emotions lessen and you have more time and energy to put into trying to solve the problem or improve the situation. Fighting reality, whatever it may be, only brings up more negative emotions for you to deal with. Can you identify things about your loved one that you're fighting? If you have a hard time identifying situations, think about the times when you have thoughts such as "It's not fair," "It shouldn't be this way," "Why us?" and so on:

- _____
- _____
- _____
- _____
- _____

Since your loved one is working to practice radical acceptance with situations of his own, you may want to discuss the situations you're having problems accepting, since some of them may overlap. You can actually work on this skill together by discussing the things you are having a hard time accepting about your loved one, about his illness, and about what the illness means for your lives. Thinking about the situations you wrote in the blanks above, can you come up with some statements that will help you to radically accept those situations? You can do this either alone or with the help of your loved one.

- _____
- _____
- _____
- _____
- _____

So radical acceptance can help you better support your loved one. But what if you are providing support to such an extent that it's actually having a negative impact on your own life?

STOP WALKING ON EGGSHELLS

You've probably heard the phrase "I feel like I'm walking on eggshells." It's possible you've said it or thought it yourself. Quite often, family and friends of people with bipolar disorder complain that they feel like they're walking on eggshells (or tiptoeing around, trying not to rock the boat, and so on) because the person with bipolar can become explosive at the drop of a hat, and they never know what to expect from her. All of this effort to accommodate the person with bipolar disorder can damage relationships and be detrimental to the friends and family involved. And as long as you make special accommodations for the person with bipolar disorder, she won't learn to live a high-quality life in which she is fully functioning. Let me give you an example.

■ Trudy's Story

Trudy, a twenty-four-year-old woman with bipolar disorder, was on a disability pension because of her illness, and she still lived at home with her mother, Antonia, and father, Cornelius. Trudy didn't pay rent, and in fact, Antonia and Cornelius supplemented her income by paying for her car, car insurance, and gas, as well as for things like cigarettes when she had spent her income for the month. Trudy's parents admitted they didn't like having to support their adult daughter financially, especially when she had an income of her own. But they found that refusing Trudy's requests for money would usually result in Trudy losing her temper and becoming verbally abusive, throwing things, or threatening suicide. The same would happen if they tried to get Trudy to assume some responsibility around the house, like doing chores such as vacuuming or doing dishes. They felt bullied into giving her what she wanted.

Can you think of similar examples where you've found yourself walking on eggshells or bending over backward to accommodate your loved one?

_____

_____

_____

_____

_____

Many people with bipolar disorder have a great deal of difficulty with anger, and we've already looked at the problems they can encounter with regulating their emotions in general. However, when friends and family continuously walk on eggshells to accommodate their loved one, the person with bipolar disorder never has to learn how to manage her emotions more effectively. In addition, she learns a precious lesson: that she doesn't *have* to learn to manage her emotions. In fact, by not learning these skills, she discovers that she actually gets her needs met, whether this is having someone give her money, clean up after her, or take care of other responsibilities on her behalf. The downside to this, of course, is that family and friends feel taken for granted or manipulated. This dynamic inevitably leads to resentment and, in the long run, burns people out. It damages relationships. What emotions come up for you when you're walking on eggshells?

- ■ _____

- ■ _____

- ■ _____

I would encourage you to share this list of emotions with your loved one. That way, she can clearly see the emotions that are triggered in you when you're tiptoeing around her to avoid provoking her.

Walking on eggshells around your loved one prevents her from learning the skills she'll need to live a healthier, more functional life. If Trudy never gets used to taking on responsibilities at home or interacting appropriately with others, for example, she'll be unlikely to find and keep a job. Persistent unemployment won't help her self-esteem or confidence. Similarly, it will be very difficult for Trudy to move out and become independent if she hasn't learned the skills required to live on her own, including how to take care of a house, how to cook, how to budget, and so on.

So you can see that it's very important for you to continue to treat the person with bipolar disorder like an adult (or that you treat her as an adult as she grows into one, if your loved one is a teenager). Yes, she does have bipolar disorder. But she also may have children she must care for, a job she must continue to work at, school to complete, or relationships she must nurture. In other words, even though she has bipolar disorder, she also has other responsibilities, and she must learn that the world isn't always going to stop when she's not feeling well. (Sometimes, if she needs to be hospitalized, it may seem to her as though the world is stopping. But this won't happen every time.) So the person with bipolar disorder has to learn to use skills to help her continue to function to the best of her ability, even when her mood starts to sink or when she starts to feel a bit speeded-up.

Looking again to Trudy and her parents, things did improve. I taught Trudy the various skills you've read about in this workbook to help her tolerate and manage her emotions more effectively. At the same time, I worked with Antonia and Cornelius, helping them to slowly make changes in their relationship with Trudy so that the relationship was more balanced and satisfying for all three of them. Trudy was able to take on more responsibilities, while Antonia and Cornelius were able to decrease their responsibilities and engage in more activities that were enjoyable for them.

When Symptoms Begin to Arise

Now that you've been working on your communication skills, one very important thing for you and your loved one to go back to discussing is how you can further help her with her symptoms. Quite often, bipolar is an illness that impacts not just the person experiencing symptoms, but those around her as well. Friends and especially family are affected as they try to negotiate their interactions with their loved one and do their best to support her in healthy ways. Because this illness has so many symptoms that can be harmful, it can be extremely helpful if you have a plan in place to deal with contingencies of the disorder. It may be especially helpful if you focus on symptoms that your loved one has experienced in the past. Talk to her about this to see if you can collaboratively come up with some ideas, and then write them in the space provided. I've started you off with some examples:

- *Give someone she trusts access to her bank accounts or credit cards so that measures can be taken to prevent her from overspending when symptoms begin to arise.*

- *When symptoms of hypomania come up, allow someone to monitor her medications so she doesn't stop taking them.*

- *When symptoms of depression are evident, have her AA sponsor call someone if she misses her meeting without informing anyone.*

- *When symptoms of depression begin to arise, have her request that her doctor prescribe only small amounts of medication at a time so that she'll have less chance of overdosing. Or she might allow someone to monitor her medications to ensure she is unable to abuse them or use them to attempt suicide.*

- _____

- _____

- _____

- _____

- _____

THERE IS HOPE

Having bipolar disorder doesn't have to be the end of the world. New medications are coming out regularly, although of course this is only half of the solution. But if your loved one has been working his way through this workbook and practicing the skills presented here, there certainly is hope that he will be able to improve the quality of his life and that bipolar disorder won't control him to the degree that it perhaps once did.

You can support your loved one, using the skills presented here and throughout the rest of this book, in learning to limit the extent to which he is controlled by his illness. After this chapter, I've provided a list of resources to assist you and your loved one in the ongoing work you will both have to do in order to live life to its fullest, in spite of bipolar disorder.

Resources for Bipolar Disorder

ADDITIONAL RESOURCES FOR BIPOLAR DISORDER

If you're interested in learning more about bipolar disorder and skills that can help you and those close to you to cope effectively with the impact of the disorder, look into these useful resources.

Books

Miklowitz, David. 2002. *The Bipolar Disorder Survival Guide: What You and Your Family Need to Know.* New York: Guilford Press.

Ramirez Basco, Monica. 2006. *The Bipolar Workbook: Tools for Controlling Your Mood Swings.* New York: Guilford Press.

Redfield Jamison, Kay. 1995. *An Unquiet Mind: A Memoir of Moods and Madness.* New York: Random House.

Websites

Bipolar News
   The online home of the *Bipolar Network News* newsletter, this site also provides up-to-date research findings on bipolar disorder.
   www.bipolarnews.org

The Mood Disorders Society of Canada
   This is a Canadian website providing information regarding bipolar disorder, as well as providing links to other resources about the illness.
   www.mooddisorderscanada.ca

Pendulum.org

> This is a comprehensive website providing information about bipolar disorder and up-to-date research on the illness. You'll find information about effective psychotherapy treatments for bipolar disorder, bipolar disorder events and conferences, recommended books and movies, personal stories, chat rooms, and online support groups.
> www.pendulum.org

Bipolar Significant Others

> This is an informal organization for significant others of people with bipolar disorder (family members and friends). Members of the site exchange support and information about bipolar disorder by e-mail and discuss issues related to the impact of the illness on families and intimate relationships.
> www.bpso.org

Bipolar.com

> Here's another comprehensive website providing information about the illness, treatment options for bipolar, tips for living with bipolar disorder (such as balancing sleep and other helpful information), as well as information for family and friends of people with bipolar disorder.
> www.bipolar.com

ADDITIONAL RESOURCES FOR DIALECTICAL BEHAVIOR THERAPY

DBT is a valuable tool to help you live more effectively with bipolar disorder. The topic is rich, so if you'd like to learn even more about DBT, check out some of the resources below.

Books

Fruzzetti, Alan E. 2006. *The High-Conflict Couple: A Dialectical Behavior Therapy Guide to Finding Peace, Intimacy, and Validation.* Oakland, CA: New Harbinger Publications.

Linehan, Marsha M. 1993. *Skills Training Manual for Treating Borderline Personality Disorder.* New York: Guilford Press.

Marra, Thomas. 2004. *Depressed and Anxious: The Dialectical Behavior Therapy Workbook for Overcoming Depression and Anxiety.* Oakland, CA: New Harbinger Publications.

McKay, Matthew, Jeffrey C. Wood, and Jeffrey Brantley. 2007. *The Dialectical Behavior Therapy Skills Workbook: Practical DBT Exercises for Learning Mindfulness, Interpersonal Effectiveness, Emotion Regulation, and Distress Tolerance.* Oakland, CA: New Harbinger Publications.

Spradlin, Scott. 2003. *Don't Let Emotions Run Your Life.* Oakland, CA: New Harbinger Publications.

Websites

DBT Self-Help

This is a DBT self-help website providing the answers to commonly asked questions about DBT, as well as handouts and articles on DBT and mindfulness.
www.dbtselfhelp.com

TrueRecovery

A DBT self-help website providing reading material, questions, and answers about DBT, and a forum to post questions and comments about skills.
www.truerecovery.org

ADDITIONAL RESOURCES FOR DEPRESSION AND ANXIETY

Bipolar disorder involves both depression and anxiety, so you might want additional information and help in dealing with these related states.

Books

Bourne, Edmund J. 2000. *The Anxiety and Phobia Workbook*. 3rd ed. Oakland, CA: New Harbinger Publications.

Greenberger, Dennis, and Christine A. Padesky. 1995. *Mind Over Mood*. New York: Guilford Press.

Knaus, William J. 2006. *The Cognitive Behavioral Workbook for Depression*. Oakland, CA: New Harbinger Publications.

McKay, Mathew, Martha Davis, and Patrick Fanning. 2007. *Thoughts and Feelings: Taking Control of Your Moods and Your Life*. Oakland, CA: New Harbinger Publications.

Strosahl, Kirk D., and Patricia J. Robinson. 2008. *The Mindfulness and Acceptance Workbook for Depression*. Oakland, CA: New Harbinger Publications.

ADDITIONAL RESOURCES FOR MINDFULNESS

Practicing mindfulness can help enormously with the symptoms and emotions of bipolar disorder. It can also help in your everyday life, whether you're symptomatic or not.

Books

Kabat-Zinn, Jon. 1990. *Full Catastrophe Living: Using the Wisdom of Your Body and Mind to Face Stress, Pain, and Illness*. New York: Random House.

Kabat-Zinn, Jon. 1994. *Wherever You Go, There You Are: Mindfulness Meditation in Everyday Life*. New York: Hyperion.

Williams, Mark, John Teasdale, Zindel Segal, and Jon Kabat-Zinn. 2007. *The Mindful Way Through Depression*. New York: Guilford Press.

AMERICAN MENTAL HEALTH ORGANIZATIONS

No matter where you're located, these organizations can offer insight, guidance, and information about living with bipolar disorder.

Organizations

The National Institute of Mental Health (NIMH) is a scientific organization dedicated to research focused on the understanding, treatment, and prevention of mental disorders and the promotion of mental health.
www.nimh.nih.gov

Depression and Bipolar Support Alliance (DBSA) provides up-to-date, scientifically based tools and information about the impact and management of mental illnesses such as bipolar disorder. DBSA supports research to promote more timely diagnosis, to develop more effective and tolerable treatments, to discover a cure, and to help ensure that people living with mood disorders are treated equitably.
www.dbsalliance.org

National Alliance on Mental Illness (NAMI) provides support, education, and advocacy. They provide a helpline for people with mental health problems (800-950-6264), as well as providing support groups for people with mental illnesses and their families.
www.nami.org

Mental Health America (MHA; formerly known as the National Mental Health Association) is an organization that strives to educate the public about ways to preserve and strengthen mental health. In addition, the agency advocates for access to effective care and an end to discrimination against people with mental health problems and addictions and provides support to individuals and families living with mental health and substance use problems.
www.nmha.org

CANADIAN MENTAL HEALTH ORGANIZATIONS

Whether you live in Canada or not, these organizations can provide valuable support and resources on living with bipolar disorder.

Organizations

Canadian Mental Health Association (CMHA) provides a wide range of specialized mental health programs and services, such as court support programs and case management tailored to the needs of the individual.
www.cmha.ca

Centre for Addiction and Mental Health (CAMH) is a public hospital located in Toronto, Ontario. It provides direct patient care for people with mental health problems such as bipolar disorder, as well as addictions. CAMH is also a research facility, as well as an education and training institute that provides health promotion and prevention services across the province of Ontario.
www.camh.net

Mood Disorders Association of Ontario provides peer-support programs for people with mood disorders such as depression and bipolar disorder, as well as education and information about mood disorders for people with these illnesses and their families, professionals, and the public.
www.mooddisorders.ca

References

Altman, S., S. Haeri, L. J. Cohen, A. Ten, E. Barron, I. I. Galynker, and K. N. Duhamel. 2006. Predictors of relapse in bipolar disorder: A review. *Journal of Psychiatric Practice* 12(5):269–282.

American Psychiatric Association. 2000. *Diagnostic and Statistical Manual of Mental Disorders*. 4th edition, text revision. Washington: American Psychiatric Association.

Beck, A. T. 1976. *Cognitive Therapy and the Emotional Disorders*. New York: Plume Books.

Beck, A. T., G. Emery, and R. Greenberg. 1985. *Anxiety Disorders and Phobias: A Cognitive Perspective*. Cambridge: Basic Books.

Benazzi, F. 2007. Bipolar disorder: Focus on bipolar II disorder and mixed depression. *Lancet* 369(9565):935–945.

Bourne, E. J. 2000. *The Anxiety and Phobia Workbook*. 3rd edition. Oakland, CA: New Harbinger Publications.

Brach, T. 2003. *Radical Acceptance: Embracing Your Life with the Heart of a Buddha*. New York: Bantam Books.

Campos, J. J., R. G. Campos, and K. C. Barrett. 1989. Emergent themes in the study of emotional development and emotion regulation. *Developmental Psychology* 25(3): 394-402.

Copeland, M. E. 2001. *The Depression Workbook*. Oakland, CA: New Harbinger Publications.

Denisoff, E. 2007. Cognitive behavior therapy for anxiety. PowerPoint presentation at the Toronto Advanced Professional Education Cognitive Behavioural Therapy certificate program, Toronto, Ontario.

Dimeff, L. A., K. Koerner, and M. M. Linehan. 2006. *Summary of Research on DBT*. Seattle, WA: Behavioral Tech.

Ekman, P., and R. J. Davidson. 1993. Voluntary smiling changes regional brain activity. *Psychological Science* 4(5):342–345.

Frank, E., and M. E. Thase. 1999. Natural history and preventative treatment of recurrent mood disorders. *Annual Review of Medicine* 50:453–468.

Ghaemi, S., J. Ko, and F. Goodwin. 2002. "Cade's disease" and beyond: Misdiagnosis, antidepressant use, and a proposed definition for bipolar spectrum disorder. *Canadian Journal of Psychiatry* 47(2):125–134.

Goldberg, J. F., J. L. Garno, A. C. Leon, J. H. Kocsis, and L. Portera. 1999. A history of substance abuse complicates remission from acute mania in bipolar disorder. *Journal of Clinical Psychiatry* 60(11):733–740.

Goldstein, T. R., D. A. Axelson, B. Birmaher, and D. A. Brent. 2007. Dialectical behavior therapy for adolescents with bipolar disorder: A 1-year open trial. *Journal of the American Academy of Child and Adolescent Psychiatry* 46(7):820–830.

Green, M. J., C. M. Cahill, and G. S. Malhi. 2007. The cognitive and neurophysiological basis of emotion dysregulation in bipolar disorder. *Journal of Affective Disorders* 103(1–3):29–42.

Gutierrez, J. M., and J. Scott. 2004. Psychological treatment for bipolar disorders: A review of randomized controlled trials. *European Archives of Psychiatry and Clinical Neuroscience* 254(2):92–98.

Harvard Medical International. 2004. The benefits of mindfulness. *Harvard Women's Health Watch* 11(6):1–3.

Hayes, S. C., with S. Smith. 2005. *Get Out of Your Mind and Into Your Life*. Oakland, CA: New Harbinger Publications.

Henquet, C., L. Krabbendam, R. de Graaf, M. ten Have, and J. van Os. 2006. Cannabis use and expression of mania in the general population. *Journal of Affective Disorders* 95(1–3):103–110.

Hirschfeld, R., J. B. W. Williams, R. L. Spitzer, J. R. Calabrese, L. Flynn, P. E. Keck Jr., L. Lewis, S. L. McElroy, R. M. Post, D. J. Rapport, et al. 2000. Development and validation of a screening instrument for bipolar spectrum disorder: The Mood Disorder Questionnaire. *American Journal of Psychiatry* 157(11):1873–1875.

Kabat-Zinn, J. 1994. *Wherever You Go, There You Are: Mindfulness Meditation in Everyday Life*. New York: Hyperion.

Kabat-Zinn, J., A. O. Massion, J. Kirsteller, L. G. Peterson, K. E. Fletcher, L. Pbert, W. R. Lenderking, and S. F. Santorelli. 1992. Effectiveness of a meditation-based stress reduction program in the treatment of anxiety disorders. *American Journal of Psychiatry* 149(7):936–943.

Keltner, D., and J. Haidt. 1999. Social functions of emotions at four levels of analysis. *Cognition and Emotion* 13(5):505–521.

Kutz, I., J. Z. Borysenko, and H. Benson. 1985. Meditation and psychotherapy: A rationale for the integration of dynamic psychotherapy, the relaxation response, and mindfulness meditation. *American Journal of Psychiatry* 142(1):1–8.

Leahy, R. L. 2007. Bipolar disorder: Causes, contexts, and treatments. *Journal of Clinical Psychology: In Session* 63(5):417–424.

Levitt, J. T., T. A. Brown, S. M. Orsillo, and D. H. Barlow. 2004. The effects of acceptance versus suppression of emotion on subjective and psychophysiological response to carbon dioxide challenge in patients with panic disorder. *Behavior Therapy* 35(4):747–766.

Linehan, M. M. 1993a. *Cognitive-Behavioral Treatment of Borderline Personality Disorder.* New York: Guilford Press.

Linehan, M. M. 1993b. *Skills Training Manual for Treating Borderline Personality Disorder.* New York: Guilford Press.

Linehan, M. M. 2000. *Opposite Action: Changing Emotions You Want to Change.* Seattle, WA: Behavioral Tech.

Linehan, M. M. 2003a. *From Chaos to Freedom: Getting Through a Crisis Without Making It Worse; Crisis Survival Skills; Part One—Distracting and Self-Soothing.* Seattle, WA: Behavioral Tech.

Linehan, M. M. 2003b. *From Chaos to Freedom: Getting Through a Crisis Without Making It Worse; Crisis Survival Skills; Part Two—Improving the Moment and Pros and Cons.* Seattle, WA: Behavioral Tech.

Linehan, M. M. 2003c. *From Chaos to Freedom: This One Moment; Skills for Everyday Mindfulness.* Seattle, WA: Behavioral Tech.

Linehan, M. M. 2003d. *From Suffering to Freedom: Practicing Reality Acceptance.* Seattle, WA: Behavioral Tech.

Magill, C. A. 2004. The boundary between borderline personality disorder and bipolar disorder: Current concepts and challenges. *Canadian Journal of Psychiatry* 49(8):551–556.

Malhi, G. S., B. Ivanovski, D. Hadzi-Pavlovic, P. B. Mitchell, E. Vieta, and P. Sachdev. 2007. Neuropsychological deficits and functional impairment in bipolar depression, hypomania and euthymia. *Bipolar Disorders* 9(1–2):114–125.

May, G. 1987. *Will and Spirit: A Contemplative Psychology.* New York: HarperOne.

McKay, M., J. C. Wood, and J. Brantley. 2007. *The Dialectical Behavior Therapy Skills Workbook: Practical DBT Exercises for Learning Mindfulness, Interpersonal Effectiveness, Emotion Regulation, and Distress Tolerance.* Oakland, CA: New Harbinger Publications.

McMain, S., L. M. Korman, and L. Dimeff. 2001. Dialectical behavior therapy and the treatment of emotional dysregulation. *Journal of Clinical Psychology* 57(2):183–196.

Miller, J. J., K. Fletcher, and J. Kabat-Zinn. 1995. Three-year follow-up and clinical implications of a mindfulness meditation-based stress reduction intervention in the treatment of anxiety disorders. *General Hospital Psychiatry* 17(3):192–200.

Oatley, K., and J. M. Jenkins. 1992. Human emotions: Function and dysfunction. *Annual Review of Psychology* 43:55–85.

O'Brien, J. T., A. Lloyd, I. McKeith, A. Gholkar, and N. Ferrier. 2004. A longitudinal study of hippocampal volume, cortisol levels, and cognition in older depressed subjects. *American Journal of Psychiatry* 161(11):2081–2090.

Ramirez Basco, M. 2006. *The Bipolar Workbook: Tools for Controlling Your Mood Swings.* New York: Guilford Press.

Rizvi, S., and A. E. Zaretsky. 2007. Psychotherapy through the phases of bipolar disorder: Evidence for general efficacy and differential effects. *Journal of Clinical Psychology: In Session* 63(5):491–506.

Roehrs, T., and T. Roth. 2001. Sleep, sleepiness and alcohol use. *Alcohol Research and Health* 25(2):101–109.

Salloum, I. M., and M. E. Thase. 2000. Impact of substance abuse on the course and treatment of bipolar disorder. *Bipolar Disorders* 2(3 pt. 2):269–280.

Segal, Z. V., J. M. G. Williams, and J. D. Teasdale. 2002. *Mindfulness-Based Cognitive Therapy for Depression.* New York: Guilford Press.

Simon, N. M., M. W. Otto, S. R. Wisniewski, M. Fossey, K. Sagduyu, E. Frank, G. S. Sachs, A. A. Nierenberg, M. E. Thase, and M. H. Pollack. 2004. Anxiety disorder comorbidity in bipolar disorder patients: Data from the first 500 participants in the Systematic Treatment Enhancement Program for Bipolar Disorder (STEP-BD). *American Journal of Psychiatry* 161(12):2222–2229.

Stoll, A. L., P. F. Renshaw, D. A. Yurgelun-Todd, and B. M. Cohen. 2000. Neuroimaging in bipolar disorder: What have we learned? *Biological Psychiatry* 48(6):505–517.

Strakowski, S. M., M. P. DelBello, D. E. Fleck, and S. Arndt. 2000. The impact of substance abuse on the course of bipolar disorder. *Biological Psychiatry* 48(6):477–485.

Teasdale, J. D., Z. V. Segal, J. M. G. Williams, V. A. Ridgeway, J. M. Soulsby, and M. A. Lau. 2000. Prevention of relapse/recurrence in major depression by mindfulness-based cognitive therapy. *Journal of Consulting and Clinical Psychology*, 68(4):615–623.

Thase, M. E. 2005. Bipolar depression: Issues in diagnosis and treatment. *Harvard Review of Psychiatry* 13(5):257–271.

Thase, M. E. 2006. Pharmacotherapy of bipolar depression: An update. *Current Psychiatry Reports* 8(6):478–488.

Tolle, E. 2006. *A New Earth: Awakening to Your Life's Purpose.* London: Penguin Books.

Van Laar, M., S. van Dorsselaer, K. Monshouwer, and R. de Graaf. 2007. Does cannabis use predict the first incidence of mood and anxiety disorders in the adult population? *Addiction* 102(8):1251–1260.

Vawter, M. P., W. J. Freed, and J. E. Kleinman. 2000. Neuropathology of bipolar disorder. *Biological Psychiatry* 48(6):486–504.

Velyvis, V. 2007. CBT for Bipolar Disorder. Spoken remarks at the Toronto Advanced Professional Education Cognitive Behavioural Therapy certificate program, Toronto, Ontario.

Williams, J. M. G., Y. Alatiq, C. Crane, T. Barnhofer, M. J. V. Fennell, D. S. Duggan, S. Hepburn, and G. M. Goodwin. 2008. Mindfulness-based cognitive therapy (MBCT) in bipolar disorder: Preliminary evaluation of immediate effects on between-episode functioning. *Journal of Affective Disorders* 107(1–3):275–279.

Williams, J. M. G., J. D. Teasdale, Z. V. Segal, and J. Kabat-Zinn. 2007. *The Mindful Way Through Depression*. New York: Guilford Press.

Zaretsky, A. E., S. Rizvi, and S. V. Parikh. 2007. How well do psychosocial interventions work in bipolar disorder? *Canadian Journal of Psychiatry* 52(1):14–21.

Sheri Van Dijk, MSW, is a psychotherapist in private practice and at Southlake Regional Health Centre in Ontario, Canada. She specializes in treating psychiatric disorders, including bipolar disorder, using dialectical behavior therapy, cognitive behavioral therapy, and mindfulness practice.

Foreword writer **Zindel V. Segal**, Ph.D., is the Morgan Firestone Chair in Psychotherapy and a professor of psychiatry at the University of Toronto. He is also director of the cognitive behavioral therapy unit at the Centre for Addiction and Mental Health, and a founding fellow of the Academy of Cognitive Therapy. He continues to advocate for the relevance of mindfulness-based clinical care in psychiatry and mental health.